Teresa of Ávila
THE BOOK OF MY LIFE

Teresa of Ávila

THE BOOK OF MY LIFE

Translated by Mirabai Starr

Foreword by Tessa Bielecki

NEW SEEDS

BOSTON & LONDON

2007

New Seeds Books
An imprint of Shambhala Publications, Inc.
Horticultural Hall
300 Massachusetts Avenue
Boston, Massachusetts 02115
www.newseedsbooks.com

9 8 7 6 5 4 3 2 1

First Edition

Printed in the United States of America
Designed by Gopa & Ted2, Inc.

⊗ This edition is printed on acid-free paper that meets the
American National Standards Institute Z39.48 Standard.
Distributed in the United States by Random House, Inc.,
and in Canada by Random House of Canada Ltd

Library of Congress Cataloging-in-Publication Data
Teresa, of Avila, Saint, 1515–1582.
[Libro de la vida. English]
Teresa of Ávila: the book of my life/translated by Mirabai Starr;
foreword by Tessa Bielecki.—1st ed.
p. cm.
Includes bibliographical references.
ISBN-13: 978-1-59030-365-8 (hardcover: alk. paper)
1. Teresa, of Avila, Saint, 1515–1582. 2. Christian saints—Spain
—Avila—Biography. 3. Avila (Spain)—Biography.
I. Starr, Mirabai. II. Title.
BX4700.T4A15 2007
282.092—dc22
[B]
2006029830

For Ganga Das,
keeper of my heart

CONTENTS

Foreword

TERESA OF ÁVILA had that mysterious quality the Spanish call *duende,* which is characteristic of gypsies, flamenco guitarists, and dancers. *Duende* is raw, primitive, tempestuous energy, a vulnerability to inspiration burning in the blood. Fiery, wild, and utterly original, *duende* cannot tolerate neat, tidy categories; cramped forms; or human limitations of any kind. *Duende* makes us ready to be devoured in the heroic struggle for individuation and genuine freedom.

In the Arab world, when *duende* enters and transfigures any music, dance, or epic poem, the people cry out "*Allah! Allah!* God! God!" How close this is to the Spanish "*Olé! Olé!*" Perhaps these cries have the same source, since the Moors, a Muslim people of mixed Berber-Arab descent, invaded Spain in 711 and lived there for almost eight hundred years. Ferdinand and Isabella finally expelled them in 1492, less than twenty-five years before Teresa's birth. The Moors left behind not only the magnificent Alhambra ("the red castle") to dominate the city of Granada and the Spanish imagination; they bequeathed to Spain—and through this country to the Western world—a rich legacy, inherited but not acknowledged by Saint Teresa.

Duende is usually associated with artists, musicians, dancers, and poets. Teresa was all of these and more, for she was also a mystic, that is, one who knows God by experience. With the inspiration of *duende,* Teresa made mysticism into music, poetry, art, and an ecstatic dance with the Beloved, while she also walked the path of suffering like every creative genius.

Teresa was a prolific writer, a great leader, and a teacher of the art of prayer. In 1970, almost four hundred years after her death, she was finally recognized as the first woman Doctor of the Church. She also stands out as the only woman in the history of the Church ever to reform a religious order of men.

What does Teresa have to do with us in the twenty-first century? Not many of us can be writers, found a school of spirituality, or reform a group of men. Yet Teresa serves as a vital prototype for a spiritual thrust that is desperately needed in our broken world.

Teresa was so vibrant, she fascinated those around her and has continued to fascinate down through the centuries. She was a dynamic personality: wild as a child, wild as she grew from an adolescent into a ravishing young woman, wildest of all as she reached middle age and set out on her quixotic adventures through her native Spain. She was stunning to look at, with shining black hair, beautiful teeth, an unusual face, a figure that was more substantial than slender. She was outgoing, cheerful, charming, and a scintillating conversationalist. People from all walks of life listened to her—men and women, bishops and mule drivers, theologians and laypeople, dukes and duchesses, even King Philip himself. Teresa enjoyed both talking and silence. She enjoyed being alone and having a good time.

She was a natural leader. As a child, she had an ingenious capacity for inventing new games and playing the starring role: the knight, the fairy godmother, the martyr burned at the stake. As an adult, she played these roles for real. "I was strikingly shrewd when it came to mischief," she confessed. She loved to laugh and laughed often. When she did, everyone else around her laughed. She liked perfume and fine clothes, chivalry, romance, and the color orange. Many men in Ávila were in love with her. "Teresa de Ahumada? With her fine mind, shapely legs, and ample dowry," people said, "she'll marry whomever she chooses." This was rare freedom in an era of arranged marriages.

Teresa's life was such high drama, we should indulge our wildest imaginings. See the all-engulfing solitude of the Castilian plain; the ninety stone turrets of the formidable walls of Ávila; the sharp, jagged peaks of the Sierra de Gredos against the skyline. Hear the musical sounds of Teresa's voice, as well as her tambourine, castanets, and drum, which she played even as a nun. Imagine sitting down with her for a good visit, basking in her wide embrace, her gaiety, and the depth of her wisdom, for Teresa was a woman of substance as well as charm.

Visualize her Jewish grandfather degraded by the Inquisition, stripped to the waist and paraded through the streets of Toledo in a humiliating procession through the jeering crowds; her five brothers sailing to South America and fighting for the conquest of Peru, Colombia, Argentina, Ecuador, and Chile; her beloved friend and helpmate, Saint John of the Cross, escaping from his nine-month imprisonment with the help of the Virgin Mary and a mongrel dog.

Imagine the beautiful, black-eyed Teresa at a party, at prayer, or doing penance; laughing over the lizard that crawled up her arm and landed in the face of her friend Antonio Ruiz; weeping over the death of her beloved father ("It seemed my soul was being wrenched from me"); or composing little verses to sing at celebrations. Watch her travel back and forth across the Spanish countryside in a rickety covered wagon, joking with her rustic muleteers, or giving astute spiritual guidance to the wealthy merchants who often accompanied her. See her captivating half the men in Spain—including the king—not as a young, eligible girl, but as a middle-aged mother foundress (*La Madre Fundadora*) who needed help from high places and got it, but not without paying the high price of pain.

Teresa was an earth mother and an earthy mystic, a poet and a brilliant administrator, a shrewd politician and a faithful friend, who walked a dangerous tightrope between the polarities of life yet held the delicate balance between human and divine, fast and feast, ecstasy and common sense.

Reading the lives of spiritual giants, I am often frustrated by the polished accounts of their eventual transformation that tell me almost nothing about the arduous years it took to get there. That's why the "raw and unwieldy" life of Teresa is so refreshing. "This book is the memoir of a life in the middle of unfolding," explains Mirabai Starr. "A story of the coming of age of a mystic." We learn how to cope with our own struggles when we see how Teresa struggled with hers: a "raging addiction" to romance novels, "falling dangerously in love," eighteen years of aridity when she never dared to pray without a book. How can we not identify with Teresa when she admits so humbly that she gets so angry she "want[s] to eat everyone up, without being able to help it?"

Teresa did not become an integrated human being all at once, any more than we do. Her transformation was a gradual process that took her entire lifetime. And like us, Teresa made many mistakes, some serious. She knew fear, failure, and human weakness; loneliness, illness, and exhaustion; the joy of sympathy and the pain of misunderstanding, especially from friends who "took the biggest bite" out of her. Before she could soar like an eagle, she had to crawl on her belly like a snake— literally, as she slowly began to move again after an excruciating paralysis that lasted three years. Throughout her sufferings, Teresa was humbly and heroically aware of her destiny and God's designs, and she clung to these tenaciously. She grew into a giant, a *conquistadora* of the spiritual life, a Doctor of the Church, and a saint for all seasons.

Please don't think that the tale of her founding of Saint Joseph's Convent is not relevant to your own life. As I've written elsewhere, Teresa teaches us how to make our own dreams reality. Though her dream was the reform of a religious order, the elements she describes are universal: the need for taking risks and displaying "holy daring," leaving our comfort zones, and cultivating courage in the face of doubt and fear. Notice how often Teresa says, "I was afraid" or "I didn't know what to do."

I have loved this great woman for decades and want the whole world to love her and benefit from her spiritual and human wisdom. When I did my research on this saint, I struggled through the literal translations of her works. These translations suffer from the fact that Teresa wrote in haste and under difficult circumstances, never rereading what she'd written. The literal Teresa is so verbose that her pearls get lost. I've often blurted out in my frustration, "Woman, you need a good editor!"

Enter Mirabai Starr. With her own contemplative depth, her experience of so many of the world's spiritual traditions, and a philosophical background Teresa never had, she translates Teresa's writings the way they deserve to be. Mirabai is not Catholic or Carmelite, and I think that gives her a fresh perspective. She's also the first woman to translate Teresa's work, and that helps.

Don't be misled when Mirabai says, "I confess to taking a few liberties with the translation." It was my task to check her version against a more literal translation for authenticity. Mirabai did more than "stay true to every nuance of Teresa's voice." She's truer than true, even more Teresa than Teresa was! I'm convinced that Teresa herself guided Mirabai's effort and now laughs down from heaven, *"Que bueno, mi hija!* That's how I really wanted to say it!"

I love "hearing" Teresa in more contemporary language. Given her personality, if she were alive today, this is surely how she would speak to us. Mirabai makes Teresa alive for our ears and our era. I love the way she compares her translating to the restoration of a medieval tapestry: untangling and reweaving every sentence "so that the underlying picture [becomes] clear and bright." For example, Mirabai has replaced Teresa's cumbersome and sometimes useless chapter introductions with short, pithy titles that accurately convey what we are about to read: Twenty Years of Turbulence, Prisoner of the Parlor, A Glimpse of the Underworld. Dividing the book into three parts also helps us steer our way through Teresa's many digressions.

Great works of spiritual literature are truly transformational tools for the reader. Mirabai Starr's gift for contemporary translation makes the jewel of Teresa's autobiography an even greater tool as well as treasure. If you have never read Teresa before, I envy you your first discovery. If you are familiar with her writings, I rejoice in your deeper study. Mirabai's searing and soaring translation helps us see Teresa with new eyes, hear her with new ears, and feel her with new hearts.

—Tessa Bielecki

Acknowledgments

IN MANY WAYS I consider this book a team effort by the two Teresas and me. The first Teresa, of course, is Teresa of Ávila. At the risk of sounding overly metaphysical, I have to say that I felt the presence of the saint every day as I was composing her translation. I would light the candle at my desk, gaze at her framed image for a moment, and off we'd go. It was effortless and joyous, as if we were galloping together along a sandy beach on swift horses, the sea air rushing through our hair.

The other companion was Tessa Bielecki, a Carmelite hermit and living mystic. I first encountered Tessa through her exquisite books on Teresa of Ávila, her patron saint: *Teresa of Ávila, Mystical Writings*; *Holy Daring*; and *Ecstasy and Common Sense.*

Then a miracle happened. I wrote to Tessa and she wrote back. A few months later, as she was passing through my hometown of Taos, New Mexico, en route from her hermitage in Colorado to the Zen Center in Santa Fe on the day of the Indonesian tsunami, she stopped at my house for breakfast. The meal lasted until four o'clock in the afternoon. On many levels, we are still eating. Our mutual love of the one Tessa calls "the wild woman of Ávila" brought us home to each other's hearts.

Tessa read every word of the manuscript. She blessed and praised it, and she also applied her sharp editorial eye and helped tighten and brighten it. When the first draft of the translation was complete, Tessa came from Colorado and spent five days with me on what we fondly referred to as our "Teresa retreat." We went over the manuscript together, Tessa filled in some of the gaps in my Catholic education, and I clarified some of my choices as a translator. We cooked and ate healthy food together, took walks in the mountains with the dogs, and in the evenings watched the eight-part Spanish television series on the life of Saint

Teresa and wept together. It was heaven. It is to Tessa Bielecki that I offer my deepest thanks.

As much as I may strive to be a recluse, I am not. Many people weave the fabric of my daily life and encourage me in this work. I am grateful to them all, beginning with my family. My mother, Susanna Starr, has been an ongoing source of support on every level: emotional, spiritual, and material. She models the unique balance of earthy practicality and cosmic consciousness that Teresa of Ávila represents. My brother, Roy Starr, and my sister, Amy Starr, bless me every day with their love and faith in me and the pure goodness of their hearts. I look to my daughter, Daniela Whitehorse, as a living example of what it is to be fully kind and deeply sane in a wounded world. And to the eternal memory of my beloved daughter, my shining star and guardian angel, Jenny Starr, thank you.

Many friends have touched my life during the nine months of this writing. My dear Jenny Bird, extraordinary singer-songwriter, read the manuscript and made some incredibly astute observations and suggestions. More importantly, she wrote and recorded an exquisite song from Saint Teresa's bookmark prayer.

Father Dave Denny revealed himself as a true companion in the love of sacred poetry. Father Bill McNichols remains my ever-faithful friend and spiritual guide in a land that has no name and requires none. Father John Dear, Liz McAlister, and Susan Crane shared their prophetic voices of hope and the example of their lives of nonviolent action, teaching me to offer the fruits of contemplation to service in the world. Nancy Casey knows the secret language and speaks it with me. Thanks to the great lady of art and spirit, Anne Hawley, and to Natalie Goldberg, lifelong friend and mentor, who never stops teaching me exactly what I need to know. To the wise and caring John Lamkin, thank you. Thanks to Reverend Bob Thompson, Dr. Alexander Shaiah, and that wild holy man, Larry Torres, for sharing their loving knowledge of the Christ.

Thanks to my generous and insightful agent, Sarah Jane Freymann, who makes everything come out right. And thanks to my New Seeds editor, Dave O'Neal, who had the wisdom to let the saint speak for herself. And thank you Dan Frank and Rameshwardas for polishing the mirror.

I would like to thank Ram Dass, who first showed me through example that Jewish-born American practitioners of the Eastern traditions can and indeed must embrace the Christian mystics and Christ himself. Thanks, too, for being in my life during these past few years of profound pain and wild joy. To Neem Karoli Baba, Maharaj-ji, quintessential holy man and fool of God, thank you for lighting my way all these years. *Sub ek!*

Finally, I would like to thank my husband, Ganga Das Jeff Little, for the ten thousand ways, small and vast, that he makes everything I do possible. For nine months, over morning coffee, Ganga Das listened to every word I wrote. He opened his mind and heart, let all preconceptions go, and heard these words with a freshness of attention that continually amazed and humbled me. His responses to Teresa's teachings guided my steps. I love you, Ganga Das.

INTRODUCTION

A MEDITATION ON THE TRANSVERBERATION

You slip away from the others and into your private chamber. You fall to your knees at the altar you keep there and gaze at your favorite painted icons, your cherished sacred statues. You feel it coming on, watch in patient fascination as the familiar, mysterious feeling washes over you. It gathers all your fragmented parts and lifts you out of yourself.

There is a stirring at your left side. Very close. You turn in slow motion to see what it is. A small angel is standing next to you. As clear and distinct as your bed, as the window above your bed, as the hills beyond the window.

He is beautiful. Exquisitely formed, androgynous. His face is made of fire. You briefly wonder what angelic category he might belong to. You have read somewhere that there are several. You conclude he must be of the highest order. He has not told you his name. It doesn't matter.

Then you see the spear in his hand, and you know it is meant for you. Meant to annihilate you. This is what you asked for. The spear is made of gold, and its tip is on fire. With a small smile, almost playful, he lifts his glorious weapon and plunges it into your heart. Again and again he thrusts, until he has penetrated your innermost core.

When at last he withdraws his spear, it feels as though he is carrying the deepest part of you away with him. You are left blazing, entirely consumed by love of God.

You swoon. You moan. The pain is unbearable. The pain is so glorious, you never want it to abate. Now you will not be content with anything less than total union with your divine Beloved.

Yes, this anguish is spiritual, not physical. True, your loins remain intact, your flesh unpierced. But the body shares this beautiful wound.

When you try to tell the others what happened to you, they think you're lying. You're just being melodramatic (again). "You want people to think you're some kind of mystic," they say. "This is delusional," they declare. "Dangerous."

"Beloved," you beseech your God, "please give them a taste of your sweet love."

You want the whole world to burn as you do. You want to see everyone illuminated.

THE LIFE

The great sixteenth-century Spanish contemplative, Teresa of Ávila, has been celebrated for more than three centuries for her mystical experiences. She did not actually have any, however, until she was nearly forty years old.

Teresa was the granddaughter of a *converso*, a Jew forced by the Inquisition to convert to Christianity on pain of death. Her "tainted" blood, combined with her distinctly unfeminine intellect, political daring, and wild visions, made her the target of severe persecution throughout her life. She was not an obvious saint.

Born in 1515, Teresa entered the convent with a high degree of ambivalence at the age of eighteen. At twenty, she professed her vows more as an act of rebellion than one of devotion. These choices literally almost killed her. But, after having seen her thirty-three-year-old mother die in childbirth when Teresa was twelve, marriage was not an appealing alternative.

For the next two decades, Sister Teresa struggled with a dry and tedious inner life contrasted with intensely gregarious impulses. She wanted to want God. But she wanted even more to be liked by other human beings. Endowed with natural beauty, charm, intelligence, and humor, Teresa was the center of attention in any situation—among her own family, entertaining visitors in the convent parlor, convincing powerful men to agree with her point of view.

Then one day Teresa entered an oratory and happened to notice a statue of Christ scourged at the pillar. She glanced at his sweet, suffering face, and it brought her abruptly to her knees. Suddenly, she was sobbing. She pressed her forehead to the floor and cried out to him, "Please, my Beloved, give me the strength to adore you! Do not ever let me forsake you again!"

After years of being incapable of "squeezing out a single holy tear," Teresa could not stop crying. Her whole life leading up to that moment felt trivial and misguided. She saw that she had manipulated her own journey while God waited patiently for her to hand over the reins and let him drive. She had never truly surrendered. She had never really loved him.

Now the love that flooded her threatened to annihilate her. And the more she felt herself consumed by this love, the more she longed to be consumed. "I refuse to get up from this spot until you give me what I want!" she told him, not unlike the vow of the Buddha under the Bodhi Tree a millennium before her. The torrent of tears washed away any last trace of self-reliance. She placed herself unconditionally in God's hands.

From that moment on, Teresa experienced an unrelenting series of raptures, visions, and voices. Word of the unconventional nun and the dramatic favors she was receiving from God spread throughout Spain and invoked the suspicion of the Inquisition. The resulting investigation ultimately yielded the jewel of spiritual literature we have come to know as *The Book of My Life*.

This book is the memoir of a life in the middle of unfolding. It is a story of a mystic's coming of age. Like Teresa herself, it is both exuberant and profound. She often wrote under the influence of the divine ecstasy she was extolling. Teresa's aim was to instruct rather than to entertain. And yet the sheer joy with which she expresses her passion for God and the delight she takes in lyrical metaphors and earthy imagery makes it a pleasure to read. She did not write it to impress us with her holiness but to document her experiences so the authorities could examine them and decide her fate. Her courage was rewarded, though not without tremendous controversy and persecution.

Teresa believed in the power of books to serve as tools of transformation. She herself experienced a significant "conversion" experience reading the *Confessions* of Saint Augustine. When the Inquisition banned many of her favorite books on prayer, it was if they had imposed life sentences on all her best friends. She was inconsolable until she heard the voice of God promising to replace these beloved texts with "a living book." However, she also grew to see the limitations of language and the need to sit in the silence of unknowing.

The "learned men" who scrutinized Teresa's life story were hypervigilant for any traces of diabolical delusion and repeatedly proclaimed that Teresa's experiences came from the spirit of evil. They need not have bothered. Teresa subjected her own visions to rigorous self-inquiry. Only after examining each spiritual encounter with the laser of her intellect and praying fervently for guidance did she rest in the certainty that God instilled in her soul.

Teresa tried to be patient and humble whenever she was denounced, but she occasionally expressed a refreshing burst of annoyance. "I don't understand these fears," she writes in chapter 25. "Why do we run around crying, 'The devil! The devil!' when we can be saying, 'God! God!' and make the devils tremble?" She goes on to frankly declare, "Without a doubt, I fear those who fear the devil more than I fear the devil himself."

Through a deepening intimacy with Christ in prayer, Teresa came to trust that the divine favors she was receiving were pledges of love from God. They were promises of the union to come, meant to ignite her heart and dissolve her soul in his. The more she tried to obey her superiors and suppress these supernatural experiences, the more they increased in both frequency and intensity.

It's worth noting that Teresa's life really took off where her autobiography ends. At the age of forty-five, after finishing this writing, Teresa embarked on a journey of radical reform, traveling all over the rugged Spanish countryside, founding convents and monasteries dedicated to a life of voluntary simplicity and contemplative practice. In spite of a lifetime of chronic illness, Teresa lived to age sixty-seven. She was canonized in 1622.

The *Life* is divided into three primary sections. The first is an account of her childhood and youth. She shares her wild escapades and her struggle to be true to God. The second section is a teaching on the four waters of prayer. It was added later at the command of one of the men who was reading the work. The third section recounts the details of Teresa's many visions, voices, and raptures, interspersed with instruction on navigating the interior life and including a brief history of the founding of Saint Joseph's, the first reform monastery.

While Teresa's devotion to her Roman Catholic faith was never in question, her autobiography transcends religious dogma and attains a universal status that makes it accessible and meaningful to any seeker from any tradition. *The Book of My Life* takes its rightful place as one of the greatest spiritual testimonies of all time.

THE DECISION

My friend, Father Bill, gave me the task of translating Teresa of Ávila's *Life*. I had deftly avoided this work for years and launched directly into a translation of her mystical masterpiece *The Interior Castle* after the publication of my translation of *Dark Night of the Soul* by Teresa's beloved protégé, Saint John of the Cross. I was satisfied that I had gotten the Spanish mystics out of my system.

Teresa wrote the story of her life in her forties, while she was in the midst of being pummeled by the very experiences she was reporting. It had always felt a little raw and unwieldy to me. That's why I had chosen to translate *The Interior Castle* instead; it is a refreshing distillation of Teresa's finest teachings on contemplative prayer. She wrote it at the end of her life, when she had ripened spiritually and emotionally.

I try to do what Father Bill tells me. It's hard to explain why. He is a Catholic priest, while I am a Jewish practitioner of Buddhist meditation, a devotee of a Hindu guru, and a trained philosopher who has trouble believing in a personified deity. Yet I identify with Teresa in more ways than one. Teresa deeply bonded with certain men who had the unique distinction of seeing her soul, that is, seeing something authentic about who she was and what her work in the world might be. Father Bill *sees* me.

Plus, I cannot deny my lifelong connection to the Spanish mystics. They speak my language. Not only my spiritual language, the language of love-longing, of the emptiness that is plenitude, of the fire that annihilates and the garden that gives refuge. It is also the literal Spanish that

I love. I first learned Spanish when I was twelve years old and my counterculture parents uprooted our family from suburban New York and took us on a year-long odyssey through Mexico that ended in New Mexico. I savored the new words the minute I first felt them in my mouth.

Northern New Mexico was colonized by settlers from Spain. Because of the unique topography of these mountain valleys, the people here were isolated for centuries and their language did not evolve along with mainstream Castilian. I grew up in a community where the people still speak a version of the sixteenth-century Spanish I'm now translating. And their spirituality feels similarly ancient. I have had the honor of attending various religious rituals in our area that feel like more medieval European pageants than contemporary Catholic liturgies.

Still, doing another translation was not exactly what I had in mind when Father Bill brought me the Spanish-language copy of Teresa of Ávila's *Vida*. It wasn't only that I was afraid of being pigeonholed as the contemporary translator of the Spanish mystics and never being able to do anything else. In light of the current political and ecological travesties I saw unfolding around me, I was also concerned about the relevance of early Renaissance religious treatises. How about unleashing some of my scholarly training on something that might contribute to reconciling conflicting belief systems and bringing some hope for peace to this wounded world?

After grappling and resisting for a few days, I gave in and agreed to translate Teresa's autobiography. Here, I realized, was a woman whose entire story models what it is to walk a path of courage and nonviolence. I could do a lot worse. It was as if the heavens had opened and a voice boomed, "Finally!" A feeling of quiet joy washed over me.

In that moment, I let my other literary aspirations go. My plans for writing the gorgeous novel, the universal memoir, the teachings of Mirabai Starr. I uncurled my fist and released them all. With this surrender came a deepening peace. And a startling excitement. I knew I had come home.

This feeling never left me for a minute during the ensuing nine-month journey through the *Life*.

A LEXICON OF VISIONS AND VOICES

Being a woman in sixteenth-century Spain, Teresa did not have access to formal education. In her struggle to find words to express the ineffable and not offend the "learned men" she was writing for, she adapted existing language of the spirit and ended up inventing her own. The unique voice that emerged ultimately earned Teresa the distinction of being named one of the first female Doctors of the Church.

It was vitally important to Teresa that her religious experiences be seen as firmly planted in the soil of the Holy Mother Church. She wrote during the Counter-Reformation, when the Church was suspicious of anything that resembled Protestant theology. Teresa knew she was playing with fire when she insisted on the possibility of a direct relationship with the Divine, independent of the intermediaries of clerical officials who, she openly acknowledged, probably lacked personal experience of these interior states.

To this end, Teresa meticulously mapped and cataloged her visions, voices, and raptures, which she gathers together under the title of "divine favors." She identifies three types of visions, ranking from the lowest to the highest order: corporeal, imaginative, and intellectual. Other than her famous supernatural encounter known as the "transverberation," when an angel appeared to her in physical form, Teresa rarely experienced corporeal visions. Most of her visions were intellectual; a few were imaginative.

Whereas a corporeal vision involves the sensory experience of an actual physical presence outside one's own body, an imaginative vision evokes a physical form that unfolds on the subjective stage of the inner eye. Teresa's stunning vision of Christ's hands, for example, is an imaginative one. Later he showed her his face. Finally, she saw his entire glorified body. She understood that her imagination was not strong enough to receive him all at once, so in his mercy, he revealed himself little by little.

An intellectual vision is a secret transmission of supernatural teachings directly to the mind. Over and over, Teresa experienced God transporting her ordinary consciousness and communicating a transcendent knowledge of divine truths. She regularly asserts that what he taught her cannot be confined to ordinary language and yet insists that it is far clearer and truer than anything we can know with the faculty of discursive reason. Often she simply experienced the undeniable presence of Christ beside her.

One of the most common of the divine favors Teresa received took the form of locutions. I have replaced this conventional theological designation with the more approachable term "spiritual voices." These auditory visions were specific. She heard Christ speaking words of comfort, reproach, and prophecy. Teresa derived more confidence from these messages than any human being could have instilled in her. She regularly acted on the instructions she received in prayer.

Beginning with her "second conversion" at age thirty-nine in front of a statue of the suffering Christ, Teresa experienced frequent states of rapture. Often when she was engaged in silent prayer, she would become transported. The faculties of sense and reason would grow still. Her body would be rigid, her breath shallow, and her pulse almost imperceptible. She was paralyzed by ecstasy.

Teresa felt powerless to resist the onslaught of these "flights of the spirit." They were a continual source of embarrassment to her. In spite of her reputation for exotic altered states, Teresa was a profoundly practical woman. She had little patience for flashy spiritual phenomena. While most of her raptures occurred in the privacy of an oratory or the sanctuary of the convent choir, sometimes she was overcome with ecstasy while stirring a pot of lentils and would become transfixed in the middle of the kitchen.

Throughout most of her life, Teresa worried about the source of her experiences. She consistently subjected her visions, voices, and raptures to rigorous inquiry in an effort to determine whether they came from the spirit of evil or the spirit of God. It did not help that the men in charge of her spiritual development regularly declared that she was being deluded by the devil.

Still, each time she checked, Teresa emerged triumphant. Her proof that the origin of her experiences was in fact divine was that they left her with a sense of lasting peace and increasing love of God that the spirit of evil could never evoke.

A contemporary reader might speculate that Teresa's visions, voices, and raptures were pathological. I'm reluctant to reduce Teresa's experiences to mere evidence of psychosis. The fine line between genius and mental illness has been applied to mystics, artists, scientists, and other great thinkers for centuries. In some ways, the discussion is gratuitous. Regardless of whatever posthumous diagnosis we might be tempted to give her, Teresa left us a legacy of some of the most stunning spiritual insights in all of religious literature. She has served as an inspiration, guide, and source of solace to countless pilgrims of the inner wilderness, and her teachings are as relevant today as ever before.

CONTEMPLATIVE PRAYER

In the tradition of Christian mysticism, there is an important distinction between meditation and contemplation. Meditation is active. The practitioner focuses on a particular sacred image or phrase as a method for gathering the awareness and gently pulling it inward. Contemplation is passive. It is a state of grace that descends when the practitioner of prayer has carved out a space inside herself through the intentional cultivation of stillness.

Christian mysticism also distinguishes between vocal prayer and mental prayer. Vocal prayer comes from the vast liturgy of the Church, which has ordained certain prayers for certain rituals. Mental prayer is contemplative prayer. It is a surrender of form and a letting down into formlessness. The practitioner of mental prayer sits in prolonged silence and waits on the presence of God.

Teresa speaks of three levels of contemplative prayer. The first is recollection, when we allow our ordinary concerns to drop away and our attention to become one-pointed. Our thoughts may chatter for a while, but then they grow quiet. Our senses grow still. There is an ingathering of the faculties of memory, will, and imagination and the soul becomes "recollected."

Into this emptiness, the Prayer of Quiet may come. This is not a state we can make happen through the use of will. It is a divine gift. A feeling of deep peace and quietude washes over us like a warm wave. The

Christian mystics describe this as an exceedingly delicate, subtle state. It is sweet and restful. It is timeless.

In the Prayer of Quiet, we are still identified, though very lightly, with the individual self. We are aware of the presence of that which transcends our individuality and may feel a longing for deeper connection with that which we experience as the source of love.

In the Prayer of Union, any sense of an individualized self slips away. The soul is consumed by the Divine. Lover and Beloved become one. God, the mystics remind us, wants union with the soul as much as the soul yearns to unite with him. This state of prayer may be fleeting, says Teresa, but its impact endures. The Prayer of Union effects irrevocable changes in the soul.

To describe the lifelong relationship to the practice of prayer, Teresa uses the imagery of a garden and the four waters that sustain it. As beginners on the path of contemplative practice, we must engage in the hard work of lowering our buckets into the well and drawing the water by hand to nourish the garden of the soul. It requires intention and determination. It is labor-intensive and not always gratifying. This is the first water of prayer.

If we persevere, we progress to the second water, in which we learn to turn the crank of a waterwheel that pulls the water through a system of aqueducts designed for greater efficiency. Although it still demands effort on our part, it is not as laborious as the beginning stage. The water flows more easily, and the soul can rest for a while in the Prayer of Quiet.

The third water corresponds to a bubbling spring or flowing stream that waters the garden from within. Throughout the mountain communities of northern New Mexico, farmers water their fields using an elaborate system of irrigation ditches called *acequias*. This method for growing crops has its origins in Renaissance Spain and has not changed in more than four centuries. The only task of the gardener is to direct the flow of the water. The garden begins to bear fruit. The soul eats and grows strong.

The final stage of prayer is union with the Divine. This fourth water is pure grace. It falls from the sky like a gentle rain, soaking the garden and causing everything beautiful to burst into blossom. This state brings such joy and peace that no amount of worldly trouble can shake the soul's equanimity. She feels so saturated with grace that she is certain her garden will never be dry again.

A Note on the Translation

I CONFESS to taking a few liberties with the translation, but I tried to stay true to every nuance of Teresa's voice. Like someone who restores medieval tapestries, I mostly untangled and rewove every sentence so that the underlying picture became clear and bright. An abiding love of language, its beauty and power, drove this work.

It goes without saying that translating mystical poetry and prose is more than an aesthetic exercise. I'll say it anyway: great works of spiritual literature have the potential to raise the consciousness of the reader. They become transformational tools. I did not invent this notion. All the world's great wisdom traditions have a practice of approaching sacred writing as prayer.

By immersing ourselves in the language of the spirit, our spirits can be directly touched, lifted, healed. This enlightenment is not guaranteed, but exposure to the light of spiritual writing opens the door to that possibility. Then we are not reading *about* something remote and unattainable; we are having an *experience* of it. This is my hope for the people who read this book.

In keeping with the convention of Spanish mysticism, I use the feminine pronoun when referring to the soul (the lover) and the masculine when talking about God (the Beloved) and do not capitalize God-pronouns. I sometimes substitute "missing the mark" and "transgression" for *sin*. I call the *devil* "the spirit of evil."

Please note that Teresa, who was ordered to write her life story against her will, tried in vain to disguise the details so she would not be recognized. She does not identify places or people by name. I have gleaned these specifics from footnotes and incorporated them into my translation.

As I worked my way though the Spanish text, I became fascinated by the dynamic relationships that develop between Teresa and the men who had authority over her: confessors, spiritual directors, government officials, even Inquisitors. Her intelligence, charm, and ripening sanctity win them over before our eyes.

Over the course of the *Life*, we witness how Teresa manages to make her most formidable opponents into her most trusted friends; her superiors become her devotees. She addresses them as "my father" and "my son" in the same breath. We can even detect that a few of them might be falling more than a little bit in love with her.

Wherever feasible, I tried to use inclusive language in my word choices. In the interest of making this treasure of religious literature accessible to anyone, regardless of religious affiliation or lack thereof, I selected more general terms for some of the particular Catholic terms and titles. In the *Life*, Teresa directly addresses her superiors who ordered her to document her unconventional experiences so they could scrutinize them. Where she often speaks to someone she calls "your Reverence," I simply say "you."

Finally, hoping to avoid alienating a vast number of potential readers, I have reduced Teresa's ten thousand self-deprecating statements about being a "wretched worm" to a fraction of that. It's still too much for many of my feminist friends and relations. But excising these statements any more radically than I have would mean not letting Teresa be Teresa.

We must be careful not to dismiss her constant claims of unworthiness as being nothing more than a problem of self-esteem. This attitude is a religious artifact, yes, and a cultural one, true. It's also authentic. Teresa knew herself. She experienced her path as precarious and often driven by self-interest. And she wanted more than anything to break the bonds of the small self and lose herself in the ultimate reality she called God.

TERESA OF ÁVILA

THE BOOK OF MY LIFE

PROLOGUE

IF ONLY SOMEONE would invite me to make a detailed list of all the things I have done wrong in my life! Instead, I have been asked to freely describe my spiritual practice and to record all the blessings my Lord has showered on me. I would be so much more comfortable disclosing my imperfections, but I have taken a vow of obedience that forces me to keep those things to myself.

All I can do is to beg you who are reading this account of my life to please, for the love of God, bear in mind that it has been much more wicked than I am at liberty to say. In fact, I keep searching among all the saints, studying the stories of their awakenings, looking for even one who can serve as a role model for me.

But, no. Once God called them, they never turned away from him again. I, on the other hand, grew even worse. I seem to have made it my personal mission to do whatever I could to deny every blessing he has bestowed on me. I knew that I should strive to serve him better, but I also knew that I myself was powerless to offer my Beloved what he deserved.

May he who has waited so long for me be forever blessed!

I ask him now, with the whole of my heart, to give me the grace of absolute clarity and perfect truth, so that I may write this account of my life as I have been asked to do. I have felt for a long time that my Lord wanted me to write this, but I have not dared to begin. Until now.

May this writing be an offering of praise and glory to my Lord. May it help my spiritual guides to know me better and so to better support my spiritual development. May I find the strength now to give back even a fraction of the great gifts I have received from God.

And may he be adored by all things, forever.

Amen.

PART ONE

My Turbulent Youth

A Child's Passion for God

THERE WAS NO VALID REASON for me to be so wicked. My parents were righteous people who revered God. And God granted me the option of being good as well. I had all the help I needed to curtail my negative tendencies. But I was incorrigible.

My father loved good books. He had some that were written in Spanish, so his children could read them, and they had a positive influence on me. My mother made sure that we all said our prayers and offered devotion to our Lady and to certain saints. When I was around six or seven years old, exposure to these holy things began to stir something in me.

It helped that I never saw either of my parents act with anything other than integrity. They were both blessed with many virtues. My father, for instance, had great compassion for the poor and sympathy for the sick. He was kind to his servants and could not bear to keep slaves. In fact, when one of his brother's Moorish slaves was staying at our house, my father treated her like one of his own children. He couldn't stand it that she was not free, he said. My father spoke only the truth. Nobody ever heard him swear or gossip. He was a profoundly decent man.

My mother, too, was a deeply virtuous woman and absolutely honest. She struggled with illness throughout her life. Even though she was incredibly beautiful, she never paid attention to her looks. In fact, by the time she died at age thirty-three, she was already dressing with the dignity of a much more mature woman. My mother was deeply serene and exceptionally intelligent. She endured terrible trials during her time on this earth, but she died in the fullness of Christ's love.

We were a family of three sisters and nine brothers. By the grace of God, all were as virtuous as our parents. Except for me. Even so, I was my father's favorite. There actually might have been some reason for this at one time. Before I started rebelling against God, I believe that God had given me some very good inclinations. It causes me such pain now to remember how I took these blessings for granted and did not make use of them.

I loved all of my brothers and sisters, and they loved me. They certainly never stood in my way or prevented me from serving God. I had one brother, close to my own age, whom I loved best of all. We used to read the lives of the saints together. When I read about certain women saints who endured martyrdom for the sake of God, I concluded that death was a small price to pay for the utter joy they were given in return when they were whisked away to heaven.

I desperately wanted to die like this. Not out of holy devotion, at least not that I was aware of, but from sheer urgency to get hold of the sublime fruits that my books promised were stored up for me. My brother and I would discuss how we could best make martyrs of ourselves. We decided to head off to the country of the Moors, begging bread along the way, and ask them to please, for the love of God, chop off our heads. I believe that our Lord had given us, even at such a tender age, the courage to follow up on our plan. The only thing stopping us was the fact that we had parents.

You know how it is said that both pain and glory are eternal? My brother and I used to spend hours pondering this together. "Forever!" we would say. "Forever! Forever!" It seems that my frequent repetition of this phrase knocked on God's door and offered me a lasting glimpse of the Way of Truth when I was only a small child.

When I finally accepted that there was nowhere I could go where I could convince them to kill me for the sake of God, my brother and I decided to become holy hermits. In the small orchard behind our house, we would pile up stones to build our hermitages. But they immediately came tumbling down, thwarting our project over and over again. Even now, as I remember how young I was when God gave me the precious gift of devotion, I am filled with sadness to see how I lost it along the way through my own carelessness.

As much as I could, which was not much at all, I gave alms to the poor. I tried to be alone whenever I said my prayers. And I prayed often. My mother had a disciplined practice of saying the rosary, and she inspired the same commitment in us. When I played with other little girls, I loved to pretend that we were building convents to live in. I think I always wanted to be a nun. But, unfortunately, I wanted other things more.

When I was around twelve years old, my mother died. When it began to dawn on me what I had lost, I was overcome by grief. Weeping uncontrollably, I threw myself at the feet of an image of our Lady and pleaded with her to be my mother now. It seems to me that even though I made this prayer with naïve simplicity, she answered me. I have found that whenever I have placed myself in her circle of mercy, the Blessed Mother has turned to enfold me. It disturbs me deeply now to see that somewhere along the way I abandoned so many of the good impulses I had begun to cultivate.

O my Beloved! It appears that you are determined to save me. May it please you to do it! You have already poured such a bounty of blessings upon me. What I don't understand is why you have allowed this dwelling of my soul, where you have chosen to live, to remain in such a terrible mess. It is not for my own advantage that I ask, but for your honor and glory.

Why am I even saying this? I already know it's my own fault. You did everything you could possibly do, from the time I was very young, to make me fully yours. I can't blame my parents either, since all I ever saw in them was pure goodness and concern for my well-being.

As I passed through childhood, I began to become aware of the many natural graces my Lord had bestowed on me. Instead of giving thanks for these gifts, I started to use them against him, as I will now explain.

FALLING DANGEROUSLY IN LOVE

WHAT I AM about to disclose is a reflection of the period, it seems to me, when I began to do myself harm. Sometimes I think it is negligent for parents not to set up every possible obstacle in the lives of their children to prevent them from being exposed to anything but virtue. My mother, as I mentioned, was a very good woman herself, but as I grew older, I did very little—almost nothing, in fact—to emulate her goodness. Instead, I seemed to be inexorably drawn toward bad things, which started to do damage to my soul.

My mother was very fond of romance novels and so was I. But they did not have the negative effects on her that they had on me. For one thing, she never allowed them to interfere with her work. Her children, on the other hand, were always stealing time to read them. My mother allowed this indulgence, partly because it kept us occupied and so lightened her own load a little, and partly because she herself found sweet escape from the many trials she suffered in the pages of those books.

This pastime of ours annoyed my father to such a degree that we went to great lengths to make sure that he did not catch us doing it. But what was for my mother a harmless habit became a raging addiction for me. Any impulse I had toward goodness began to cool, and I started looking for trouble. I didn't think that there was anything wrong with my wasting long hours, day and night, in such a useless enterprise as devouring these insipid tales, even though I had to hide it from my father. I became so intensely immersed in reading romances that unless I had a new book lined up behind the last one, I was not happy.

Then I started taking inordinate pride in my appearance. I dressed in the latest fashions, doused myself with perfumes, pampered my hands, and fussed with my hair. I was fastidious and vain, grasping for all the trinkets I could find to enhance my beauty. My intentions were not dishonorable in the sense that I would never have wanted anyone to offend God because of me, but I was overly concerned about how I looked and smelled and seemed. These things did not feel sinful to me, and so I spent years preoccupied with them.

My father was very careful about who was allowed into our house. But we had some questionable cousins who visited often. Oh, if only he had been careful about those cousins as well! In retrospect, I see how dangerous it is to allow children to be exposed to certain influences just at the time when the seeds of their virtues are starting to germinate. It's not that such people are wicked in themselves, but they have a way of arousing wicked desires in others. Like me.

The cousins were around my age, some a little older. We spent most of our time together. They adored me, and I made it my project to amuse with my conversation and offer my rapt attention whenever they recounted their own inane escapades. There was nothing worthwhile in these exchanges. In fact, even worse, I began to feel my soul being pulled into a vortex of evil.

If I were to offer some advice to parents, it would be this: pay attention to who it is that your children are associating with. Bad company can do a great deal of damage. And young people are naturally inclined to follow what is worst for them rather than what is best. This was certainly the case for me.

My sister Maria was much older than I was. Even though she was honest and kind and pure of heart, I learned nothing from her. Instead, I studied every kind of wickedness from an older relative of mine who was often in our house. This cousin was so frivolous and superficial that it irritated my mother to have her around. Really, I think my mother must have had some idea of what a negative effect this girl was having on me. But there were so many reasons for her to be there that it was no use trying to keep her away. We gossiped constantly and confided our deepest secrets to one another. She accompanied me in all the things I liked to do and introduced me to activities I had never dreamed of.

When I was around fourteen, I began to grow even closer to this cousin. I had never before committed a mortal sin—not so much out of fear of God as from concern about my own reputation. This obsession with my image is what prevented me from losing my honor altogether. To tell the truth, I don't think there was anything or anyone I loved enough in the whole world to justify surrendering my virtue. My innate attachment to my own honor probably would have kept me from going against the honor of God in any case. What I didn't realize was all the subtle ways in which I was sacrificing my honor every day.

I couldn't have cared less about the deeper meanings of virtue and integrity, but I did go to great lengths to make sure that my image and reputation remained intact. All I really cared about was that I not pass the point of no return. My father and my older sister were not at all pleased by my association with this cousin of mine, and they made no secret of their disapproval. But since there was nothing they could do to stop her from coming over, their protesting my friendship with her did no good at all. Besides, when it came to figuring out ways to do bad things, I was extremely clever.

If I had not experienced it myself, I would not believe how seriously one person can poison another's soul. This is particularly problematic when a person is young. Listen to me, parents, and beware! My connection with this young woman changed me completely. I lost almost all of my motivation to do good in the world. Plus, the relationship opened the door for me to associate with another person who influenced me to do even more dangerous things.

If only I had associated with worthy companions at that age! If only I had been around peers who modeled devotion to God! Then I might have retained my virtue. Then my soul might have grown strong enough not to stumble and fall. Finally, all fear of God drained out of me, and what was left was this vain concern for my worldly reputation, which tortured me. But as long as I thought no one noticed, this worry did not prevent me from doing all kinds of things to risk offending God and shaming myself.

My behavior began to take on a self-destructive quality. I cannot blame my cousins for this; it was my own fault. After a while, my own wicked inclinations were more than enough to lead me into trouble. Our servants did little to protect me from myself. In fact, they seemed to encourage my wild antics. If any of them had attempted to guide me back on track, I might have paid attention to them and avoided all kinds of grief. But they were as blinded by their own interests as I was by desire.

Still, something in me always prevented me from falling into utter disgrace. The truth is, I was an essentially modest girl who preferred the company of wholesome people. Whenever an opportunity came along to do something truly deceitful, I worried about the effect it might have on my father and my brothers. God, it seems, did not want to lose me. Against my will, he delivered me from danger. But not before I did grave damage to my coveted reputation! My private escapades were turning out to be not as private as I believed.

Not even three months had gone by since I began to experiment with these rebellious behaviors. When my father began to suspect what I had been doing, he sent me off to Our Lady of Grace, a nearby Augustinian convent. It was a place where young people like me—though far less extreme in their misdeeds—could stay out of trouble and receive an education.

We managed to keep the real reason for my leaving concealed from almost everyone except a few close relatives. They had been looking for an excuse to send me away and finally they found one: my sister had married and moved away. I had no mother. A girl in my position could not be expected to live alone without the care of an older woman. The convent was deemed the only proper place for me.

My father's love for me was so unconditional and my skills of deception so refined that he never accepted that my behavior had been anything other than harmless. And so, though I deserved it, I never fell out of my father's favor. It had not been going on long enough for me to arouse too much suspicion. I had made such an effort to conceal my sins and preserve my good name that although my relatives had some idea of what was going on, nothing could be proven.

What I forgot to take into consideration is that nothing is secret from the One who sees all things.

O my Beloved, we do such harm in this world when we forget this! Such harm when we believe that there is anything we can do to dishonor you that you will not notice! I'm sure we would avoid a great deal of suffering if we could just remain mindful of you at all times and protect ourselves, not from other human beings, but from our own negative impulses which lead us to neglect you.

For my first week at Our Lady of Grace, I was miserable. It wasn't the place that upset me, but the fear that everyone suspected what a shallow girl I was. You see, I was already growing weary of the superficial values I had been embracing. And I had never really stopped holding God in my heart. The minute I missed the mark, I was always rushing to atone for it.

In the beginning of my time in the convent, I was terribly restless. But soon I found myself happier than I had ever been at my father's house. My Beloved gave me the grace to delight people wherever I went, and so it was not long before I became a favorite of the nuns. I still had absolutely no desire to be a nun myself. In fact, I felt a tremendous aversion to the prospect. But I was pleased to see such goodness in the nuns who lived in that house. They all seemed to be pure of heart and utterly devoted to a life of prayer.

But in spite of this excellent buffer against worldly temptation, the spirit of evil managed to continue taunting me for a while. My friends on the outside unsettled me with a flurry of secret messages. This kind of communication was forbidden, however, which finally allowed me to settle into the rhythms of monastic life undistracted. The holy inclinations of my early childhood began to return. I could see what a great gift God gives us when he places us in the company of good souls. It seems to me that his Majesty was searching high and low for ways to bring me to himself.

Blessed are you, O Lord, who have put up with me for so long! Amen.

There is one thing that may serve as a partial excuse for my many faults: I believed that my intimacy with that unsavory cousin of mine would come to a natural end with her imminent marriage. My spiritual director and other people have assured me that I never did anything to truly set myself against God.

Soon God sent his light in the form of a certain nun, who oversaw the dormitory where the secular girls slept, to begin showing me the way.

III ✠

Our Lady of Grace

I BEGAN TO ENJOY talking with that nun I mentioned. Our conversations felt sacred. I loved listening to her speak about God. She was simultaneously witty and wise. She never failed to hold my interest.

"Simply reading that part in the Gospel where the Evangelist says, 'Many are called but few are chosen' is what drew me into monastic life," she told me. She described the great treasure the Lord shares with those who leave everything for him.

This excellent friendship started to displace the bad habits that had been forming in me. My thoughts drifted back toward God, and my desire for eternal things was returning. I no longer felt that terrible aversion toward the notion of becoming a nun, a feeling I had been convinced would never leave me. Whenever I witnessed one of the sisters weeping as she prayed or any other overtly spiritual demonstration, I would suffer a wave of envy. To my unending dismay, my own heart was so hardened that even if I read the entire story of Christ's crucifixion, I could not manage to squeeze out a single holy tear.

I stayed at Our Lady of Grace for a year and a half, and it did me a great deal of good. I learned to recite some beautiful prayers. I asked the nuns to intercede with God on my behalf, asking him to transform me in such a way that I would be inclined to give over my life in service to him. He had not yet blessed me with this desire. Still, while I was resistant to the idea of becoming a nun, the prospect of marriage repelled me even more. By the time I left the convent, I had reconciled myself to becoming a nun, but I had decided not to join that particular house. Their spiritual practices were a little too extreme for me. At least, some of the younger girls impressed me this way. If all of the nuns had behaved consistently, it would have been easier for me to find my way.

Plus, I had a close friend, named Juana Suarez, who lived in another convent, the Incarnation. This gave me the idea that if I was going to live as a nun, I might as well do it with her. As you can see, I was more motivated by sensual gratification and vanity than by any genuine inclination to perfect my soul. In fact, though monastic urges arose in me now and then, I couldn't persuade myself to follow through with them.

Around this time, God decided to prepare me for the life that was best for me. It's not that I had been neglecting my spiritual growth, but I obviously needed a little push. He sent me such a serious illness that I was forced to go home to my father's house. When I began to feel better, they took me to see my sister Maria, who lived in a nearby village. My sister loved me so much that if she could have had her way, I never would have left her home. Maria's husband was also very fond of me. At least, he treated me with great tenderness. This is my Beloved's grace: I am appreciated and treated beautifully wherever I go. I do nothing to earn this except to simply be who I am.

My Uncle Pedro lived partway between my father's house and my sister's. He was a sensible, virtuous man whose soul God seemed to be making ready for himself. Uncle Pedro's wife had died, and in the last part of his life, he decided to give up everything and become a monk. I believe he left this world in such a way that he is now basking in the joy of God.

Uncle Pedro wanted me to spend a few days with him and read to him. All he ever wanted to talk about and read about was the glory of God and the vacuity of the world. Even though I was not interested in his books, I pretended to like them just to please him. All my life I have labored to please people. In others this might be a virtue, but in me it has been a serious shortcoming, because I have not been discriminating about it.

O God, save me! In how many ways did you gradually cultivate my soul to be of use to you? And in how many ways did you hold me back, against my will, until I could learn to hold myself back? May you be blessed forever. Amen.

I only stayed with Uncle Pedro for a short time, but the teachings he exposed me to burned an impression on my heart. The word of God, both written and spoken, blended with my uncle's excellent company to remind me of what I had known as a small child: everything is nothing. This world is temporary. All things change and pass away.

I came to grips with the reality that my recent illness had almost killed me. This brush with death scared me. I wondered if I would have gone to hell for the things I had done. And so, even though I still did not have an authentic desire to be a nun, I concluded that I would be better off as one. Little by little, I forced myself to embrace that path.

This struggle went on for three months. I tried to talk myself into it by arguing that the trials and tribulations of monastic life could not possibly be any more difficult than the miseries of purgatory. As it is, I deserved to go straight to hell. Therefore, I reasoned, it was not such a big deal to spend my time in this world as if I were in purgatory if it guaranteed my undisputed entrance into heaven, which is all I had ever really wanted.

This important decision, then, turned out to be motivated more by humble terror than by sublime love. The spirit of evil suggested to me that because I had been raised with wealth and comfort, I would not be able to bear the hardships of religious life. But this just made me think about all that Christ had to go through, and I decided that the least I could do would be to endure a few hardships for his sake. Maybe I believed that Christ would help me to bear those things; I can't remember. I was constantly buffeted by doubts in those days.

I started suffering from high fevers and fainting spells. My health had always been precarious. It was my love of good books that sustained me. The Epistles of Saint Jerome filled me with the courage to tell my father about my decision to become a nun. Such a confrontation was as significant to me as actually putting on the habit! I was such an earnest person that once I had given my word, nothing could have persuaded me to go back on it.

My father was so attached to me that I was never successful in getting him to agree to my plan. Not even the various people I begged to talk to him were able to convince my father to let me go. The best we could get out of him was a reluctant concession that I could do whatever I wanted after he was dead. But I had no faith in my own ability to persevere. I knew that if I did not act quickly, I would lose my resolve. So I found another way to achieve my goal, as I will now describe.

IV

TAKING THE HABIT

D URING THE TIME that I was trying to convince myself to become a nun, I managed to convince my brother Antonio to become a monk. We were in agreement that the world is nothing but an illusion. We decided to take a trip to visit my friend Juana at the Incarnation, and we arranged to meet very early one morning and set out on our journey.

I had already surrendered to entering any convent in which I could best serve God. Finally, the scale had tipped and I was more interested in the good of my soul than in being comfortable. But my primary concern was for my father. I wanted so much for him to approve of my decision, and he didn't.

I remember that when I left my father's house that day, my distress was so intense that I believed it couldn't be greater if I were actually dying. I still really believe this. It felt like every bone in my body was being wrenched apart. Since my love of God did not compare to the intensity of my love for my family, the strain on my heart was almost more than I could bear. Nothing I could tell myself was enough to keep me on course. I was going to require divine assistance, which I did receive. The Lord gave me the fortitude to fight against myself, and I was able to follow through with my plan.

The moment I took the habit, the Beloved demonstrated to me the great rewards he grants to those who wage war against their small selves in service to him. But my inner battles were invisible to everyone else. No one guessed that my taking vows was motivated by anything less than pure desire. As it turned out, entering this new life filled me with a joy so complete that it has never left me. God transmuted the aridity of my soul into the deepest tenderness.

Everything about the religious life delighted me. I would be perfectly content merely sweeping the floors. All of a sudden, it would occur to me that the time I was spending on these simple tasks was the same time I used to waste indulging and decorating myself. When I realized that I was now free of these things, a new wave of joy rose in my heart. I was shocked by its intensity and could not imagine where it came from.

All I have to do is remember moments like these and I realize that there is nothing, no matter how difficult, that I would hesitate to do for my Beloved if it were put before me. Experience has shown me that if I bolster my determination for his sake alone, he will bless me not with increased certainty but with deeper doubt. Then, when I achieve my goal, the reward is all the sweeter. Not in the world to come, but in this very lifetime.

Only those who have tasted these joys can understand what I mean. I have had many such experiences. Some involved very serious matters. And so, if I were asked for my advice, I would say this: if a worthy inspiration arises in you, never hesitate to manifest it. Do not let fear rule your actions. If you give yourself over to God and practice detachment, there is no reason to be afraid that things won't turn out. God is all-powerful. May he be blessed forever. Amen.

Enough. O Supreme Good! O my Refuge! All the blessings you have given me up till now should be enough for me. After all, your mercy and your magnificence have guided me through so many winding paths to this place of safety. I am surrounded by those who live only to serve you, who inspire me to grow in greater service to you.

When I remember the profound determination with which I made my vows and the sweet satisfaction I felt when I gave myself to you, my Beloved, in holy matrimony, I can barely go on. I cannot speak of this without crying. And my tears should be tears of blood. My heart should shatter. Even that would not be enough to demonstrate the sorrow I feel for the terrible ways I have treated you since that day so long ago.

Now I think that maybe I was right to have resisted such an honor, since I have taken it for granted so badly. But you, my Beloved, were willing to wait almost twenty years for me—during which time I made poor use of your many blessings—because you knew that eventually I would come around. It seems as if I made a point of breaking every promise I made to you, although that was never my conscious intention.

Actually, when I look back on all this, I have no idea what my intentions were. All it does is prove the difference between your nature and mine, my Spouse. My only solace in the face of this shame is the knowledge that I have served as a living example to the multitudes of your tender mercies. I can't think of anyone to better illustrate the radiance of your compassion than myself, I who buried the blessings you had begun to give to me under the shroud of my bad deeds.

O my Creator! It would be useless for me to try to make excuses. I have no one but myself to blame. I could never repay you even a fraction of the boundless love you have shown me. Maybe if I had tried, my effort would have remedied this broken situation. But I did not deserve a remedy, nor have I been lucky enough to receive one. And so, my Beloved, may you take mercy on me now.

My new life brought many changes, including in my diet, which affected my health. Although I was exceedingly happy, this was not enough to cure me. I kept fainting all the time, and the frequent pains in my heart alarmed everyone who witnessed them. I spent my entire first year at the Incarnation suffering from innumerable mysterious ailments. At least my poor health did not leave me with much energy left over to offend God.

I began to spend more time unconscious than awake. My condition grew so serious that my father was absolutely determined to find me a cure. Our local doctors were out of ideas, and so my father arranged to take me to a healer who lived in my sister's village and had a reputation for successfully treating difficult diseases.

The Incarnation was not cloistered, so Juana, who was senior nun there, was able to accompany me to Maria's house, where I was to stay during my course of treatment. The healing was supposed to begin in early summer, but I left the Incarnation to go to my sister's in late fall so that I would not have to keep coming and going. During the year that I was there, I spent three months undergoing treatments so drastic that they nearly killed me. I don't know how I survived. Actually, my constitution took such a beating from these so-called cures that their effects did permanent damage, as you will see.

On the way to my sister's village, we stopped in to see my Uncle Pedro. He gave me a copy of *The Third Spiritual Alphabet* by Francisco de Osuna. This a book is all about the Prayer of Recollection. In the past year, I had realized what harm my appetite for romance novels had done to my soul, and I had begun to develop a tremendous appreciation for spiritual books. Since I did not know a thing about the practice of contemplative prayer or how to go about recollecting my senses and my thoughts, I was thrilled to find a book that told me exactly what to do.

I set out on the path of contemplation with all my might. By now, God had begun to give me the gift of tears, and I would spend hours in solitude, reading and crying. I went to confession frequently. With only my book to guide me, I did the best I could. I couldn't find a spiritual master who understood me, though I spent the next twenty years searching for one. This lack of guidance hurt me; I was constantly backsliding and almost lost my way completely. It would have been helpful if there had been someone who could at least have prevented me from offending God.

During these nine months of isolation, his Majesty began to bless me with so many spiritual gifts that I managed to navigate my soul to safety, though not as skillfully as I thought I should. My book indicated that by this point in my practice of prayer, I ought to have gone beyond any opportunity for missing the mark, but it seemed to me that this degree of consciousness was impossible. I was especially reluctant to commit grave errors during this period. Oh, if only I had always been so mindful! But I was careless about avoiding minor transgressions, and this complacency is what ruined me.

Still, the Beloved was so generous to me along my way that he actually led me to the Prayer of Quiet. Once, I even entered the Prayer of Union. At the time, I had no idea what either of these states meant or how deeply I should cherish them. If I had understood these blessings, it would have done me a great deal more good. It's true that my experience of union may not have lasted any longer than it takes to recite a single Ave Maria, but the effects were so powerful and lingered for so long that I was convinced that I had succeeded in rising above the world altogether, even though I was barely twenty years old. I remember pitying those who were still attached to earthly things, even things that were righteous.

When I was in prayer, I would try to keep Jesus Christ, our Lord and our Good, present within me. I would think about a scene in his life and then try to picture it with my mind's eye. But what I liked best was to read good books. This is because God did not give me much talent for figuring things out with my intellect or making good use of my imagination. In fact, my imagination was so clumsy that no matter how hard I tried to meditate on the Lord's humanity, I could never quite succeed.

Some people try to harness this conceptual emptiness as a way of attaining the contemplative state. Maybe if they persevere in this practice, they get there quicker. But it's an arduous and painful path. If the will has nothing to occupy it and the heart has no object to engage it, the soul is left with neither support nor motivation. Her solitude and aridity are excruciating. And her thoughts fall into utter turmoil.

People with this sort of disposition need to have a purer conscience than those who are capable of working things out conceptually. A person who ponders the nature of the world and reflects on how much he owes to the One who loves him, who suffered for his sake, will find himself equipped with the tools he needs to defend himself against his own dangerous thoughts and to avoid occasions for error. A person who is incapable of formulating concepts in prayer is at much higher risk and should compensate for this by reading more, since he has no other source of guidance.

The nonconceptual path is so harrowing that any spiritual director who compels a person to practice contemplative prayer and yet forbids such a person to support himself by reading is placing him in great peril. Even just a small amount of reading will help substitute for the mental prayer he can't seem to practice. Good books are an aid in recollection. What I mean is that if a person is incapable of engaging his intellect or imagination in prayer and is not allowed to read holy books, he will be unable to sustain his practice for very long and will probably endanger his very health and well-being.

Looking back, I can see that it was a blessing that God did not send me a spiritual teacher during that time. If he had, I don't think I would have been willing to endure this internal aridity and this inability to meditate for eighteen years. During all that time, I never dared to sit down to pray unless I had a book close at hand. My soul was as terrified of praying without a book as it would have been if thrown unarmed onto a raging battlefield. Books were my companions, my consolation, my shield against the explosion of thoughts.

If I didn't have a book, I would suffer from terrible aridity. The minute I found myself without something to read, my soul would become immediately agitated and my mind would start to wander. But as soon as I started reading, the words acted like bait to lure my soul and my thoughts began to collect themselves again. Sometimes it was enough just to know that I had a book beside me; I didn't even have to open it. Sometimes I read just a little, sometimes a lot, depending on the mercy of God.

It seems to me that as long as I could be alone with my books in those days, there was no danger of being deprived of that blessing. Actually, by the grace of God, I would probably have done just as well with the guidance of an actual teacher or some other person who could have advised me about how to flee from opportunities for error and, if I stumbled into them, how to get back out.

In those days, if the spirit of evil had attacked me head-on, I believe I would never have missed the mark again. As it is, the spirit of evil was so subtle and I was so weak that my loftiest resolutions did me almost no good. Later as I began to dedicate myself to serving God, he rewarded me for this same determination with the patience I needed to endure serious illnesses.

Again and again, I find myself in awe of God's great goodness. Again and again, my soul has rejoiced in his magnificence and his mercy. May he be blessed for everything! I have clearly seen that he has never failed to reward me, even in this lifetime, for any of my good intentions. No matter how flawed or feeble my deeds may have been, this Beloved of mine has taken them and perfected them, polishing and giving them worth. The minute I commit any errors, he hides them. Even if someone does witness my transgressions, his Majesty renders that person blind and wipes her memories clean. He sugarcoats my imperfections and makes some small virtue of mine—which he himself gave to me in the first place, practically forcing me to accept—absolutely resplendent.

I'd like to get back to what I have been ordered to do. But first, I must mention again that I lack the intelligence to offer any accurate description of how my Beloved handled me in those days. I forget to reflect on what I owe him. I forget to acknowledge my own ingratitude and weakness. May he be forever blessed, who has put up with me for so long! Amen.

V

Illness and Patience

I FORGOT to mention that during the year of my monastic initiation, I suffered terrible anxiety about insignificant incidents. For instance, people would often blame me for things that were not my fault. I did not handle this well. In fact, it caused me deep distress. The only reason I was able to endure being unjustly accused was because I was generally so happy being a nun. Sometimes the others would catch me praying alone and weeping over my sins. They would jump to the conclusion that I was discontented, and they would say so. This was not true. I loved everything about religious life.

I craved admiration and I could not bear to be misunderstood. I was meticulous about everything I did, and I considered this to be a virtuous trait. Not that my impeccable behavior should have gotten me off the hook. Believe me, I knew how to find something to please me in any situation. Nor is ignorance any excuse for my shortcomings. It is true that the Incarnation was not exactly strict; I suppose I could place some of the blame on that. But being flawed, I had a tendency to go after what I knew to be bad and neglect what was good.

There was a nun in our community at that time who was suffering from a very serious and agonizing ailment. Intestinal obstructions had created open sores in her stomach. She couldn't keep any food down. Her health rapidly deteriorated and soon she was dead. I noticed that the other sisters were terrified of this disease. But I found myself envying the nun's incredible patience. I begged God to send me whatever illness he chose, as long as it would instill that kind of patience in me. I

In joyful remembrance of my
GOLDEN JUBILEE
1957–2007
Sr. Mercedes of the Immaculate Conception

don't think I was afraid of being sick. I was so hungry for heavenly blessings that I was willing to obtain them by any means necessary.

It surprises me to recall this. Although I had not yet fallen as deeply in love with God as I have since I embarked on a life of prayer, there was enough light for me to see that temporary things are trivial and pass away. Somehow I knew that the blessings that come from letting these things go last forever.

His Majesty was listening to me. Less than two years later, I became seriously ill. It was not the same disease that had killed the nun, but I believe it was just as painful and difficult to bear. I will now tell you about something that happened during the three-year period I was suffering from this illness.

As I said, I stayed with my sister while I was waiting for my treatment to begin. When the time came, my father, my sister, and my friend Juana, with the utmost care and concern for my comfort, took me away. Juana was that nun who had accompanied me when I first left the convent and stayed by my side because she loved me so much. It was during this time that the spirit of evil began to really agitate my soul. But as you will see, God turned the whole thing into a great blessing.

There was a young priest who lived in the village where I went for my treatment. He was from a good family and was an extremely intelligent man. He was well educated but not overly so. I began to go to him for confession. Men of learning have always attracted me, but half-learned men have done great harm to my soul. I never seem to find any men who are as learned as I would like them to be. Experience has taught me that men with no knowledge at all are less dangerous than those with only a little. If they lead virtuous and holy lives, they are better off not knowing anything. Such men are not inclined to trust themselves, nor would I trust them myself, until they have checked in with men of real learning.

A real man of learning has never led me astray. Not that the half-learned men meant to deceive me; they simply didn't know any better. But I thought they did and that my only obligation was to believe them. They spoke ambiguously and gave me no boundaries. Of course, I see now that if they had been strict with me, I would have just ignored them and looked for others who told me what I wanted to hear. That's how wicked I am.

These spiritual teachers would tell me that my minor sins were no sins at all and that my major ones were only minor. This did me such harm that I feel compelled to take this opportunity to warn other seekers to avoid such relationships. But I had no excuse before God. I was well aware that I was doing things that were wrong, and this knowledge alone should have been sufficient to keep me from doing them.

I believe that God allowed these men to misguide me and lead me astray as a consequence of my own transgressions. I, in turn, led many others astray, repeating what my teachers had told me. I blundered through this blindness for more than seventeen years until a Dominican friar named Vicente Barrón disabused me of my illusions. Father Vicente was an extremely learned man. He and certain Jesuit priests scared me by convincing me that I was building my life on seriously faulty principles. I'll say more about this later.

When I started making my confessions to that priest I mentioned, he developed an extreme affection for me. Maybe this is because ever since I had become a nun I had very little to repent, especially in comparison with what I had later! It's not that there was really anything wrong with his fondness for me; the problem was that there was just too much of it.

"Not only do I understand that there is nothing I could do to persuade you to commit any grave offense against God," he assured me, "but I would never dream of trying."

We spoke a great deal about this. But I was so madly in love with God at this time that all I ever wanted to talk about was him. My passion for God was childlike, and it mystified my friend.

Because of his great desire for me, he began to confide in me. His was no small problem. It turns out that this priest had been intimately involved for a number of years with a local woman. Everyone in the village knew about the affair, but he continued to celebrate the Mass anyway. Even though he had lost his honor and his good name, no one dared to denounce him.

I felt sorry for this man because I was so fond of him. I was so superficial and blind in those days that I thought it was a virtue to be loyal and grateful to anyone who liked me. Damn such loyalty when it distracts a person from her loyalty to God! This is a common mistake people make in this world, and yet it never ceases to baffle me. Even though it is God to whom we owe gratitude for all good things, we do not hesitate to act against him, while we are reluctant to do anything that might strain our human friendships.

O blindness of the world! May it serve you, my Beloved, to replace my imperfect appreciation for worldly relationships with unmitigated gratitude for you. But I have exhibited the exact opposite behavior. That's how wicked I am.

I started asking around about my priest. That's when I began to realize what deep trouble the poor man had gotten himself into and to see that it was not altogether his fault. It turns out that this wretched woman had cast a spell on him! She gave him a little copper amulet and begged him to wear it around his neck as a symbol of their love. No one had the power to persuade him to take the thing off.

Now, I must say, I do not believe in the story of bewitchment. I am simply recounting an incident I witnessed as a warning to you men to be on your guard against women like this. Since women in general are more compelled than men are to be honest and true, a woman who is willing to sacrifice her virtue is thoroughly untrustworthy. The devil whispers in her ear, enflaming her desire, and off she goes. Such women are willing to shame themselves before God for the pleasure of following their own will.

I know I'm not perfect, but I have never tried to manipulate anyone like that. Even if I had the power to force someone's affection for me, I wouldn't want to! Fortunately, God has kept me from making this kind of mistake. If he had abandoned me to my own impulses, however, I might well have done wrong in this regard, as I have in so many others. I'm simply not to be trusted.

When I found out about the spell, I began to show this man greater affection. Although my intentions were good, my actions were bad. Bad means, no matter how small, never justify good ends, no matter how great. I mostly spoke to this priest about God. This must have benefited him to some extent, but I believe that his love for me helped him more. To please me, he ended up giving me the copper amulet, and I immediately threw it into the river.

After this, the priest was like a man awakening from a dream. As he began to recall everything he had been doing during his years of involvement with that woman, he was shocked and disappointed with himself. He felt loathing for the woman who had led him to his downfall. His intense devotion to the Blessed Mother seemed to have helped him a great deal. The feast day of the Immaculate Conception had always been very important to him. Finally, he cut off the affair once and for all. And he never tired of giving thanks to God for showing him the light.

Exactly one year after the day I met the priest, he died. He had spent a lifetime actively serving God. I never thought that there was anything incorrect about his affection for me, although it could have been purer. There were times when, if we had not been so close to God, we might have engaged in some serious offenses. But I would not have allowed myself to do anything I thought might lead to mortal sin. I think he realized this, and it made him love me all the more.

I believe that all men are attracted to women whom they perceive as being inclined toward virtue. Even women who have no aspirations beyond this world will get more from men by maintaining their integrity. I'll elaborate on this later. I have no doubt that this priest is now on the road to liberation. He died a very holy death, completely free of the errors he had committed. I guess it was the Lord's will for him to be redeemed in this way.

I stayed in that village for three months. With my delicate constitution, I suffered terribly. I barely survived the radical treatment. At the end of the two months, the cure had almost killed me. That pain in my heart, which was the reason I had gone there in the first place, was much worse. Sometimes it felt as if sharp teeth were biting into me. My pain was so intense that the people taking care of me were afraid that I was going to lose my mind. My energy plummeted. I took only liquid because I was nauseated all the time and couldn't bear to eat solid food. I ran a constant fever. They had been giving me purgatives every day for almost a month, and I was wasting away. I was so constricted that my nerves began to shrink, causing me such excruciating pain that I could not sleep day or night. I was utterly miserable.

It became apparent to my father that the healer was doing me no good, and he took me away. We went back to the regular doctors, but they had given up on me. They concluded that in addition to all my other ailments, I was suffering from tuberculosis, and there was nothing they could do for me. This diagnosis did not bother me nearly as much as did the constant pain that racked me from head to foot. The doctors themselves admitted that nerve pain is unbearable. And since my nerves had collapsed, I would indeed have been incapable of enduring the suffering if not for the realization that my condition was of my own making.

I battled all of these problems at the same time for more than three months. It was excruciating. In retrospect, it seems impossible that I survived. I am equally amazed and also grateful that his Majesty gave me the blessing of great patience. It is clear that this gift came directly from God. Reading the story of Job in *The Morals of Saint Gregory* bolstered my patience tremendously. I even slept with them! The Lord used this text to prepare me for the suffering I had to undergo. It also helped that I had begun to cultivate contemplative practice, because this enabled me to sit with things as they are. All my conversations were with God. I continually carried the words of Job in my mind: "Since we have received good things at the hand of the Lord, shall we not suffer evil things?" I repeated this frequently, and it gave me strength.

It was time for the August Feast of Our Lady. I had been in agony since April, but the last three months had been the worst. I had always been inclined to go to confession often, but now I was confessing at every opportunity. They all thought that this was because I was afraid of dying, so my father, thinking he was protecting me from mental distress, decided to forbid me from going anymore.

Oh, too much earthly love! My father was a good Catholic and a very wise man, so it was not a matter of ignorance that prevented him from seeing what good the practice of penance had been doing me. Nevertheless, despite his intention, his stance could have done me great harm.

That night I had a seizure that left me unconscious for almost four days. They administered the sacrament of unction, and from hour to hour and moment to moment, they expected me to die. Over and over, they recited the creed to me as if I could understand! At one point, they seemed to conclude that I was dead, because I actually found wax on my eyelids when I regained consciousness.

My father was terribly distressed about having prevented me from going to confession. Many tears were shed for me, and many prayers were said to God on my behalf. Blessed be the One who heard them! They dug a grave for me back at the Incarnation and were waiting a day and a half for my body. In another monastery of our order, far away, they had already performed the last rites for me.

But it pleased the Lord for me to return to consciousness. I immediately wanted to go to confession. When I received Communion, I couldn't stop crying. It was not only that I was moved and distressed by the possibility that I had in any way offended God. That remorse in itself would have been enough to save my soul. No, what upset me most was the realization that the men who had attempted to guide me had misled me and tried to convince me that my sins were minor, when in fact they had been grave. I now saw clearly that I had used this guidance as an excuse for inexcusable acts. My suffering was so unbearable, I could hardly form thoughts. Still, I think I managed to offer a complete confession of all the ways I had forsaken my God.

There is a certain blessing, among so many others, that his Majesty has given me; ever since I first began to speak with him, I have never kept back anything. If I thought I might have committed any error, even a minor one, I confessed it. But I do believe that if I had died back then without having had access to proper confession, my salvation would have been questionable. This is partly because my spiritual guides were only half-learned men and also because I myself was such a mess. There were many other reasons as well.

When I come to this point in my story, I find myself so stunned to remember how my Beloved brought me back to life that I am trembling inside. It seems to me that it would be a good thing, my soul, for you to take a look at the danger from which your Lord delivered you. That way, if love is not enough to keep you from offending him, you will at least be motivated by awe. There were a thousand times he might have let you die and when you were in an even greater state of peril than you found yourself in that day.

I do not believe I am exaggerating when I say "a thousand," although the person who has ordered me to tell my life story has repeatedly urged me to be moderate when I recount my sins. But I have already made my transgressions sound far too innocent. For love of God, I beg this man not to excuse a single one of my faults, because they only serve to reveal the magnificence of God and his willingness to suffer for our souls. May he be blessed forever! And may his Majesty be pleased to know that I would swallow myself whole before I would ever stop loving him.

VI

SAINT JOSEPH'S CURE

I EMERGED FROM that four-day fit in a state of such unbearable torment that only the Lord can know the truth of what I went through. I had bitten my tongue to pieces. Not a morsel of food had passed my lips in so long that I was too weak to swallow, and I choked when I tried to take even a sip of water. It felt like all my limbs were out of joint and my mind was in a total fog.

Not only that, but the suffering I had endured during those four days left me all twisted up like a pile of knotted ropes. I had no more ability to move my hand or foot than a dead person has, unless someone else moved it for me. Actually, I think I was able to move one finger on my right hand. I was in such a pitiful state that I could not bear for anyone to see me like that. I felt so bruised that my friends and family had to carry me around on a sheet. One person would take up one corner and another person would take up the other. This went on until Easter.

Since I couldn't bear to be touched, the only time I had any relief was when I was left alone for a little while. After resting in solitude, I began to think that I was getting well. I was very relieved whenever my pain let up, simply because I was beginning to worry that my patience was failing me. I still suffered from terrible bouts of fever and chills and unrelenting nausea.

I was desperate to return to the Incarnation, so my family finally relented and took me there. The nuns, who had been expecting to receive a dead body, were pleased to be welcoming a living woman instead. But I was in such bad shape that I looked worse than a dead person! I was nothing but skin and bones by this time, and I cannot even begin to describe how weak I was.

It took eight months for me to recover from this paralysis and the illness that accompanied it. Although I continued to improve, the paralysis lingered for almost three years. When I began to get around by crawling on my hands and knees, I praised God. I accepted all this and eventually came to bear my condition with genuine joy. After all, it was a vast improvement over what I went through at first. I had surrendered to the will of God, even if he were to leave me like that forever.

I think my greatest wish was that I could get better just so that I could practice solitary prayer again as I had been taught. It was impossible to be alone in the convent infirmary. I was unwavering in my commitment to confession. I spoke about God constantly and in such a way that everyone I talked to was uplifted and amazed by the patience the Lord had given me. It was obvious that this was a gift from the Beloved's hand, because without it I could not possibly have endured such terrible suffering with such pure contentment.

In prayer, God granted me the grace of his mercy. This was a wonderful blessing, because it helped me to realize what it is to love him. I began to feel the holy virtues flowing back into me, although as it turned out, not strongly enough to hold me up in righteousness.

I made it my practice to avoid speaking badly of anyone, ever. Whenever I was tempted, I would simply remind myself not to say anything about someone else that I would not want someone to say about me. I was uncompromising in my commitment to this value. Of course, I was not perfect, and certain difficult situations came up that strained my resolve to the breaking point. Still, this was my customary way of behaving, and those who spent time with me were so struck by it that they made it their practice too. People realized that when they were with me, they could turn their backs and be perfectly safe. This was true not only for the women I lived with at the Incarnation but also for my friends, my relatives, and my students.

But I have set a very bad example in other areas, and I'm going to have to be accountable to God for those. Please forgive me, your Majesty, for all the trouble I have caused. Know that my negative actions do not in any way reflect my positive intentions.

My longing for solitude continued. I still loved to read good books. The only conversation I found worthwhile was conversation about God. Whenever I encountered anyone who wanted to talk about God with me, it gave me more delight and sheer recreation than any worldly pleasures (which are actually empty) ever could. I took communion and made confession as often as possible. I remember that sometimes I avoided prayer because I was afraid of facing my disloyalty to God and the terrible pain this would cause me. The very thought that I might have done anything to offend my Beloved was a severe punishment in itself.

This anxiety intensified to such a degree that I do not know what to compare it to. It was not a matter of fear, because I was just as likely to suffer from this kind of distress when I considered the blessings the Lord had given me in prayer as when I reflected on the mistakes I had made. If I thought about all he had done for me, I couldn't help but notice how little I had offered in return. I couldn't bear to face this, and I would cry over my many faults.

But my tears only made me angry with myself. Had my remorse stopped me from falling whenever an opportunity presented itself? Were all my resolutions and effort doing me any good? This weeping of mine struck me as fraudulent. All it did was highlight my imperfection, because tears of repentance are a gift from God and I was wasting them.

I always tried to confess my transgressions as soon as I committed them, and I did everything I could to return to a state of grace. But the problem was that I did not know how to cut off my sinful inclinations at their root. Nor were my confessors much help in the matter. If they had told me that these long religious conversations of mine were thinly veiled indulgences, I would have stopped them immediately. I would never have consciously risked missing the mark for even a single day.

In prayer, I would be overcome with awe of God. A sign that I was motivated more by love than by fear was that I never thought about retribution. My anxiety was always enfolded by love. The whole time I was sick, I was hypervigilant over my conscience, careful to avoid anything resembling spiritual error. Dear God, how I yearned for good health so that I might serve you better! This desire itself became the cause of my undoing.

I was so young when I became seriously paralyzed. As soon as I realized that earthly doctors were unable to cure me, I turned to heaven for healing. Because even though I carried my illness with joy, I still preferred to get better. I sometimes thought that if I were to recover my health only to go out and miss the mark all over again, it would be better to stay sick. But I still believed that I could be of greater service to my God if I were well. This is how we deceive ourselves: we do not surrender entirely to God's will, even though he is the one who knows what is best for us.

I began to offer devotions during Mass. I stuck to prescribed prayers, because I distrusted alternative expressions of worship. Women, especially, love to invent ceremonies. I could never stand these rituals. It has been confirmed to me since then that such practices are superstitious and inappropriate.

I chose the glorious Saint Joseph as my master and advocate and entrusted myself to him completely. I found that this great father and lord of mine solved the problem of my health and also delivered me from bigger issues, like the loss of my soul and my honor. He freely gave me greater blessings than I could ever ask of him.

Even now, I can't think of a single instance in which he has neglected to give me anything I have asked for. It is amazing to see all the mercy God has shown me and the perils, both physical and spiritual, from which he has rescued me through this blessed saint. The Lord seems to have given other saints the grace to fulfill certain needs, but in my experience, this glorious saint comes to our aid in all areas.

When Christ walked this earth, Joseph was his guardian; as a boy, Jesus called him "father" and obeyed his commands. It seems to me that Christ wants us to know that in heaven he still does everything Joseph asks. Other people I have advised have experienced a similar response when they commended themselves to this saint.

I used to observe Saint Joseph's feast with great ceremony. I was obsessed with the details. Although my intentions were good, I can see now that I celebrated this holy day with more vanity than spirituality. Another negative trait of mine was that whenever the Lord gave me the grace to do anything well, I would do it imperfectly instead, replete with mistakes. I was highly skilled at being finicky and vain! May the Lord forgive me.

I wish I could convince everyone to be devoted to this glorious saint. I have experienced the innumerable blessings that come through him from God. I have never known anyone who sincerely revered him and offered particular vows to him who did not make spiritual progress. Saint Joseph comes to the aid of those who commend themselves to him. Year after year, I have made some request of him on his feast day and he has always granted it. If my appeal were twisted in any way, he would straighten it out for me.

If I were a person with the authority to do so, I would not hesitate to describe in great detail the many favors this magnificent saint has given to me and to others. But since I am constrained by my order to write about certain things at great length and to minimize others, I will have to keep this part much more brief than I would like. In other words, I am going to have to act like someone who has no sense of discrimination and doesn't know what is good!

For the love of God, I ask anyone who does not believe me to put my claims about Saint Joseph to the test. Then you will see for yourself the great goodness that comes when you offer devotion to this sublime patriarch. How could anyone think about the Queen of Angels and how she suffered for the child Jesus and not give thanks to Saint Joseph for the way he helped them both? People of prayer should foster special affection for him. If you cannot find a guide to teach you contemplative practice, appeal to Saint Joseph, and I assure you that this wondrous master will not lead you astray.

I pray that I have not made a mistake in daring to speak of Saint Joseph like this. While I have always made a great display of my devotion to him, I have never managed to successfully imitate and serve him. He cured me of my paralysis and gave me the power to stand up and walk again because of who he is. I, on the other hand, have misused this gift because of who I am.

Who could have predicted that I would fall so soon after receiving so many gifts from God? After his Majesty blessed me with the very virtues that awakened my desire to serve him? After I had found myself almost dead and in grave spiritual danger? After he had raised me up, body and soul, filling everyone with amazement that I had survived?

What is this, my Lord? We live a perilous life. Here I am, writing this account, and through your grace and mercy, I could easily join Saint Paul in saying (though I would not say it half as well), "For it is not I now who live, but you, my Creator, who lives in me."

It has been quite a few years now that, as far as I can understand, you have held me by the hand. In every way, little and big, I have always wanted to place your will before mine, and I have repeatedly resolved to do so. Over the years, you have tested these desires and resolutions of mine. Without even being aware of it, your Majesty, I must have disappointed you again and again.

There is nothing I would not do for love of you. In fact, you have already helped me to accomplish many things. I don't desire this world or worldly things. Nothing seems to make me happy unless it comes from you. Everything else feels like a heavy cross. Maybe I'm wrong. Maybe I don't really want what I say I want. But you know, my Beloved, that I am not lying. I am afraid, with good reason, that you may give up on me again. I am well aware how totally dependent I am on your grace to compensate for my lack of strength and virtue and to help me not give up on you.

Please don't abandon me, my Beloved! Not now, while I am thinking all these things about myself. I really don't know what makes us want to keep living when life is so uncertain. I used to think, my Lord, that it would be impossible for me to forsake you, and look how many times I have done so. I can't help but be afraid, because when you withdrew from me even just a little, I fell flat on my face.

May you be forever blessed! Even though I have neglected you, you have continuously offered me your hand and helped me back up. Often, my Lord, I refused that hand of yours. Often, my Lord, you would call me again, and again I would refuse. This is what I would like to talk about next.

VII ✠

PRISONER OF THE PARLOR

THIS IS WHEN I began to indulge in distraction after distraction, conceit on top of conceit, vice compounded by vice. I gave in to so many subtle and destructive temptations during this time, and my soul drifted so far away on the tides of vanity that I was afraid to approach God again. Prayer is an intimate friendship with the Divine, and I did not feel worthy of such intimacy. My shame grew in proportion to the abundance of my errors. The more I transgressed, the less comfort and joy I was able to derive from holy things.

It was clear to me, my Beloved, that my joy was failing me because I was failing you. The spirit of evil, disguised as humility, led me into the most insidious deception of all: fear of prayer. I felt utterly lost. I considered myself to be the most wicked person alive. I concluded that I would be better off giving up on silent contemplation and starting to pray like everybody else. It was time to stop conversing privately with God and instead recite the vocal prayers exactly as I had learned them. After all, any outward display of silent prayer only deceived others into thinking I was good and holy, when in fact I was the opposite.

My decline in virtue had nothing to do with the house where I lived; it was not their fault. I managed to manipulate everyone's good opinion of me, but I didn't mean to. I would never dream of pretending to be a good Christian! I have had many faults, but I have never, praise God, been an egomaniac or a hypocrite, as far as I know. The minute I ever felt the stirrings of arrogance inside myself, it would make me so upset that the devil would flee in consternation and I would be left better off.

Maybe if God had chosen to tempt me in this area as severely as he has in others, I would have developed an overly inflated concept of my own holiness, but he has kept me from falling into this trap. May he be forever blessed! The truth is, I was much more troubled by the notion that people would be fooled by my outward appearance of goodness than that they would see me for who I knew myself to be inside.

There were several reasons why nobody noticed how bad I was. What they observed was that even though I was very young and vulnerable to countless opportunities for missing the mark, I frequently removed myself from the group to pray in solitude. I read a lot and spoke exclusively about God. I liked to have pictures of Christ everywhere, and I requested a chapel of my own that I could fill with sacred objects. I refused to ever speak badly about another person. I did many other things that made me appear to be virtuous. The truth was, I was vain and worldly; I liked it when people held me in high esteem.

Because of my spiritual conduct, they gave me as much freedom as they gave to the older nuns. Even more! They had a great deal of confidence in me, because I never took liberties. I asked permission for everything. I did not sneak out at night to talk to outsiders through crevices in the wall or to hold private discussions with other nuns. I don't think I could ever have brought myself to participate in such secret exchanges, nor did I try, because the Lord held me by the hand.

I tried to consider the ramifications of things. It seemed to me that it would be wrong for me to do anything that would compromise anyone's reputation by engaging in clandestine encounters. After all, they were the ones who were good and I was the bad one. As if any of those other things I was doing were so virtuous! The truth is, though I often acted inappropriately in different areas, it was never as intentional as that kind of misbehavior would have been.

It was probably inappropriate for me to live in a convent that was not cloistered. The lives of those who have not taken a vow of enclosure are less circumscribed than those of cloistered nuns. Most women are good, and enjoying more freedom would not make them any less good. But I am bad, and the only reason this latitude did not lead me straight to hell was that the Lord used his own special ways and remedies to save me from peril.

It seems to me that the more autonomy people are given in spiritual community, the greater their risk of missing the mark. For those who are inclined to be wicked, broad liberty is not an antidote for their weakness but rather a further step on the path to hell. This is not the case in the convent where I live now. There are many women here who serve the Lord in a completely genuine manner. His Majesty cannot fail to help them on their way. Ours is not one of those open convents either; we practice rigorous spiritual discipline here. I'm talking about other religious houses I have been familiar with.

This kind of thing breaks my heart. When a spiritual community engages in the activities of the world, the residents tend to forget their religious obligations. Then the Lord has to call to each of them in a particular way—not once, but over and over—until each remembers why she is there. May God save them and not let them confuse virtue with sin, as I have done so many times!

This is not an easy thing for people to see. The Lord has to take the matter into his own hands. If parents would heed my advice, they would think twice about sending their daughters to a convent, assuming the girls will automatically walk in the way of God, when in fact they are likely to get into more trouble than they would out in the world. They should at least look out for their daughters' reputations.

Parents would be better off letting their children marry someone of a lower status than they would be sending them to convents of this kind. If the young women are genuinely inclined toward devotion, then may God lead them away from what is dangerous and toward all that is good! Otherwise, they might as well stay home. If they want to be wicked there, they cannot hide it for long. In a monastic setting, such behaviors can be concealed for a very long time until, eventually, the Lord himself reveals them.

These girls not only hurt themselves, but their actions have a negative effect on others. Often, though, it's not their fault. The poor creatures are simply trying to fit in. Some girls join a spiritual community hoping to escape this cycle. They think that by withdrawing from the world they will avoid worldly pitfalls and so be able to serve God undistracted. But the next thing they know, they find themselves in ten worlds combined and they don't have any idea how to get out and remedy the situation.

Youth, sensuality, and the spirit of evil conspire to incline these young women toward worldly attachments and to convince them that these things are somehow acceptable. They remind me of those poor atheists who blind themselves to the sacred and then try to convince everyone else that the path they are following is the correct one. But all along a voice deep inside them is whispering the truth.

Oh, what terrible harm! What terrible harm comes to religious people who do not live what they profess. I am speaking now as much of men as of women. There are two paths available to those who enter a religious life: the way of virtue and devotion, and the opposite of virtue and devotion. Unfortunately, both paths seem to be trodden equally. No, I'm wrong; they are not trodden equally. Many more people walk the irreligious path, because it is the broader road and much easier to navigate for those of us inclined to miss the mark.

The true spiritual life is so rare that those who hear the call and begin to follow it ought to be more afraid of the members of their own community than of all the demonic forces that exist. They should carefully conceal their true desire for friendship with God. It is safer to discuss the false connections that the spirit of evil stirs up in religious houses.

I don't know why we are so shocked to hear about all the bad things that happen in spiritual communities. After all, those who are supposed to be modeling virtue to the rest of us have generally drifted so far away from the ancient wisdom that the spirits of the saints have abandoned us. May his Divine Majesty be pleased to remedy this situation as he sees fit.

And so I was misled into thinking that it was harmless for me to indulge in the pseudospiritual conversations I enjoyed so much. It was only later that I discovered that this kind of companionship could be dangerously distracting. I didn't see why such an ordinary custom as receiving visitors at the convent and discussing so-called religious things with them should do my soul any more harm than it did other nuns who were perfectly decent people. I failed to consider that they were better people than I was and what was safe for them was not safe for me. Still, I have no doubt that there is an element of trouble for everyone in this practice, because even if it does not cause damage, it is at least a waste of time.

Once, in the early stages of my acquaintance with someone, the Lord chose to show me that these kinds of relationships were not good for me. He broke through the core of my thick blindness to teach me and show me the way. Christ himself appeared before me, fierce and direct, to tell me exactly what it was that troubled him about these interactions. I saw him more clearly through the eyes of my soul than I ever could have with my physical eyes. This vision had such a powerful impact on me that even now, twenty-six years later, I can still seem to see him standing here. I was so stunned and disturbed by this experience that I never again wanted to see the person who triggered it.

It did me no good to maintain the belief that it was impossible to see with any eyes other than those of the body. It was the spirit of evil that made me think such a thing. It made me wonder if my vision of Christ was a figment of my imagination or, worse, a demonic phenomenon. But I couldn't shake the conviction that this vision came from God and I had not imagined it.

Since the stern form in which Christ had appeared was not pleasing to me, however, I forced myself to lie to myself and I didn't dare discuss the matter with anyone. The spirit of evil returned full force, convincing me that there was no harm in my relationship with that person, and that far from damaging my reputation, our interactions could only enhance it. So I started having these intimate spiritual conversations with him again, and later I received other visitors in the same way.

I wasted years in this insidious diversion. When I was doing it, it never seemed to me to be as bad as it really was, although I sometimes had a clear sense that I was doing something wrong. Still, no one ever distracted me quite as badly as the person I've been speaking about. I was excessively fond of him.

There was another time when I was with that same person, and we saw something like a large toad coming toward us but moving much more swiftly than toads generally do. Other people who were there saw it too. I could not imagine where such a creature could have been hiding and how it could have emerged like that in broad daylight. None of us had ever seen anything like it before. This incident had such a powerful effect on me that it must have concealed a deeper meaning. I have never forgotten this experience either.

O great God! You warned me in so many little ways and with such tender compassion, and how much did I benefit from your efforts? Hardly at all.

There was an older nun in the house where I lived, a distant relative of mine who had been there a long time, whose spiritual practice was extremely disciplined. "These parlor discourses of yours are not healthy," she would warn me sometimes. Not only did I refuse to listen to her, but I became annoyed that she was making something innocent into some kind of scandal.

I mention all this to demonstrate how bad I was and how great God is, since I fully deserved to be punished for my outrageous ingratitude. This way, if it is God's will and pleasure that anyone read this book, they can take it as a warning and not have to make the same mistakes I made. I beg you, for the love of our Lord, don't get caught up in this noxious kind of recreation.

May his Majesty be pleased to allow me to make up here for the many people I have led astray in the past. In the midst of danger, I would assure them that there was nothing wrong. Of course, I would never willingly deceive anyone. My faulty guidance was nothing but an artifact of my own blindness. Without ever dreaming that I was doing so, I was setting a terrible example and causing a great deal of harm.

It is a very common temptation among beginners to try to help other people before they have learned how to take care of themselves. In those early days, when I was still very sick, I fell into that trap. Luckily, the outcome was positive. Because I loved my father so much, I wanted him to benefit from the blessings that I was enjoying from the practice of prayer. There seemed to me no greater gift to share.

So I did my best, by indirect means, to persuade him to pray. I gave him books on the subject. As I have said, my father was a very good man, and this practice captured his heart. Within a few short years, he had made so much progress that all I could do was praise God for it. I was very much encouraged by this. It's not that my father did not suffer great trials along his path, but he handled them with tremendous patience and perseverance. He visited me often, because it comforted him to discuss divine things.

Meanwhile, I was becoming more and more of a wreck. I was no longer praying. I couldn't bear to see that my father still thought I was practicing what I preached. I had somehow convinced myself that refraining from prayer was more truly humble than praying. This became a serious temptation for me and almost caused my ruin. At least when I was practicing prayer, I might offend God one day, but the next day I had the opportunity to recollect myself and turn away from other occasions for missing the mark.

A year had passed since I last prayed, and I finally decided it was time to tell my father the truth about my own practice. When that blessed man came to visit me, it broke my heart to see him laboring under the illusion that I was communing with God as I had before. I admitted that I was not practicing prayer anymore, but I did not tell him the real reason why. I used my ill health as an excuse. Although I had recovered from the worst of my ailments, I have suffered from various maladies, some quite serious, ever since.

Lately, my problems have not been quite as severe, but they still bother me. For instance, I have suffered from nausea and vomiting every morning for twenty years. I cannot eat a thing until afternoon, sometimes even later. Ever since I began taking communion more regularly, I have had to make myself throw up at night before I go to sleep, using feathers or some other trigger, which is terribly uncomfortable. But if I let the nausea go on, I feel even worse.

Nor am I ever entirely free from aches and pains, especially in my heart. Sometimes they are quite intense. The fainting spells, which used to be continuous, are now more rare. And it's been eight years since I was cured of that mysterious paralysis and the high fevers that accompanied it. These illnesses seem so insignificant to me now that I've begun to rejoice in them, thinking that maybe they have served my Beloved in some way.

Since my father never lied himself, he believed me when I told him that I had quit practicing prayer because of my health. By this time, in light of the nature of the things we discussed, I shouldn't have been lying either. I knew quite well that there is no excuse for giving up prayer, but to make my story more convincing, I added that it was all I could do to keep up with my regular religious duties. Not that one needs much physical strength for a practice that demands nothing more than showing up with a loving and constant heart.

Our Lord always provides opportunities for prayer if we choose to take them. I say "always" because, even though sickness and other troubles may sometimes hinder our free access to hours of solitude, there are plenty of other times when we are healthy and can make up for that. We can also pray in the midst of our ordinary activities. And we can even harness our pain itself as a genuine opportunity for prayer by offering up the very thing from which we are suffering and remembering the One for whom we suffer it.

All we need to do is accept our ill health and the thousand other things that happen to us. Prayer is an exercise of love. It is a mistake to believe that if we have no time alone we cannot practice prayer or, for that matter, that when we do have time alone we will use it to pray. With a little care, we can draw great blessings from the occasions when the Beloved sends us trials that deprive us of time we had set aside for prayer. When my conscience was clear, I had no trouble uncovering these blessings.

Because my father loved and respected me, he believed everything I said. In fact, he felt sorry for me. But he had reached such a high state of prayer that he began to spend less and less time visiting me. He would leave shortly after arriving. He felt that to linger was a waste of time. Since I was busy wasting time on various vanities, I did not take this very seriously.

My father was not the only person I tried to lead into a life of contemplative prayer, even though I myself was more interested in trivial matters. When I noticed certain nuns reciting vocal prayers, I taught them how to practice silent prayer. I would help them along and share my books with them. As I have mentioned, ever since I first began to pray, I have had this desire for others to serve God. It seemed to me that since I was no longer serving my Beloved as I knew I should, the least I could do was to not waste the knowledge his Majesty had given me and help others to serve him through me. Look how blind I was! I was trying to save others while letting myself get completely lost.

Around this time, my father became very ill and eventually died. I went home to take care of him. Vanity had rendered my soul sicker than disease had rendered my father's body. However, I must say that during the entire period when I was wasting time showing off in the convent parlor, I never, to my knowledge, committed any grave error. If I had believed I was in any way offending God, I would have stopped immediately.

My father's illness was deeply distressing to me. I hope that I repaid him a small part of all he did for me when I was sick. In spite of my grief, I forced myself to stay busy. Even though in losing him I was losing all the goodness and comfort in my life, I was determined not to let my anguish show, and so I behaved as if I didn't have a care in the world until the day he died. I loved that man so much that as I saw his death approaching, I felt like my own soul was being ripped from my body.

I cannot help but praise the Lord for the good death my father died. He welcomed death. After receiving extreme unction, he offered us final words of wisdom. "Please, my children, pray for God to have mercy on my soul," he said. "And serve God always. All things come to an end," he reminded us.

Then he began to weep. "I would have liked to have been a friar," he said. "I regret not having served God in that way."

I see now that God gave my father a glimpse of his impending death a full two weeks before he died. Until that time, while he was certainly not feeling well, I don't think he believed that he was dying. But afterward, even though he felt much better and his doctors assured him that he was going to be fine, he ignored them and got to work putting his soul in order.

My father's primary affliction was a severe and unrelenting pain in his spine. Sometimes it was so acute it was like torture. Since the image of Christ carrying the cross on his back was so meaningful to my father, I suggested to him that maybe his Majesty wanted him to share some of the pain that Jesus endured. He took such comfort in this notion that I never heard him complain again.

For the last three days of his life, my father was mostly unconscious. But on the last day, the Lord brought him to full consciousness. We were amazed. We began to recite the creed aloud with him. He remained alert until halfway through, and then he just quietly slipped away. There he lay, looking like an angel. It seems to me that my father had a truly angelic character and soul.

I'm not sure why I've told you all this, except that maybe I still feel guilty. With the legacy of goodness my father left, in terms of the quality of both his life and his death, I should have made more of an effort to improve myself. "There is no doubt that your father went directly to heaven," the highly educated Dominican Father Vicente Barrón said. He had been my father's confessor for many years and he praised the purity of my father's conscience.

Father Barrón was a very good man, a man in awe of God. I went to him for confession and he was a real help to me. He took great care to point out to me the dangerous spiritual waters I was heading for and set my soul back on track. He had me meet with him every two weeks, and gradually I began to open up to him and tell him about my path of prayer.

"Never give up this practice, because it can do you nothing but good," he told me. So I began to engage in prayer again, and I have never ceased.

This did not stop me, however, from continuing to miss the mark. My life felt very heavy to me, because prayer illumined all my faults. God was calling to me in one ear, and the world beckoned in the other. All the things of God filled me with joy, but the things of the world held me captive. It seems to me now that I was struggling to reconcile two fundamental opposites: the life of the spirit and the pleasures and distractions of the senses.

It was very difficult for me to practice prayer, because my spirit was not the master but the slave. I was not able to shut myself inside myself, which was my whole method of prayer, without shutting a thousand follies in with me. I spent many years engaged in this struggle. Looking back, I'm amazed at how I could have put up with this and never given up one mode in favor of the other. Well, what I do know is that by this time, there was no turning back. The power to abandon prayer was no longer in my hands because he who desired me and wished to bless me with great mercies was holding me in his.

O God, help me! If only I could recount all the times you rescued me from myself over the years and how I kept going right back into opportunities for error. If only I could describe how you preserved my reputation when I was in danger of completely ruining it.

Through my actions, I continued to demonstrate what kind of person I really was. But the Lord kept covering up my faults and uncovering some small virtue, as if I had any, and magnifying it in the eyes of others, causing them to hold me in high esteem. Even though my mischief was sometimes blatantly obvious, nobody took it seriously; they focused on the good things instead. This is because the Knower of All Things saw that later, when I would speak about serving him, I would require some credibility. And in his supreme generosity, my Beloved chose not to look upon my sins but instead on my constant desire to serve him and the sorrow I suffered in lacking the strength to manifest it.

O Lord of my soul! How could I ever pay tribute to the mercy you bestowed on me during those years? How could I ever express my gratitude for the moments when I turned against you and you swiftly brought me back, through the most extraordinary repentance, to taste your sublime gifts? Truly, my King, you chose the most delicate and painful punishment I could possibly have endured. You knew exactly what would break my heart open; you chastised my faults with great favors.

I do not believe I am speaking nonsense here. Although when I recall how ungrateful I was in those days, I almost wish that I *could* lose my mind and not have to reflect on how wicked I was!

In my condition, it was far more painful to receive divine favors when I had committed some grave offense than it would have been to be castigated. A single favor of this kind troubled and bewildered and exhausted me more than a dozen illnesses and ordeals put together. Even though I made more mistakes than I could ever atone for, it still seemed to me that when I was suffering I deserved it, and at least it gave me the opportunity to pay a little something for my bad behavior. But to see myself receiving fresh blessings after failing to appreciate the grace I had already been given was a kind of torture to me.

I think anyone who has any knowledge and love of God must feel this way. All we have to do is reflect on the ultimate good and we can't help but notice how far we are from it. As I took stock of my feelings, I saw that I was always on the brink of falling into error. This awareness triggered tears of anger. At the same time, I knew that my desire was strong and my resolve was firm.

It is a terrible thing for a soul to be alone in the midst of such danger. It seems to me that it would have been very helpful to me to have someone to talk to about all of this. If I lacked sufficient shame before God, maybe I would have felt ashamed enough in front of another human being to adjust my behavior and avoid falling into error again.

This is why I would advise anyone who practices prayer, at least in the beginning, to cultivate connection and companionship with like-minded souls. This is very important, because we can help each other make progress on the path of prayer and bring each other even greater benefits. After all, in ordinary human friendships, people seek each other out to relax and indulge in idle chatter, which may not be very good, and they find mutual sympathy and comfort in these attachments. So I don't see why we would ever discourage people who are beginning to love and serve God from getting together to discuss the trials and joys of the spiritual path. There are certainly plenty of both!

If the friendship you desire to have with his Majesty is authentic, I don't think you need to worry about ego. When you notice the first egotistical stirrings, disclose them and you will emerge victorious. I believe that when you discuss the trials and joys of the spiritual life for the sake of your friendship with God, you will benefit yourself and whomever you are sharing them with. Your own wisdom will increase, and without even knowing how you did it, you will contribute to the wisdom of your friends.

If you have detected spiritual arrogance in yourself, you are likely to notice it coming up not only in these conversations about the practice of prayer but also during any religious ritual that moves you to deep devotion in front of other people. This does not mean you should refrain from all spiritual practices for fear of being egotistical. Nothing should ever tempt you to abandon your path.

I cannot overemphasize how important these friendships are, especially for souls whose virtue is not yet fully ripened, since there is no lack of either enemies or friends to incite them to do wrong. This vigilance about spiritual pride seems to me to be an invention of the spirit of evil, who finds our anxiety very valuable. The spirit of evil takes this concern and twists it so that those of us who truly love and serve God try to hide our spiritual inclinations, while less righteous souls are encouraged to proclaim their wicked ways far and wide. These days, offenses against God are so common that people not only find them easy to justify but actually seem to revel in them.

Maybe what I am writing sounds foolish. If this is the case, I would invite you to tear it up right now. But if what I have to say rings true, then I beg you to augment my simple understanding with your deeper knowledge. People are so lazy regarding the things of God that those of us who love and serve him need to back each other up if any of us are going to make any progress on the path. It is generally considered to be a fine thing to buy into the vanities and comforts of the world, and nobody thinks twice about these indulgences. On the other hand, the minute someone gives herself to God, she has no shortage of critics. We need companions to defend us against this kind of persecution until we grow strong enough to protect ourselves and not become discouraged by suffering. Without this companionship, we find ourselves in deep difficulty.

I think this must be why some holy men and women used to withdraw to the desert. There is a kind of humility in not trusting exclusively in ourselves but in turning to others in the hope that God will help us all. Charity increases when it is shared. A thousand blessings flower from this kind of sharing. If I had not directly experienced the benefits of this type of exchange, I would not dare advocate it.

It is true that I am the weakest and most wicked of anyone ever born. But I believe that someone who humbles herself, no matter how strong she might be, and trusts another who has more experience than she in these matters has nothing to lose. I know that if the Beloved had not revealed this truth to me and provided me with access to other people who were practicing prayer, I might have continued rising and falling until I plunged into hell.

Believe me, I had plenty of friends to help me fall. But when it came to rising, I found myself so completely alone it's a wonder I did not remain stuck where I had fallen. I praise the mercy of God, for he is the One who gave me his hand. May he be blessed forever and ever. Amen.

VIII ✠

TWENTY YEARS OF TURBULENCE

I REALIZE THAT it must make my readers uncomfortable to hear me go on and on about a person as wretched as I was. But it is not without reason that I have lingered so long on this period of my life. How could you not disdain me for being so obstinate and ungrateful to the One who bestowed so many blessings on me? If only I were allowed to tell you about all the times I disappointed my Beloved by failing to lean on the pillar of prayer.

I spent almost twenty years on this turbulent sea, falling and rising, only to fall again. My life was so far from perfection that I barely took any notice of my minor spiritual mistakes. I was concerned about committing grave errors, but not enough to remove myself from the temptations that might lead to them.

You cannot imagine what a painful way of life this was. I found neither joy in God nor gratification in the world. In the midst of enjoying worldly pleasures, I would feel sorrow remembering all I owed to God. Yet when I was trying to be with God, my worldly attachments would agitate me. This battle was so painful that I don't know how I managed to endure it for a single month, let alone for so many years.

I can clearly see, however, the great mercy the Lord showed me during this time. Even while I was busy consorting with the world, he gave me the courage to keep practicing prayer. I say "courage" because I cannot think of a thing that requires more courage in the whole world than to betray the King, knowing that he knows what you're up to the entire time and yet never removing yourself from his presence! Of course, we are all in the presence of God all the time, but it seems to me that those who practice prayer are present with him in a special way. They are continually aware of him. For others, several days may go by without any awareness that God sees them.

It is true that there were times during those years when I gave myself entirely to prayer and sometimes went for many months—once even a whole year, I think—without offending God. Since I am obligated to tell the whole truth here, I must admit that I did make a sincere effort not to commit any transgressions against him. But since I have few memories of the good days, there must not have been very many of them.

Still, not many days went by without my devoting long hours to prayer, unless I was very sick or very busy. Actually, I felt closer to God when I was ill. I tried to get the people who took care of me to draw nearer to him too. I spoke to them constantly about God and beseeched him on their behalf.

And so, except for that one good year I mentioned, I spent the first eighteen of the past twenty-eight years in this inner strife. The conflict was between yearning for God and attraction to the world. The war has not exactly subsided during the remainder of those years, as you will see, but the causes have been different. Also, since these other battles have been fought in the service of God and with greater understanding of the emptiness of the world, everything has gone smoothly. I will tell you about that later.

The other reason I have gone into all this at such length, besides to point out how merciful God has been to such an ungrateful wretch as I, is so that my readers may see what great blessings God showers on souls who devote themselves to a life of prayer, even if their discipline is less than perfect. If they persevere through failures and temptations and the thousand obstacles that the spirit of evil throws in their path, I have no doubt whatsoever that the Beloved will lead them into safe harbor, as he has done for me (at least, so far). May it please his Majesty that I never lose my way again!

Many holy men have written and spoken about the good that comes from practicing prayer. By the way, when I say "prayer," I'm talking about contemplative prayer. Glory be to God for such goodness! I know that I am far from humble, but even I would not be presumptuous enough to deal with this subject unless these saintly souls had already opened the door. I can only share what I have experienced. And what I know is that however sinful a person may be, once she has begun to practice prayer, she must never give it up.

Prayer is the means by which we can repair all that is broken. Without prayer, it is almost impossible to make amends. Oh, may the spirit of evil not tempt you, as it has tempted me, to give up prayer out of false humility! Instead, let's believe the words of the One who told us that if we sincerely regret our mistakes and return our full attention to God, he will meet us with the fullness of his friendship and grant us again the blessings he gave us before, maybe even more generously than ever if our repentance warrants it.

If you have not yet begun to practice prayer, I beg you, for the love of God, not to pass up such a great blessing. Fear has no place at this table, only love. Even if you don't make much progress, and even if you don't expend the level of effort that would seem to merit the gifts and delights God lavishes on those who do, you will still begin to glimpse the road that leads to paradise.

And if you persevere, I believe with all my heart that God, who never fails to reward those who take him as their friend, will have mercy on you. As I see it, contemplative prayer is simply an intimate sharing between friends. It's about frequently taking time to be alone with the One we know loves us. If the friendship is to endure, the love must be honored and tended. The will of the two friends needs to be in harmony. The Lord, of course, is perfect, and he loves us perfectly. But our human nature is still sensual and selfish, and we are not yet capable of fully contributing to this excellent friendship. We may endure deep pain when we realize how different we are from the One we love.

Oh, how infinitely good you are, my God! It seems that in our encounter, I see both you and myself. O Delight of the Angels! When I think of you, I long to be completely consumed by you. How true it is that you graciously suffer the one who suffers to be with you. Oh, what a good friend you make, my Lord! How you bear us and comfort us. You patiently wait for us to rise to our true nature, and in the meantime, you accept us as we are. You take into account, my Lord, all the times we have loved you, and in one moment of atonement you let all our transgressions go.

This is so clear in my case. I cannot fathom, my Creator, why everyone does not try to connect with you in this bond of friendship. Why won't the wicked come to you so that you can make them good? All they need to do is to invite you to be with them for at least two hours a day. It doesn't even matter if they are incapable of being with you but are caught up in a thousand revolving thoughts and distractions, as I used to be. Simply making the effort to be in your company may be all they can do at the beginning, sometimes even later on.

You, Beloved, defend us against the onslaught of evil spirits, diminishing their strength every day. Finally, you give us sweet victory. And so, O Life of all that lives, you do not sacrifice anyone who trusts in you and longs to be your friend. You sustain the health of our bodies and give vitality to our souls.

Why are some people afraid to practice contemplative prayer? I don't understand what it is that scares them. The spirit of evil benefits from our fear by making the truth seem like an evil thing. The spirit of evil wants to frighten us away from reflecting on the sacred qualities of suffering and glory, on the ways we have lapsed and how we might rectify our relationship with God, on the trials and the sorrows Christ endured for us.

These are the things I would dwell on when I was praying. During the whole time I was navigating those dangerous waters I've been telling you about, this remained my focus in prayer. But I had trouble keeping my attention on God. I was more interested in when the hour I had allotted myself for prayer would be over than I was in abiding in quietude with my Beloved. I spent more time listening for the clock to strike than I did with lofty thoughts. I often would have preferred to take any heavy penance laid on me than do what was necessary to recollect myself and practice prayer.

They say that I am an exceptionally brave woman, far braver than most, but I sometimes had to gather all the courage God gave me to show up and pray. I'm not sure if the force of resistance was a technique used against me by the spirit of evil or if it was just a consequence of my own bad habits, but sometimes I felt such overwhelming sadness when I entered the chapel that I could hardly bear it. But once I made the effort, the Beloved helped me. After meditations like these, I was filled with a deeper sense of peace and delight than when I prayed because I wanted to.

Prayer has been the remedy for all my troubles. If the Lord has put up with someone as flawed as I am, why should you be afraid, no matter how wicked you think you may be? I don't care how bad you are, you could not possibly stay bad for as many years as I did after receiving so many blessings from God. The only reason the Lord tolerated me for so long was because I yearned for him and strove to set aside some time and place for him to be with me. I did not always feel like praying, but either because of the power of my struggle or the grace of God, I persevered and have derived indescribable benefits from it. Seeing me, how could you despair?

If someone like me, who has made it a habit not to serve God but to offend him, has found prayer to be such a worthy and necessary practice, then why would those of you who are truly inclined to serve God hesitate to engage in it? It can do no harm; it can only bring positive results. Do you want to add more trials to those you must already suffer in this life? Do you want to close the door on God's face, preventing him from gifting you with the joy of contemplative prayer?

If so, I feel sorry for you. You may well be serving God, but you are doing so at a terrible cost to yourself. Don't you know that God himself pays the price for those who practice prayer? In exchange for our small effort, God rewards us with serenity and delight, giving us the energy to bear whatever trials may come our way.

Later I will tell you much more about the sweet blessings the Beloved gives to those who persevere in prayer. All I can say for now is that prayer is the doorway to the kinds of exquisite gifts he has given me. If we keep that door closed, how can he give us what we need? He may be wanting to grace the soul with delight and take his delight in her, but he can't get in. Unless he finds the soul solitary, empty, and longing for his love, there is nothing he can do. We put all these obstacles in his way and make no effort to remove them. And we want God to do us favors!

To demonstrate God's great mercy and to highlight the good it did me not to give up prayer and reading, I will tell you about the violence with which the spirit of evil waged war on my soul and the loving-kindness the Beloved used to win it back. It's important that my readers understand this and make every effort to avoid the perils I unwittingly fell into. For the love of God and for the great love he has for us, protect yourself against opportunities for error. Once we are caught, we are besieged by enemies and are too weak to defend ourselves.

If only I could describe to you the captivity my soul suffered in those days. I fully understood that I was a prisoner, but I didn't know why. I found myself unable to trust my guides when they made light of things that I felt in my soul to be wrong. When I went to a particular confessor to discuss a certain scruple that was bothering me regarding the conversations I was having with guests in the convent parlor, he dismissed it. This man insisted that even if I were brought into the highest contemplative state, such things would not be inappropriate.

But by this time, I was already starting to withdraw from these dangers, even though I still had not given up the activities that led to them. Because of my devotion to the practice of prayer and the desire for God that my spiritual guides witnessed in me, they thought I was doing exceedingly well. But my soul understood that she was not fulfilling her debt to the One who had done everything for her.

Looking back, I feel sorry for the suffering my poor soul had to endure with little help from anyone other than God. Encouraged by my confessors to indulge in my own pleasures and distractions, my soul stumbled into all kinds of trouble.

Sermons were no small torment to me, because I loved them too much. Whenever I heard someone preach with passion and skill, I felt a wave of affection rise up in me that I was powerless to suppress. Very few sermons were so bad that I did not listen to them with eager pleasure, even when other people said that the preaching was inept. But if the preaching was good, it gave me inordinate satisfaction. Once I had embarked on the contemplative path, I never grew tired of speaking about God or hearing others speak about him. Still, even though I drew deep comfort from a good sermon and a skillful preacher, it also tormented me, because it made me see how far I was from where I wished to be.

I beseeched the Beloved to help me. But I failed to put the whole of my trust in God and relinquish all traces of trust in myself. I searched earnestly for a remedy; I tried everything. But without the fundamental realization that I was powerless and that the only thing I could rely on was God, my efforts were useless.

I wanted life. I could clearly see that what I was doing was not living, but wrestling with the shadow of death. There was no one to give me life, except God. And he had already brought me back to himself so many times, only to have me forsake him all over again, that he finally seemed to be giving up on me. Who could blame him?

TEARS OF CONVERSION

B Y NOW, my poor soul had grown weary. But no matter how much she wished she could rest, the bad habits I had developed would not let her.

Until one day, when something happened that changed everything. I was about to walk into the chapel when I noticed a statue the Incarnation had borrowed for an upcoming festival. Someone had set it aside in preparation for the celebration. It was an image of Christ scourged at the pillar. The sight of it was so moving that it shook me to the root of my being and stirred the depths of devotion in me. I became acutely aware of what Christ had suffered for us and how little gratitude I had ever offered him in return.

Suddenly, it felt like my heart was breaking. In a flood of tears, I threw myself down at his feet, beseeching him to give me the strength to adore him and never to forsake him again.

I had always felt a special bond with the glorious Magdalene. Often, especially when I was taking Communion, I would reflect on her conversion. This is when I knew for certain that the Lord was inside of me. Resting in this, I would place myself at his feet, confident that he would never reject my tears. I didn't know what I was talking about. But he was gracious, and he allowed my tears to flow. How quickly I would then forget the feeling that prompted them! And I would implore that glorious saint to intervene with the Beloved on my behalf.

But that day when I encountered the statue outside the chapel, it went much deeper. I had lost all trust in myself and had placed myself unconditionally in God's hands. I think I told him then that I would not get up again until he gave me what I wanted. I am convinced that this surrender did me great good, because from then on I made dramatic progress.

This was the method I used in prayer: since I was no good at intellectual meditation, I would strive to picture Christ within me. It worked best for me to visualize him in those moments when he was most alone. It seemed to me that when he was lonely and forsaken, he would be, like anyone in great need, more open to receive me. I had many simple thoughts of this kind.

The scene of Christ praying in solitude in the garden was a special comfort to me. I would go there with him to keep him company. I would think about the anguish he experienced, and I would wish with all my heart that I could wipe the sweat from his face and alleviate his pain. But awareness of my own transgressions prevented me from actually doing it. I stayed with him as long as my thoughts would let me. But a thousand distractions tormented me.

For many years before going to bed, after I had commended myself to God so that I would sleep well, I would spend a little while pondering Christ's prayer in the garden. Actually, I started this habit before I even became a nun, because someone had told me that it was a good way to atone for my transgressions. I see now that this custom was a great benefit to me, because without my even realizing what was happening, it was preparing me for the practice of prayer. Just as I could never forget to make the sign of the cross before bed, I became totally used to picturing this episode in Christ's life.

Now, to get back to what I was saying about the way my distracting thoughts used to torment me. The wandering mind is a hazard of non-vocal prayer. Without the support of the discursive intellect, we can either make great progress or become utterly lost. The soul who does advance goes far, because she is carried by love. But there is a high price to pay for this kind of progress, except for those souls whom the Lord decides to bring very quickly to the Prayer of Quiet. I have known some souls like these.

For those who walk the path of silent prayer, a book can be a useful devise to prompt recollection. I have also found it helpful to gaze at meadows, flowers, and water. Creation reflects the Creator. These things have awakened me and brought me back to recollection, as a book would.

They also remind me to be grateful and good. My mind was so dense that I could never imagine sublime things until the Beloved showed them to me in a way I could understand.

My ability to picture things in my mind was so poor that I could never engage my imagination unless I had seen the thing I was trying to visualize. Other people are able to use their imaginations to recollect themselves in prayer, but mine is of no use to me. I could *think* of Christ as a man, but I couldn't really *see* him.

No matter how much I read about Christ's beauty or how many pictures I saw of him, I was like a blind person or someone sitting in the dark. If such a person is speaking with another and feeling him beside her, this is enough to convince her that he is actually there, even if she can't see him. This is what I experienced when I thought about our Lord.

That's why I have always been so fond of pictures. I really feel sorry for people who purposely abandon images. Obviously, they do not love the Lord, because if they did they would enjoy looking at his picture, just as they would delight in seeing portraits of the ones they deeply love on this earth.

Around this time, someone gave me a copy of the new translation of the *Confessions* of Saint Augustine. The Lord must have ordained this, because I never asked for this book, nor had I ever seen it. I have great affection for Saint Augustine. Our Lady of Grace, the first convent where I lived when I was still a layperson, belonged to his order. And he was a sinner, like me.

I drew great comfort from saints who once were sinners, before God brought them back to himself. I thought they could help me on my way. If the Lord forgave them, there was hope that he would forgive me. The thing that left me inconsolable was that God only had to call them once and they returned to him. But I slid back so many times that I was exhausted. Still, when I reflected on his love for me, I would regain my courage. Even though I was plagued by doubts about myself, I never doubted the mercy of God.

O God, help me! I am astonished to see how unresponsive I was in the face of all the help you gave me. It terrifies me to see how little I could ever accomplish on my own. A thousand attachments prevented me from following through on my intention to give myself entirely to God.

As I began to read the *Confessions*, I perceived my own story written there. I couldn't help but entrust myself to this glorious saint. When I came to the passage about how he heard the voice in the garden and was in that moment converted, I felt in my heart that the Lord was speaking directly to me. Overcome by wordless weariness, I dissolved into tears and remained that way for a long time.

O God, help me! How a soul suffers when she loses the freedom to be who she truly is. What torment she endures. I am amazed to see that I survived such pain. Praise be to God, who gave me life when I was on the brink of such a deadly death.

I think that his Divine Majesty must have heard my mournful cries and been moved by my tears. He bolstered my soul with new strength. I started yearning to spend more time alone with him. I lost all my taste for sinful things; the space they left behind filled immediately with new love of God. I was sure that I loved him. At least, I thought I did. But I didn't have the slightest notion what that love was truly about.

It seems to me that I was not quite ready to surrender myself completely to his service when all of a sudden his Majesty began to bless me all over again. Without my presuming to ask, the Beloved seemed determined to bestow on me the sweet devotional gifts that other souls labor so rigorously to experience. He poured comfort and joy into my soul, while all I ever wanted was forgiveness for my wrongdoing and the grace to honor him. Knowing how seriously I had transgressed, I would never have dared to wish for such favors and consolations. But he showed me abundant mercy and compassion. He drew me into him and allowed me to bask in his presence. I knew that I never could have entered this place unless he himself had brought me there.

The only time in my life I remember asking God for relief was once when my soul felt dried up. But as soon as I realized what I was doing, I became deeply distressed at my own lack of humility, and my very shame triggered the grace I was longing for! It's not that I thought there was anything wrong on principle with asking for consolation in prayer. It's just that I felt that only those who are ready, those who have tried with all their might to love God and to do good works, deserved to make such a request.

These tears of mine struck me as girlish and ineffectual, because they did not win me what I desired. But I see now that they were beneficial. After those two occasions of being so powerfully moved, overcome by distress over my sins and deep soul-weariness, I began to leave my wicked ways behind and to devote myself more constantly to contemplative prayer. I did not give up those harmful old habits completely, but God helped me to gradually turn away from them.

All his Majesty was waiting for was some measure of preparation on my part. Then the spiritual blessings continued to blossom in me, as I will now describe. But it is very unusual for our Beloved to grant such grace to someone whose conscience is as impure as mine was.

X ✠

First Favors

I NEED TO TELL YOU about my first fleeting yet undeniable tastes of God. Sometimes, when I was visualizing Christ inside of me or even if I was just reading, the unexpected presence of God would sweep over me in such a dramatic way that I could not possibly doubt that he was within me or that I was enfolded by him. This was not any kind of vision; I believe they call it "a mystical experience."

In this state, the soul seems to be suspended totally outside itself. The will still loves. The memory is practically empty. And the intellect, though not completely lost, ceases to function, standing in amazement of all it suddenly understands. It seems that God wants the mind to know that it knows nothing at all of what he is communicating.

Before this, I would frequently experience a deep devotional tenderness; this is something we can partly attain, I think, through our own efforts. It is a God-given gift that belongs neither totally to the senses nor completely to the spirit. I have noticed that we can sometimes trigger this state by reflecting on our own insignificance and on the awesome greatness of God. It also helps to think about how much Christ has done for us, about the intense pain of his Passion and the sorrows of his life, and to rejoice in the recognition of his good works, his nobility of being, and his boundless love for us. If we really want to make progress on the path, there are many other blessings that we may often stumble upon, even when we are not seeking them.

When we engage in spiritual practice with love, our souls are uplifted and our hearts are softened, which may stimulate a gentle upwelling of tears. Sometimes our tears seem forced; other times it seems like the

Beloved is drawing them out of us and we cannot resist him. His Majesty appears to reward us for our small efforts by blessing us with the sweet relief of weeping for love of so great a Lord. This does not surprise me; the soul has ample reason to find comfort in a love that surpasses all understanding. Here the soul finds solace; here she finds joy.

A comparison comes to mind at this point, and I think it's a good one: the joys of prayer must be something like the joys of heaven. Souls in heaven perceive only as much as the Lord allows them to perceive, in proportion to the merits they earned when they were alive. Realizing how small her virtues are, each soul is content with whatever place is given to her. There is an even greater difference between one heavenly joy and another than there is between various spiritual delights here on earth.

Following those moments in which God opens the heart during the early stages of the spiritual path, the soul truly feels that she has been more than compensated for her service to him and that there is nothing left for her to desire. She would be more than correct. Remember, a single instance of these holy tears is so powerful that it cannot be purchased with all the trials in the world.

While we seem to play some part in attaining this state of tenderness, we can accomplish nothing without God. And what greater reward is there than to be given evidence that we are in some small way pleasing our Beloved? Let anyone who has come this far recognize our debt of gratitude and praise God. For it seems that God has chosen us for his kingdom and that if we do not turn back, he will take us into his own house.

We should try to avoid false humility, which I'll say more about later. For instance, we may think it's humble to pretend not to notice that the Beloved is bestowing sweet gifts of grace upon us. Let me make something perfectly clear: God is giving us these blessings irrespective of our merits. Let us thank his Majesty for them! If we do not acknowledge what we are receiving, our hearts are not awakened to love. The more we remember our poverty, then the richer these gifts make us feel, rendering our humility more genuine and advancing our spiritual progress.

Another mistake the soul makes is to be afraid of grace. We assume that we are unworthy of receiving divine favors. Then, when the Beloved begins to grant these blessings, we worry about spiritual pride. We need to trust that the One who gives us these gifts also gives us the grace to discriminate when the spirit of evil tries to tempt us in this way, making us strong enough to resist the temptation. All we need to do is walk in simplicity before God, striving to please him alone.

We seem to love other human beings most when we remember the kindness they have shown to us. Now, it is righteous—in fact, it is laudable—for us to remember that we owe our being to God, who created us from nothing and sustains us. It is correct and commendable for us to reflect on Christ's Passion and his death, which he suffered for each of us living today, long before we were created. Why, then, would it be wrong for me to notice and understand and frequently ponder that, when all I used to talk about was trivial, now the Beloved has granted me the desire to speak only of him?

Here is a jewel that has been given to us in love. When we remember that we have it, how can we fail to be aroused to love the One who gave it to us? Love is the fruit of prayer that is grounded in humility. Wait until we receive other, even more precious gifts! Some souls who serve God, for instance, are rewarded with an abiding detachment from the things of the world and even from themselves. Acknowledging God's boundless generosity, such people are undoubtedly moved by even deeper gratitude and inspired to be of even greater service. They must be aware that they have nothing to do with any of these blessings.

Personally, I would have been more than satisfied to have received a single spiritual jewel. And yet the Beloved chose to bestow more riches than I could ever begin to desire on a soul as undeserving as I!

We must be sure to draw from every blessing the fresh strength we need to be of service. And we must always be grateful. For the Lord gives us these treasures on the condition that we make good use of his gifts. If we do not rise to the high state to which he lifts us, he will take it all away again and we will be left poorer than before. Then his Majesty will give those jewels to someone else who will display them properly and use them both for her own benefit and for the good of all.

How can people make good use of their riches and spend them generously if they don't even realize that they are rich? In my opinion, it is impossible, given human nature, for anyone to have the courage to do

great things if he is unaware that he is favored by God. We are patheti-
cally attached to worldly things. Unless we realize that we already have
divine things in our possession, how can we succeed in detaching ourselves and walking away from the attractions of the world? By pledging
heavenly gifts to us, the Beloved replenishes the strength we ourselves
have drained through our transgressions.

Until we have some promise of God's love, we will have trouble bearing the universal disapproval and persecution suffered by those of us on
fire with living faith. Our nature is so dense that we tend to go after
whatever we see dangled in front of us. And so, it is these favors from
God that ignite and strengthen our faith.

Of course, it may well be that I am erroneously measuring others
against myself. Others may find that the truth of perfect faith is enough
to inspire them to do perfect things, whereas I am such a poor wretch
that I need much more. In fact, I need everything.

Everyone must speak for herself. All I can do is tell you what happened to me, as I have been ordered to do. If the person who is reading
this does not approve, he can just tear it up. He knows better than I what
is wrong with it. But I implore him, for the love of the Lord, to publish
what I have said about my miserable little life up to this point. I hereby
grant this permission to him and to all my other confessors. They are
welcome to publish this now, in my own lifetime, so that I will no longer
be deceiving the ones who believe there is some good in me. Insofar as
I understand myself at all, I assure you that this would give me great
comfort.

I do not, however, authorize the publication of anything I say from
this point on. If they show the next part to anyone, please do not tell
who it is that wrote it or whose experiences it is describing. This is why
I do not mention myself by name and why I have conveyed all this in
such a way that it would be difficult for most people to identify me. For
the love of God, I implore you to honor my privacy. If the Lord gives me
the grace to say something good here—in which case, of course, it is his
and not mine at all—then the authority of such learned and serious men
as you should be sufficient endorsement.

I am not learned nor have I led a good life. I have not even had
instruction from learned men—or from anyone else, for that matter.

Only those who commanded me to write this know what I am working on, and they are not here to guide me right now. I almost have to steal time to write, and I do so with some reluctance because it gets in the way of my spinning. We are a poor monastery here, and there is so much work to be done.

If the Lord had given me greater intellectual capacity and a better memory, I might have benefited from the things I've heard and read. But I have retained very little. And so, if I have said anything right, it is because the Lord has willed it for reasons all his own. If, however, I have said something wrong, the fault is entirely mine and you can simply strike it out.

Regardless of the merits of the things I say, there is no advantage to revealing my name. During my lifetime, of course, it would not be appropriate to talk about anything good that I might have done. And after I am dead, there would be no point in mentioning my association with such things, since to do so would only devalue their goodness. Besides, who would ever believe that such a lowly person as I would be involved in such exalted matters?

I do have confidence that for the love of God, you and the others who read this manuscript will respect my wishes. That's why I am expressing myself so freely. Otherwise, I would have terrible qualms about telling anything other than my sins, which I have no hesitation in admitting. As for the rest, just being a woman is enough to make my wings droop, let alone the fact that I am such a wicked one!

Since you have insisted that I give some account of the favors God gives to me in prayer, it is up to you to make sure that what I say is in conformity with the truths of our holy Catholic faith. If it is not, I am willing for you to burn this immediately.

And I will say what has happened to me so that if it conforms to these truths, it might be of some use to you. If it does not conform, then you will disillusion me, and if it turns out that I am not gaining what I think I am, at least the spirit of evil will not gain it. The Lord knows well that I have always been a seeker of the light.

No matter how clearly I wish I could speak about contemplative prayer, it will remain obscure to anyone who has not experienced it. What I will do is describe certain obstacles people commonly encounter along the path and some other dangerous things the Lord has shown me through experience.

Recently, I have been discussing these things with men of great learning and other people who have spent years living spiritual lives. They acknowledge that although I may have navigated my path poorly and often stumbled, his Majesty has given me more experience in twenty-seven years of practicing prayer than most people receive in thirty-seven or even forty-seven. Of course, their progress is probably the result of regular penance and consistent virtue.

May he be blessed for everything, and may he make good use of me! My Lord well knows that all I want is for people to praise him and magnify his name when they see that he has planted a garden of sweet flowers on such a dirty, stinky pile of manure. And may he grant that I not pull these beauties back up by their roots through my own unconsciousness and fall right back into being the way I used to be. I beseech you, for the love of our Lord, to pray for me, since you know me far better than you have allowed me to reveal myself here.

✠ PART TWO

The Four Waters

XI ✝

The Garden

Let's talk now about the ones who are beginning to become servants of love. This is exactly what happens to us, I think, when we take up the path of prayer with determination and follow he who has loved us so much. This is such a high station that the very thought of attaining it transports me with a strange exaltation. If we conduct ourselves correctly during this early stage, all insipid fears vanish.

O Lord of my soul and my Good! There are souls so determined to love you that they gladly abandon everything else to focus on nothing but loving you. Why don't you want them to immediately ascend to a place where they may receive the joyful gift of perfect love?

Wait, I said that wrong. What I ought to be complaining about is that we ourselves don't want this grace. If we fail to reach for this state of sublime dignity, it's our own fault. Don't we realize that the perfect possession of true love of God brings every blessing with it? We are so slow and so stingy about giving ourselves completely to God, why should his Majesty desire to give us something so precious as perfect love? We need to pay the price of rigorous self-preparation.

It is clear to me that there is nothing on earth with which we could ever purchase such a divine blessing. Yet if we do all that we can, if we avoid getting attached to worldly things and concentrate exclusively on heavenly things, as the saints have demonstrated, then I believe without a doubt that this great gift would swiftly be given to us. The problem is, we think we are giving all that we have to God when all we are offering him is the interest (or the fruit) while withholding the capital (or the orchard itself).

We may surrender to our poverty, and this is a good thing, but then we often obsess on having enough of what we've given up. Sometimes we even scheme about how we are going to store up some extra or cultivate relationships with people who will ensure that our needs are met. All this does is put us in a greater state of anxiety, and maybe even danger, than we suffered before we "freed ourselves" from bondage to our possessions.

We may also renounce our self-importance when we embark on the spiritual path in pursuit of perfection. Yet the minute someone challenges our good name to the slightest degree, we forget that we have offered up our personal status to God and try to snatch it right back out of his hands, so to speak. Hadn't we just finished appointing him Lord of our wills? This happens with everything else too.

What a charming way we have of seeking God's love. Our hands are already full of our own attachments. We make no effort to lift our affections above this earth and carry them to fulfillment, and yet we demand spiritual comforts. These two desires, the divine and the personal, strike me as being mutually exclusive. Since we are incapable of giving ourselves up whole, we will not receive the whole of the heavenly treasure. May it please the Lord to give it to us drop by drop, even if receiving it costs us all the trials in the world.

Whenever God gives a person the grace and the courage to strive for this blessing with all her heart and soul, he is bestowing the greatest mercy. God does not deny himself to anyone who perseveres. Little by little, he increases her courage, ensuring that she will reach her goal. I keep saying "courage" because in the beginning the spirit of evil erects many obstacles to prevent us from setting out on the path. The spirit of evil knows that if it lets this one soul get away, it is sure to lose many others.

I truly believe that if a beginner strives, with the help of God, to reach the summit of perfection, she will not reach heaven alone but will bring many souls home with her. Like a good captain, she will deliver everyone in her care to God. The spirit of evil creates so much chaos along the way that if the soul has any hope of not turning back, she will require not a little courage but a lot—and plenty of help from God as well.

Let's take a look at the early stages of the path. For those who are determined to pursue this blessing and emerge from this adventure victorious, the beginning is the most difficult part. The soul struggles and God responds with a flow of grace. In the more advanced degrees of prayer, our primary task is simply to enjoy God. Still, whether we find ourselves at the beginning, middle, or final stage of our path, we all carry our crosses, even though no two crosses are alike. All who follow Christ must walk the path he walked if they don't want to get lost. Blessed be the trials that even in this lifetime are so abundantly rewarded!

At this point, I'm going to have to resort to metaphor. Since I am a woman and only writing what I have been ordered to write, I hesitate to speak this way, but it is difficult to get the language of the spirit just right, especially for someone like myself, who is uneducated. And so I will have to find some alternative means for expressing myself. It may be that my metaphors are ineffective, in which case you can use my foolishness as the opportunity for a good laugh.

It seems to me that I have read or heard of this metaphor somewhere. But since my memory is so poor, I have no idea where it comes from or what it was meant to illustrate. So I am content to borrow it for my own purposes for now.

Let the beginner think of herself as a gardener who is preparing to plant a garden for the delight of her Beloved. But the soil is barren and full of noxious weeds. His Majesty himself pulls up the weeds and replaces them with good seed. Bear in mind that the minute the soul sets out on the path of prayer and service, God has already begun to cultivate her soil in this way.

Like good gardeners, our job is to tend those plants with loving care, striving to get them to grow. We labor to water them so that they will not wither but instead bud and bloom, emitting the most sublime fragrance and giving this Lord of ours great pleasure. This inspires him to enter often into our garden and enjoy himself amid the array of virtues.

Let's see now how this garden needs to be watered. In this way, we will understand what we have to do, the price we have to pay to do it, whether the gain exceeds the cost of labor, and how long we might expect to have to work before our efforts come to fruition.

It occurs to me that our garden can be watered in four ways. We can pull water up from a well; this is a lot of work. Or we can turn the crank of a waterwheel and draw the water through an aqueduct; I have tried this method, and I know that it is not as labor-intensive and yields more water. Or we can channel the flow of water through irrigation ditches; this results in deeper saturation of the soil and lasts longer, which makes less work for the gardener. Or the water may come directly from an abundant rain; this is when the Lord waters the garden himself, without any effort on our part, and this is by far the most effective method of all.

It is important to me to apply these four ways of watering the garden to the four degrees of prayer to which the Lord in his great kindness has sometimes raised my soul. Remember, water is the only way to maintain the garden; without it, everything will die.

May it please his Goodness that I manage to speak in such a way that it might be of some use to one of the men, in particular, who has ordered me to write this. In four months, this man has made more spiritual progress than I have made in seventeen years. He has prepared himself better, so without any labor on his part, his garden is watered in all four ways, although he only receives the last kind of water in drops. At this rate, you will soon be submerged! If this man finds my description amusing, he is more than welcome to laugh at me.

We might say that beginners in prayer are the ones who draw water from the well. As I have mentioned, this requires a lot of labor. Accustomed to a life of distractions, they exhaust themselves trying to recollect their senses. Beginners need to practice withdrawing their attention from what they see and hear. They should sit in solitude and reflect on their past life.

As I will explain later, everyone needs to spend some time thinking about her past, but the extent to which each person must do this varies. In the beginning, this kind of reflection is painful. The practitioner is not sure if she genuinely regrets her transgressions. The clearest sign of repentance is her burning desire to serve God. All she needs to do is meditate on the life of Christ and her intellect will exhaust itself.

And so, there are certain things we can do to advance on the path, but we must always remember that everything we do is with the help of God. Without his support, as everyone knows, we cannot think a good thought. This phase corresponds to fetching water from the well. May

God grant that there is water in it! All we can do is our part; dipping our bucket and drawing it up to water the flowers.

God is so good that even if the well is dry, he sustains the garden without water and makes our virtues flower anyway. Like good gardeners, we do whatever lies in our power and leave the rest to him. His Majesty has a purpose for everything, and this aridity may ultimately be to our advantage. What I mean here by *water* are tears of love-longing, or at least a tenderness of interior devotion.

But what happens when many days go by and all the gardener experiences is dryness, distaste, and total lack of desire to even bother to draw water? Only the thought that what she is doing gives service and pleasure to the Lord of the garden keeps her from giving up. She needs to carefully guard whatever merits she has gained so far from the tedious labor of letting the bucket down into the well shaft and hauling it up empty over and over. Often she will find that she cannot even lift her arms for this work or come up with a single worthy notion. When I speak of trying to draw water from a well, what I mean, of course, is engaging the intellect in meditation.

What then? Well, then the gardener rejoices! She is consoled and considers it an incomparable blessing to be able to work in the garden of such a great Emperor. Her purpose is to please him, not herself, and knowing that her labor is pleasing to him, she praises God with all her heart. The Master has confidence in the gardener because he sees that, without any compensation, she so carefully tends what has been entrusted to her.

Let her also help Christ to carry his cross. Let her remember that the Lord lived with this cross all his life. Do not let her ever abandon the path of prayer or seek God's kingdom here on earth. Even if this aridity lasts throughout her whole life, let her resolve never to let Christ fall under the weight of his cross. The time will come when the Lord will repay her all at once. She does not need to be afraid that her labor is going to waste. She is serving a good Master, and he's keeping his eye on her. She must ignore her negative thoughts, remembering that the spirit of evil tried to use such tricks on Saint Jerome in the desert.

These trials take their toll. I should know; I endured them for many years, and I know how extraordinary they are. Whenever I was able to squeeze a drop of water from the sacred well, I considered it to be a mercy from God. Such labor seems to me to require more courage than many worldly tasks combined. But I have clearly seen that God does not fail to reward us generously, even in this lifetime. A single hour tasting his glory more than compensates me for all the anguish I have suffered in persevering for so long in prayer.

I believe that the Beloved sends these trials in the beginning, and many other temptations later, to test his lovers. Before he is willing to lay great treasure inside us, we need to prove that we are capable of drinking from his chalice and carrying his cross. It seems to me that his Majesty puts us through all this to remind us of our insignificance. The blessings he will give to us later are so exalted that he wants us first to experience our own imperfection so that what happened to Lucifer won't happen to us.

Is there anything you could possibly do, my Beloved, that is not for the greater good of the soul? You know that she is already yours. She places herself in your power. She will follow you wherever you go, even to death on the cross. And she is determined to help you bear that cross and never leave you alone with it.

Those who see this kind of determination in themselves have absolutely nothing to fear. Spiritual people, do not be distressed. Once you have been placed in such a high state that all you really want is to leave the cares of the world behind and commune in solitude with your God, the majority of your work is done.

Praise the Lord for this, and trust in his goodness; he never fails his friends. Cover the eyes of your mind, and banish thoughts such as "Why has God given that person an experience of devotion after only a few days of practicing prayer and nothing to me when I have been hard at work for so many years?" Let us trust that it's all for our own good. Let his Majesty lead the way along the path he chooses.

We do not belong to ourselves anymore; we belong to God. He grants us an immeasurable blessing when he gives us the desire to dig in his garden and be in the presence of the Lord of the garden, who is certainly present within us. What difference does it make to me if he gives me water from the well to nurture some of these plants and flowers while others thrive without it?

Your will be done, O Lord. Help me never to forsake you. Whatever virtues you have, in your great kindness, bestowed on me, let them not be lost now. Since you suffered, my Beloved, I am willing to suffer. Manifest your will in me in every way. And do not give anything as precious as your love to anyone who only serves you expecting to get something in return.

I know from experience that those whose souls progress are the ones who set out on the path of contemplative prayer with determination and persuade themselves to ignore whether the Beloved is giving them the blessing of tenderness in devotion or is withholding it from them. If they succeed in detaching from self-gratification—neither rejoicing when the Lord gives them these favors nor becoming discouraged when they are taken away—they should have no fear of falling back, even when they stumble. The foundation of their building rests on solid ground. They understand that the love of God is not about tears or tenderness or relief but serving him with humility, fortitude, and righteousness. Otherwise, all they do is take, without giving anything in return.

Poor women like me, on the other hand, are weak. Lacking fortitude, it seems appropriate to me that we would be led with holy favors. These gifts are leading me even now, instilling me with the strength I need to endure some of the trials God has given me to suffer. But it appalls me to see prominent, well-educated, and highly intelligent men making such a fuss because God has not given them devotional experience. I don't mean that if God does choose to grant them this consolation they should not accept it and cherish it, because if this happens, it is God's will.

But if they are not moved by devotion, they should not wear themselves out trying to conjure it up. They should understand that if his Majesty is not giving it to them, they don't need it. They should take control of themselves and move on. They need to see their desire for consolations in prayer as a fault. Not only have I witnessed this, but I have proved it true. Such cravings are the artifact of imperfection; they reflect a lack of both freedom of spirit and the courage to overcome adversity.

I am emphasizing this because it is very important to cultivate such freedom and determination. This is less of an issue for beginners than it is for those who have made some progress. Many people start on the spiritual path but never reach the end. I think that this is because they refuse to embrace the cross at the outset. Believing they are accomplishing nothing, they become despondent. They cannot bear it when the intellect ceases to function. They do not realize that when the mind is stilled, the will is growing strong and robust.

We need to realize that the Lord does not care about the things we worry about. They may seem like faults to us, but they are not. His Majesty already knows our misery and our inadequacy better than we could ever know ourselves. He also knows that all we really want is to think of him and love him always. It is our determination that he desires. The suffering we create for ourselves has no other purpose than to disquiet our souls. Then if we fail to profit from an hour of prayer, we waste four more hours fretting over it.

Sometimes the problem actually stems from a physical condition. I have a great deal of personal experience in this matter and, having carefully analyzed it and discussed it with spiritual people, have confirmed that what I say is true. We feel so miserable that our poor little imprisoned souls end up sharing in the misery of the body. Changes in the weather and our natural bodily cycles prevent us from doing what we really want to do and cause us all kinds of suffering. This is not our fault.

The more we try to force ourselves at times like these, the worse our condition becomes and the longer it lasts. We need to use discernment and take care not to smother the poor soul. We need to acknowledge when we are sick. Then our spiritual practice may have to be adjusted. Sometimes these changes will be necessary for several days. Let us suffer our exile as best we can. It is a sad thing when a soul in love with God realizes that she is host to such a wretched guest as the body, which prevents her from doing what she really wants.

The reason I mentioned the need for discernment is that sometimes it is the spirit of evil that is causing the problem. Just as it is not always a good idea to torture the soul into doing what she is incapable of doing, it is not always appropriate to give up on prayer the minute we encounter severe turmoil and distraction.

We do have alternatives. We can engage in certain external activities, such as works of charity or spiritual reading. Sometimes, of course, we are not even well enough for these. In that case, let us serve our body out of love for God, remembering all the times the body has served the soul. A genuinely holy conversation can function as an authentic spiritual practice. Our guides might also recommend that we spend some time in nature.

Experience is a great teacher because it helps us to see what is best for us and to realize that God can be served by everything we do. *His yoke is easy.* It is of the utmost importance that we not drag our souls, as they say, but lead them gently. In this way, we will make much better progress.

I don't care how many times I repeat myself, I must return to this essential advice: do not let feelings of emptiness or distracting thoughts distress you or disquiet your soul. Do you desire liberation? Do you wish you weren't always so troubled? Then do not be afraid of the cross. You will see how the Lord helps you to carry it. Then you will make joyful progress and find blessings everywhere you look.

It is clear that if the well is dry, we cannot put water into it. Still, it is equally true that we should never stop dipping our buckets. Because when there is water there, God uses it to multiply our virtues.

XII ✝

Lifting the Bucket

I KNOW THAT I digressed quite a bit in the previous chapter, but that's because I felt that what I had to say was very necessary. What I have been trying to explain is that we can accomplish a great deal through our own efforts and help ourselves to experience deep devotion during this initial phase of the spiritual path.

When we think and reflect on what Christ suffered for us, we are moved by compassion. The sorrow that arises may bring tears, and there is an inexplicable sweetness in this. Thinking about the glory we are hoping for, the love Christ demonstrated for us, and the miracle of his resurrection, we are filled with a joy that is neither wholly spiritual nor entirely sensory. But it is a virtuous joy. And the corresponding sorrow is equally worthy.

There is virtue and worth in everything that awakens devotion, even if it comes in part through the labor of the intellect. Of course, this devotional blessing cannot be earned or obtained unless the Beloved chooses to bestow it. If God has not yet raised a soul higher than this, it is best for her not to strive to elevate herself. All she will do is thwart her own progress and suffer harm. Please take special note of this danger.

There are many things the soul can do in this state to awaken love. She can make resolutions to serve God and engage in other acts that stimulate the growth of virtue. There is a book called *The Art of Serving God*, which does a fine job of explaining these things. It is appropriate reading for those who are at this stage in which the intellect is still an active participant in spiritual practice.

The soul can picture herself in the presence of Christ in all his sacred humanity and build up the fire of love. She can keep him close to her always, talking to him, asking him for the things she needs, and confiding her troubles. When she feels joy, she can rejoice with him, but she must never let the good times make her forget him. She should try to communicate with him, not through prescribed prayers, but with the words of her own heart that express her desires and needs.

This is an excellent way to make rapid progress. Any soul who strives to remain in Christ's precious company, who is sincerely grateful for this intimacy, and who truly finds herself in love with this Lord who has done so much for us is a soul I consider to be evolved.

This is why we should not be distressed when we are not moved by devotion. We should simply thank God, who allows us to want only to please him, even if our efforts seem less than successful. This practice of carrying Christ in our consciousness is beneficial at all phases of the spiritual path, especially in these first degrees of prayer, and it quickly advances us to the second. It also safeguards us against the perils with which the spirit of evil may confront us in the later stages.

So this is what we can do for ourselves. Anyone who tries to do more than this, struggling to elevate the spirit to obtain a taste of a divine sweetness that is not freely given, risks losing everything he has gained so far and jeopardizing future growth. These blessings belong to the realm of the supernatural. If he puts the intellect to sleep prematurely, he finds his soul desolate in a dry desert. Since the entire edifice is built on humility, the nearer we draw to God, the more we must cultivate this virtue. If we don't, everything will be ruined. Our Lord is already doing too much for us by drawing us into his presence, considering how imperfect we are; I see that it is arrogant for us to desire to ascend higher.

I'm not suggesting that we shouldn't raise our consciousness by reflecting on sublime things such as the wonders of heaven and the great wisdom of God. Personally, I never had the ability to reflect in this way, as I have mentioned, and besides, I was too wretched to try. God gave me the grace early on to recognize how much courage it requires for me to even reason my way through worldly things, let alone ponder divine things.

But other people can benefit from this practice, especially if they are educated. Education, in my opinion, is like a treasure that can only enhance this practice, as long as the learning is grounded in humility. I witnessed this phenomenon only a few days ago among some educated men who have only recently begun to practice prayer and have already made remarkable progress. This only reinforces my conviction that educated men should become spiritual men. I will say more about this later.

When I say that we should not raise ourselves up to God until he raises us himself, I am speaking the language of the spirit. Anyone who has experience will understand me. If I am not making myself understood, I don't know what more I can say about it.

In mystical experience, the intellect ceases to function because God suspends it. If God gives me the grace and the help to explain it better, I will elaborate on this later. For now, please understand that we should not take it upon ourselves to shut down the mind. If we stop using the intellect, we will be left frozen and stupid, accomplishing nothing.

When the Lord suspends the intellect and stems the flow of thoughts, he himself gives it something to astonish and occupy it. Without any thought, the mind understands more in the length of time it takes to recite the creed than we could possibly learn in an entire lifetime through our own human efforts. To presume that we can keep the faculties of the soul busy and the mind quiet at the same time is ridiculous.

Even if I am misunderstood, I will say it again: this effort to suspend the intellect is not very humble. It may not constitute a terrible mistake, but it is certainly a waste of time and energy. And it's an exercise in frustration. The soul is left like a person who is about to leap forward and is suddenly pulled back by someone else. She feels like she has depleted all her strength and has not achieved what she set out to achieve with it.

Anyone who wishes to take a look at this will detect that small lack of humility I mentioned reflected in the small spiritual progress made here. Humility has this excellent quality: when it is present in any act, the act never leaves the soul with that sense of frustration. I think I have explained this clearly, but maybe I have only clarified it for myself. May the Lord open the eyes of the ones who are reading this. May he give them the experience they need to understand it, even if just a little.

For many years, I read a lot of things and didn't understand anything I read. Even though God was blessing me, for a long time I couldn't come up with the words to describe his blessings. This was no small trial.

Then, in a single moment, his Majesty amazed me by teaching me everything all at once!

There is one thing I can say for sure: I spoke with many spiritual people about my experiences, and they tried their best to explain what the Lord was giving to me so that I would be able to talk about it, but I was too dense to understand them. Or maybe since his Majesty has always been my greatest teacher, it was the Lord's wish that I had only him to thank for my understanding.

May he be blessed for everything! It upsets me to confess the truth about all that he has given to me. I neither requested nor desired these things. In fact, I have never even been curious about their significance, although it would have been a virtue to try and understand them. As it was, I was far more interested in trivial matters. And yet God gave me a moment of such dazzling clarity that I suddenly understood everything that had happened to me and was able to explain it all in a way that astonished me even more than it did my spiritual directors (since I was far more aware of my own stupidity than they were). Since this happened only a short time ago, I will not try to understand beyond what he has already taught me, unless it is a matter of conscience.

I repeat my warning one more time: it is very important for the spirit not to ascend unless the Lord raises it up. If he does, we will know it instantly. This effort is especially damaging for women, because the spirit of evil can more readily delude us. Still, I am certain that the Lord would not allow any harm to come to someone who was humbly striving to reach him. Instead, she is more likely to profit from the very experience the spirit of evil used to throw her off course.

Many people travel the path of beginners, and the advice I have offered is exceedingly important. This is why I have elaborated to such an extreme. I admit that other writers have explained all this much better. In fact, it has embarrassed me to attempt this at all, although not as much as it probably should have.

May the Lord be blessed for everything, who wills and consents for such a creature as I to speak about his lofty and sublime graces!

XIII ✠

JOYFUL ABANDON

1 **I**T OCCURS to me now to mention certain temptations that I have noticed tend to assail beginners. I myself have grappled with many of these and I think I have some important advice to offer.

As you embark on the spiritual path, try to remember to walk with joyful abandon. Some people think that if they relax a little, their devotion will fall apart. Of course, there's nothing wrong with being self-aware so that you avoid letting arrogance lead you into habitual patterns that dishonor God. There aren't many people who are so perfect that they can afford to let down their guard against the snares of human nature altogether.

So until we are wholly virtuous, some vigilance is necessary. Throughout our lives, it's important to be mindful of our own insignificance, because this hones our humility. But there are many good reasons to engage in recreation, as I have said. For one thing, it enables us to return to prayer reinvigorated. We just need to use a little discretion in everything we do.

2 · Be confident! Don't hold back your heart's desires. Believe in the power of God. With his help, we will gradually reach the station that the saints attained. We just need to keep striving. If the saints had not been singular in their desire and steadfast in their determination, applying themselves little by little, they would never have risen to such a high state.

His Majesty is the friend and lover of courageous souls, as long as they walk with humility and shed self-importance. I have never seen such a soul hanging back on the path. Nor have I ever noticed a cowardly soul, especially one who hides behind a façade of false humility, make a fraction of the progress in many years that courageous souls make in only a few.

I am amazed by how much can be accomplished on this path by being bold and striving for great things. Even if the soul is not quite strong enough yet, she can still lift off and take flight. She can soar to great heights. But like a fledgling bird, she may tire herself out and need to perch for a while.

3 . I used to reflect often on the words of Saint Paul, who said that all things could be done through God. It was clear that I could accomplish nothing by myself. This understanding was very helpful to me. So were the words of Saint Augustine, who said, "Give me, Lord, what you ordain, and ordain what you will." I've always thought that Saint Peter didn't lose a thing by throwing himself into the sea, even though he became afraid as soon as he had done it.

This initial determination is crucial. It's also important in the early phase to move slowly, use discretion, and follow the advice of a spiritual guide. Just make sure that your guide doesn't see your soul as a toad, capable only of pursuing small lizards. And always be humble, remembering that this strength arises from a power beyond our own.

4 . It's important to pay attention to the quality of this humility. One of the ways I believe that the spirit of evil hurts people who practice prayer and prevents them from making progress is by deceiving them about the true nature of humility. It makes us worry that our desire to imitate the saints is delusional and that our longing for self-denial is self-serving. Then it tries to convince us that since we ourselves are sinners, we should look to the saints for inspiration, not imitation.

I do agree that it is wise to be discriminating about which deeds of the saints we should imitate and which we are meant to simply admire. It would do no good for a weak or sickly person to take on severe fasts or harsh penances, or to go off alone to the desert where she could find no place to sleep and nothing to eat. But we should remember that with God's help we are fully capable of detaching from the world, turning away from personal honor, and releasing our tight grasp on possessions.

Our hearts are so stingy that we're afraid we'll lose the earth beneath our feet if we turn our attention away from the body for a single moment and shift our focus to the spirit. We convince ourselves that because our meditations are frequently disturbed by concerns about the necessities of life, all we need to do is secure our material things and then we will be able to get on with the practice of prayer.

It makes me sad that we have so little trust in God and so much regard for ourselves that worries like these so easily throw us off course. The truth is, when we are not evolving on the path, a few petty annoyances are as upsetting as numerous severe trials would be to a more mature practitioner. And we presume to call ourselves spiritual!

5. It seems to me that people in this state are trying to reconcile body and soul in such a way that they obtain maximum comfort here on earth and ensure their entrance to heaven at the same time. If we walk in righteousness and hold fast to virtue, this method is fine. But we will advance at the pace of a chicken! We will never reach spiritual liberation this way. This is a good balance for householders, who need to put their worldly obligations first. As for me, there is no way I would be satisfied with that rate of progress, nor could anyone convince me of its value. Believe me, I have tried this kind of compromise, and I would not have moved forward an inch if the Beloved in his mercy had not taught me a shortcut.

6. I have always had strong desires. But as I mentioned, I have attempted to practice prayer and live for my own pleasure at the same time. If only there had been someone to encourage me to soar to greater heights, I might have been able to manifest these desires. But such a guide is very rare; most spiritual directors are excessively cautious in these matters. I believe that is one of the primary reasons that beginners do not generally make more rapid progress toward perfection. It's not the Lord's fault; he never fails. It's our own lower nature that impedes us.

7. One thing we can do is imitate the saints by seeking solitude and silence. Contrary to what we might believe, cultivating virtues like these does not endanger the well-being of the body. Sometimes the physical seems bent on thwarting the spiritual, and the minute the spirit of evil detects a little apprehension, it joins forces with these wretched bodies of ours to confound our minds. The spirit of evil would like nothing better than to make us think that our devotional practices are going to kill us or at least do damage to our health. It even suggests that crying will make us go blind.

I have been through all this and I know. But what higher health or deeper sight could we desire than to lose them both for such a cause? Since I have always been so sickly, I have had a tendency to allow my health to tie me down and keep me from engaging in full devotion. I don't pay so much attention to my body anymore.

When the spirit of evil put it into my head to worry about compromising my health with prayer, God decided to clear my thinking. "So what if I die?" I asked myself. And when I wondered if it was all right to feel so tired, I answered myself, "I don't need rest; what I need is the cross!" I was able to counter many other troubling thoughts in this way. Even though I am chronically ill, I have clearly seen on many occasions that my concerns arose either from the spirit of evil or from my own laziness. Ever since I stopped obsessing about my comfort and ease, my health has radically improved.

So it is very important not to be intimidated by our own thoughts in the early stages of the path. You can take my word on this; I know it from experience. It is my hope that simply by reading this litany of my mistakes, you will be able to avoid some of them yourselves.

8 ⌐ Here is another common temptation: since we are beginning to enjoy the serenity and growth that comes from prayer, we want everyone else to be on a spiritual path too. There is nothing wrong with this desire. But the attempt to carry it out may backfire unless you use discretion and temper your efforts so it doesn't look like you are trying to teach people. If you hope to do any good in this area, you must always act with integrity; otherwise, you may end up inadvertently trapping other souls in a snare.

I found this out the hard way, so I know what I'm talking about. When I tried to persuade others to practice prayer, they would hear me talking about the wonderful blessings that come from this practice on the one hand and then observe my own unscrupulous behavior on the other. And I was supposed to be their role model. In fact, I think I served more as a source of temptation and confusion for them. And so they had every reason to miss the mark. Later they explained to me that they could not find a way to reconcile what I preached and what I practiced. Besides, they actually believed that what was wrong was in fact right, simply because they saw me doing it myself and they respected me.

9 This is a trick of the devil, who tries to twist our virtues to justify his own wicked purposes. No matter how minor our mistakes may be, the devil gains major benefit from them, especially if we commit them in spiritual community. Since my wickedness was already excessive, the spirit of evil must have profited all the more! As it turned out, over the course of many years, only three people seem to have benefited from what I had to say to them. In the two or three years since the Beloved has strengthened me in virtue, however, many people have benefited.

This effort of trying to build up other people is a significant drawback. It can detract from our own growth. In the beginning, we need to put ourselves first. The most important thing at this stage is to take care of ourselves. We should pretend that there is no one in the universe but our soul and our God. This is a very useful practice.

10 We all feel a certain zeal for virtue. This may tempt us to judge the sins and failings of other people. The spirit of evil puts it in our minds that the distress we feel over other people's behavior stems only from a desire to protect God from being dishonored. We become so agitated by our desire to remedy the situation that we are unable to practice prayer. The greatest harm lies in our belief that this distress is a mark of our perfect virtue and passion for God. We need to be mindful of this kind of delusion. Genuine concern for the well-being of the community does not disquiet the soul in this way.

The safest path for a soul who practices prayer is to pay no attention to anyone or anything else but to focus instead on knowing herself and pleasing God. This is vitally important. If I were to tell you about all the mistakes I have seen people make in the name of good intentions, I would never be finished talking.

Let us always strive to reveal the good qualities in others and let our awareness of our own imperfections conceal their defects. We may not be able to do this perfectly at first, but we will gradually acquire great virtue by seeing everyone else as better than ourselves. Then by the grace of God—which we always need, since without God's grace nothing is possible—we will begin to grow virtuous. Actually, we should beg God to give us these virtues. He never denies anyone who makes a sincere effort.

11 This advice applies to people with very active intellects, who derive a

multitude of ideas and concepts from a single thought. For people like me, who don't work well with their minds, my only counsel is to be patient. Eventually, the Lord illuminates us and gives us worthy work to do. Those of us with weak intellects do ourselves more harm than good by trying to think our way to enlightenment.

Again, for those of you who are intellectually inclined, I would recommend that you not spend all your time thinking. Even though discursive reason has its place, and it can actually enhance the delight of prayer, intellectuals forget to observe a Sabbath once in a while and give their minds a rest from all that labor. They think it would be a waste of time. But I consider such waste a tremendous boon.

All they need to do, as I have mentioned, is place themselves in the presence of Christ. Instead of wearing themselves out trying to make logical sense of spiritual matters, they should simply speak with him and delight with him. They should lay their needs at his feet and acknowledge that he has every right to deny them his company. There is a time for thinking and a time for being. Otherwise, the soul would get tired of always eating the same food. Once we accustom the palate to non-conceptual practices, they become not only delicious but also very helpful. They nourish the soul and give her life, providing all kinds of benefits.

2. I need to keep trying to clarify things, because unless a person has a really masterful spiritual director, these matters are very difficult to understand. For someone with a sharp intellect, like the man who ordered me to write this, just touching on these subjects would be sufficient. But although I wish I could be brief, my own ineptitude prevents me from finding an adequate way to explain such important matters using a minimum of words. I suffered so much myself, I feel sorry for people who only have books to rely on. It's amazing how different what we think we understand is from what we learn later through experience.

To come back to what I was saying, let's begin to think about an episode from the Passion, let's say when our Lord was bound to the pillar. The intellect gets to work trying to come up with reasons why Christ had to suffer such pain and anguish, struggling to comprehend his loneliness and isolation. If a man is well educated and works hard with his mind, he can glean a great deal of understanding from this kind of exercise. We should all begin, continue, and end with this method of prayer. It's an excellent path to follow—and a safe one—until the Lord leads us in other supernatural directions.

13. I talk about "all of us," but there are some souls who do better meditating on other things than the sacred Passion. For just as in heaven there are many mansions, so there are many roads that lead there. Some people find it useful to imagine hell. Others benefit from thinking about death. Some have such tender hearts that they cannot bear to stay with the imagery of the Passion. They find it comforting and inspiring to dwell on the power and glory of God as manifested in his creatures. They prefer to reflect on his infinite love for us and how this love is revealed in all things. This last way is a very good way, as long as it is balanced by sometimes thinking about the life of Christ and all that he did for our sake. He is the source of all our good, past and present.

14. Beginners on the path require wise counsel to determine what they really need. For this reason, an experienced guide is indispensable. If the spiritual director does not have personal experience, he can be badly mistaken and easily lead souls astray simply because he does not understand them and therefore is incapable of helping them to understand themselves. For their part, beginners may be so thrilled that they have someone to guide them that they do not deviate from whatever he tells them to do.

I have come upon souls so tormented and troubled by the inexperience of their spiritual guides that I felt truly sorry for them. There was one person who had no idea how to act for herself anymore. Ignorant guides do a great deal of damage to body and soul. Because they do not understand spiritual things, they actually obstruct spiritual progress. One person confided in me that her guide had held her in bondage for eight years by refusing to allow her to explore beyond the state of self-knowledge. Since the Beloved had already brought her to the Prayer of Quiet, this constraint was a great torment to her.

15. We must never neglect this process of self-inquiry. No soul on this path is such a spiritual giant that she doesn't need to return again and again to the divine breast and suckle there. Do not forget this! Since this is so important, I will repeat it often. No stage of prayer is so sublime that the practitioner does not need to come back frequently to the begin-

ning. Self-knowledge is the bread we must feed ourselves along the road of prayer, continuously supplementing the sublime delicacies we are given by God. In fact, without it, we cannot be sustained.

Still, we should eat this bread in moderation. We empty ourselves of ourselves. We clearly understand that anything good in us comes not from us but from God. We remember all that we owe to such a great King, and we feel ashamed of how little we have to repay him. Fine. Do not linger there; it's a waste of time. The Beloved has placed other foods in front of us and it would be wrong to disregard them. His Majesty knows what foods are best for us to eat at what times.

16. This is why it's so important to work with guides who are well informed, exhibit good judgment, and have experienced spiritual things themselves. It wouldn't hurt if they had some formal education as well. If they cannot meet all these criteria, they should at least have experience and sound judgment. It's always possible to locate a man of learning and consult with him when particular theological issues come up. Unless a learned man practices prayer himself, all his learning is of little help to beginners on the path.

I do not mean to imply that beginners should have nothing to do with educated men. I would rather see a spirit standing on the solid ground of truth without prayer than one who prays but has no knowledge. Learning is a great thing, because learned men teach those of us who know so little and illumine our ignorant minds. When we are exposed to the truths of sacred scripture, we are able to behave the way we should. God save us from foolish devotions!

17. I should explain myself better, but I keep going off on tangents. I have always been bad at explaining myself. I don't seem to know how to say things without using too many words.

All right. A contemplative begins to practice prayer. Her spiritual guide is a fool, and he takes it into his head that she should obey him unconditionally. He does not demand this out of malice. If he is not engaged in contemplative practice himself, he will think he is doing the right thing.

Maybe she is a householder, and he tells her to ignore the tasks at hand and just pray. This would put a great deal of stress on her marriage and family. Such a spiritual director doesn't know how to arrange things or manage time in a way that conforms to reality. Because he lacks light himself, he is incapable of enlightening anyone else, even though he might sincerely want to.

While I do not believe that true knowledge is dependent on education, I do think that every spiritual seeker should make an effort to have conversations with those who have a background in studies. The more educated the person, the better. The more spiritual the one who practices prayer, the greater her need for this kind of input.

18. We should not deceive ourselves by concluding that spiritual directors who do not practice prayer are useless to those of us who do. Over the years, I have increasingly sought the counsel of learned men because I desperately needed it. I have always had educated friends. Even though many of them lack contemplative experience, they certainly do not despise the spirit nor do they ignore it. After all, the scriptures they study continuously reveal the truth of the good spirit.

I believe that the devil will never be able to deceive a soul who practices prayer and consults learned men (unless she chooses to be deceived). Real learning, accompanied by humility and virtue, is a terrifying thing to the powers of evil, because it finds them out and banishes them.

19. I've emphasized this because there is a popular opinion that unless learned men are also spiritual, they are no help to people who practice prayer. I have already said that I believe it's necessary to have a spiritual director and that if he is not a learned man, this lack of learning is a serious drawback. If an educated man has integrity, even if he has not had direct spiritual experience, it can be very useful to consult him. God will help him to explain to us what we need to know—he may even give him the spiritual experience he lacks—and he will benefit us accordingly.

I speak from experience. This has happened to me at least twice. I repeat, any contemplative who puts herself in the hands of a single spiritual director without being certain that he possesses all the virtues I have mentioned will be making a big mistake. It is a heavy enough cross to bear when we forge a relationship with a guide who lacks these spiritual qualities; if his understanding is also poor, how can we voluntarily submit to his guidance? I myself have never been able to bring myself to do this, nor do I think that kind of submission is ever a good thing.

If the beginner on the path to prayer is not a monastic but a person who lives in the world, she should take advantage of the gift of freedom to choose her own spiritual director and praise God for it. She should take her time in selecting a guide until she finds someone suitable. Meanwhile she should cultivate her own humility and desire to make spiritual progress. If she does her part in this way, the Beloved will provide the right teacher for her.

I praise God with all my heart. All women and other people who have not had the benefit of an education should be infinitely grateful to him, for he has given us access to men who have labored hard to attain truths that those of us who are ignorant know nothing about.

20. I am frequently amazed that learned men, religious ones in particular, would bother to offer me the fruits of their labors simply because I ask. Imagine, there are people who have no desire to benefit from the work of these scholars. God forbid! I witness these men bearing the intense hardships of monastic life with its many penances, its bad food, its obligation of strict obedience, and it puts me to shame. On top of all this, they endure a constant lack of sleep. Everything is a trial for them, everything a cross.

It seems to me that it would be a terrible waste for anyone to forfeit the benefits of such a life willingly. Those of us who live as we please, free from such burdens, have spiritual food dropped into our mouths, as they say. Because we spend a little more time practicing prayer, we assume that we deserve more than those who have labored long hours to reap the fruits of knowledge.

21. Blessed be you, O Lord, who has made me incompetent and useless! And bless you even more for awakening so many to awaken us. We should pray unceasingly for those who give us light. What would we do without them during these tempestuous times when so many troubles buffet our society? If some of our leaders have gone bad, the good people shine even more brightly. May it please God to hold such souls in his hand and help them to help us. Amen.

22. I certainly have wandered off the subject I meant to speak about. But for those who are embarking on such a lofty journey, everything can be harnessed to set their feet on the right path.

Let's go back to what I was saying about meditating on Christ bound to the pillar. It is good to spend some time thinking and reflecting on the pains he suffered in those moments, why, who he is, and the love with which he bore his suffering. But we should not make a habit of exhausting ourselves in pursuit of these reflections. Rather, we should stay there in his presence with our minds quiet, our thoughts at rest.

If we can, we should occupy ourselves with simply gazing at he who is gazing at us. We should keep him company, talk with him, pray to him, humble ourselves and delight in him, remember what a privilege it is to be near him. Even if we only start off our prayer in this way, our souls will derive great benefit from this practice. I know mine has.

I don't know if I have succeeded in explaining this. You will have to be the judge of that. May it please the Lord that I bring him pleasure forever. Amen.

XIV ✠

The Waterwheel

WE HAVE SEEN how at first we learn to draw water up from the well, sustaining the garden through the labor of our own hands. Now let's explore the second method that the Master of the garden teaches us to employ. Turning the crank of a waterwheel, the gardener harnesses the forces of nature to pull the water through aqueducts and obtains more water with less effort. She no longer has to work constantly, and she can rest a little. This describes the Prayer of Quiet, which is what I'd like to discuss next.

The Prayer of Quiet comes when the soul begins to be drawn into a supernatural state of interior recollection. It is not a state of prayer that she can attain through her own efforts, although it is true that it can be tiring to turn the crank that pulls the water through the aqueducts. In this method, we engage the labor of the intellect to fill the bucket of the soul. But the water comes from a higher place now, and so it requires much less work than it did to pull it up from the well. What I mean is, the water of grace is much closer now and reveals itself more clearly in the soul.

This state is an ingathering of the faculties, allowing the soul to savor the sweetness of prayer more deeply. The other faculties are neither lost nor sleeping, but they are suspended. Only the will is actually occupied. Without knowing how it happened, the will has been taken captive. More than happy to be the prisoner of its Beloved, it consents without hesitation.

O Jesus! O Lord of mine! How precious your love is to us in this place.

Your love holds our love so closely that we are incapable of loving anything but you!

The suspended faculties support the will, expanding its capacity for the enjoyment of so much goodness. Every once in a while, the other faculties can actually make trouble for the soul, even when the will is already united with God. When that happens, the soul should simply ignore them and continue basking in joy and quietude. If the will tries to bring the other faculties along, it risks losing them all.

Then the faculties would behave like dissatisfied doves. Not content with the food the owner of the dovecote feeds them—food they receive without having to do anything for it—off they go, looking for something better. But discovering that nourishment is scarce out there, they come back.

So the wayward faculties go away and then return to see what the will is enjoying so much and if it will share some with them. If the Lord tosses them a handful of food, they stop and eat. If not, they continue their search. The soul who wants to force the faculties of memory and imagination to paint a picture of what she experiences for the benefit of the will may actually be doing more harm than good. The soul needs to treat her faculties with great care, as I will explain.

Everything that happens in this state of prayer deeply consoles the soul. Even if the state lasts a long time, it doesn't weary the soul because it costs so little in labor. The intellect works very gently here and extracts much more water than it did from the well. The tears God gives us now flow with joy. Although we cherish them when they come, we do nothing to induce them.

This water of bountiful blessings and mercies that the Lord gives us makes our virtues grow more abundantly than the water we drew in the beginning stages of prayer. Now the soul is rising above her misery and glimpsing glory. This not only causes the personal virtues to flower, but it brings the soul much closer to True Virtue—that is, God, the source of all goodness. As his Majesty begins to communicate directly to the soul, he wants her to feel this communication in every fiber of her being.

Arriving at this place, the soul finds her craving for mundane things falling away. No wonder! She clearly sees that she could never experience a single moment of this sublime glory here on earth. No wealth, no power, no honor or pleasure offers even a fleeting taste of that happiness. For this joy is true joy. It is unconditionally satisfying.

It is almost impossible to find satisfaction in our ordinary reality. Earthly things always have a *no* entwined with the *yes*. In a deep state of contemplation, everything is a *yes!* The *no* comes later, when the soul realizes that the delight has passed and that she doesn't know how to get it back. But even if she were to smash herself to pieces with penances and prayers and all those other practices, it would do no good. It's up to the Lord to decide whether or not to grant her this delight.

God in his greatness wants the soul to understand now that she doesn't need messengers to communicate with him. She can speak to him herself. And she doesn't need to shout either; he is so near that all she has to do is move her lips and he will understand her.

Maybe it seems silly for me to say this, since obviously God is always with us and he always understands us. There is no doubt about it. But what our Emperor and Lord desires is that we *know* in these moments that he understands us. That we know what his presence means. That we know that he wants to begin working with our soul in a special way. The deep inner and outer satisfaction that washes over us helps us to realize the difference between worldly pleasure and heavenly joy. The void carved out by our transgressions begins to fill up with this sublime sweetness.

This joy is bewildering to the soul. It unfolds in her secret depths and she doesn't know where it comes from or how it happens. She doesn't know what to do or what to want or what to ask for. She feels as if she has found everything at once, and yet she has no idea what she has found.

Again I find myself at a loss to explain this. Many things require a framework of learning to be understood properly, and I think this is one of them. It would be helpful, for instance, if I could describe the difference between a general and a particular grace because many people are ignorant of this distinction.

There are many other things I could express more accurately if I had a bit of education. But since this is going to be read by people who will be able to detect any errors in it, I'm going to continue without worrying.

I'm well aware that I can be mistaken in both matters of theology and those of the spirit. Fortunately, since this account will end up in the right hands, I can trust that the learned men who receive it will understand what I'm trying to say and omit anything that's wrong.

Still, since we are dealing with the beginning stages of the spiritual path, I feel that it's essential to do my best to explain this experience adequately. When the Beloved first begins to grant the soul these mercies, she doesn't understand what's happening to her or what to do with herself. If God is leading her along a path of fear, as he led me, then her confusion becomes a terrible trial. It's even worse when there is no one around who understands her. That's why it can be such an intense relief to see yourself described in a book. It's affirming to discover that you are on the right path after all.

I know how wonderful it is to find out what you need to do to make spiritual progress. I have suffered terribly and wasted so much time not knowing how to proceed. I have tremendous compassion for souls who arrive at this stage only to find themselves alone. Although I have read many spiritual books that touch on these subjects, they don't really explain much. Even if the explanations were ample, an inexperienced soul will have a hard time understanding what is happening to her.

I want so much for the Lord to help me convey the effects that these supernatural things begin to have on the soul! By recognizing the effects, the soul may know whether or not the cause is the spirit of God or something else. I say "the soul may know," but I mean only insofar as we can understand heavenly things while we are here on earth. It's always a good thing to walk with caution and restraint. Because even though an experience may be the work of God, the spirit of evil can sometimes transform itself into an angel of light and an inexperienced soul might not be able to tell the difference. In fact, most souls may need to reach the pinnacle of prayer before they develop that degree of discernment.

The fact that I have so little time to give to this writing certainly does not help my ability to explain any of this very well. Therefore, his Majesty must come to my rescue. Living in a house that was so recently founded, I am inundated with community duties and other related business. I can only write in fits and spurts, and I can never really settle down into it. I wish I had more space to write, because when the Lord gives me inspiration, the words flow with great ease and clarity. Then writing is just like sketching a model that is sitting right in front of me.

But when inspiration is lacking, it doesn't matter how many years a person might have spent in prayer, my words make no more sense than if I were speaking Arabic, as the saying goes. And so it seems to me that my only hope is to enter a state of prayer while I am writing. That's when I can clearly see that I am not the one doing the writing. I'm not the one planning out in my mind what I'm going to say nor do I understand afterward how I managed to say it at all. This happens to me often.

Let's return our attention now to our garden. See how the orchard is beginning to bud. Feel how the trees will soon burst into full blossom and then bear fruit. Smell the whiff of carnation and other flowers.

This imagery is utterly charming to me. I have always loved the notion of my soul as a garden and the Beloved taking his walks in it. When I was beginning on this path, I used to beg his Majesty to intensify the fragrance of those little flowers of virtue that I could see had begun to blossom inside me. I wanted nothing for myself, and so I asked him to sustain the garden for his own greater glory. "Go ahead and cut whatever you please," I said to God. I knew that pruning would only make the flowers bloom with greater vigor.

I talk about pruning because there are times when the soul forgets all about the garden. Everything appears to be dry, and it doesn't seem like there will ever be enough water to sustain it. The soul cannot detect a single virtue inside herself. She suffers terrible tribulation because she feels like she has utterly failed to tend and water the garden that has been entrusted to her.

This aridity is the will of the Lord. Only when the gardener surrenders her self-importance does God take over, pulling up the weeds and rooting out every plant that has gone bad, no matter how small it may be. She is forced to acknowledge that if God chooses to withhold the water of grace, no amount of effort on her part is going to keep the garden growing. She must see herself as nothing. As less than nothing. Then her humility stimulates the garden to bloom again.

O my Lord and my greatest Good! I cannot say this without crying. My soul rejoices to know the truth that you choose to be fully present with us in the sacrament of Holy Communion. It is our own imperfections that prevent us from being with you all the time, since you have made it clear that you would be happy to be with us, that in fact your greatest delight is to be with the children of the earth. What does this mean? These words have always been deeply consoling to me, even when I have wandered the farthest from my path.

Is it possible that there could be a soul, O Lord, who reaches the stage at which you bestow such blessings and mercies on her and has understood your desire to be with her and yet goes right back to offending you in spite of all the gifts you have given her? It's not as if she had not received striking demonstrations of your love. The effects of this love are far too obvious to be doubted.

Yes, there certainly is such a soul, a soul who has done this not once but many times. I am that soul! Please, my Beloved, let it be that I am the only one who has been so ungrateful, who has made such terrible mistakes and shown you such flagrant ingratitude. Yet your boundless goodness has drawn out something worthwhile even from my excessive wickedness. The more faithlessly I behaved, the more brilliantly the wonder of your mercy shone. Your blessings are so abundant, I could sing of them forever!

Let it be so, my God. I beseech you. Let me sing your praises without end. You have granted your mercies to me so liberally that anyone who witnesses them is awestruck. As for me, your holy compassion transports me beyond myself so that all I can do is glorify you even more. I could not remain inside myself without you in me, Lord. I would be able to do nothing more than cut away the remaining flowers until my garden returned to the state of the dunghill it used to be.

Do not let this be, my Lord! Do not give up on the soul you have won through such intense labor, the soul you have rescued again and again from the jaws of the dreaded dragon.

Please forgive me. I have wandered off the subject again. Don't be surprised; I'm following a subject of my own. It's just that every time I go inside myself and write about all that I owe my beloved God, something greater than I takes over, triggering a flood of feelings, and I cannot resist continuously proclaiming his glory. I don't think this will displease you very much, since I believe we can sing the same song, even if the melody is a little different. You and I both know that I owe God even more praise, because he has had more reason to grant me forgiveness.

XV ✠

THE PRAYER OF QUIET

NOW LET'S get back to our subject. The satisfaction and serenity the soul experiences at this deeper stage of prayer are signs of the quietude and recollection God has bestowed on her. These feelings are accompanied by a sense of profound contentment and calm, as well as a gentle joy that permeates the faculties. Since this is the furthest the soul has ever traveled, she thinks she has nothing left to strive for. Like Saint Peter, she would gladly "make her dwelling there."

The soul in this state hardly dares to move or stir for fear that this delight will slip through her fingers. Sometimes she is afraid to even breathe. The poor little thing doesn't realize that just as there was nothing she could do to obtain this blessing by her own efforts, she is even less capable of holding on to it longer than the Lord desires her to have it.

I have already mentioned that in this initial recollection and quietude, the faculties of the soul do not cease functioning. But the soul is content just to abide with God, so the calm and quietude endure as long as the recollection lasts. The other faculties may be distracted, but the will is in union with God. Gradually, the will draws the intellect and memory back into a state of recollection. Even though the will is not yet totally absorbed, it is so thoroughly engaged (with what, it doesn't really know) that no matter how hard the other faculties may try, they cannot steal its joy and contentment. In fact, with hardly any effort, the will helps keep this tiny spark of love for God from going out.

May his Majesty be pleased to give me the grace to explain this clearly, because a multitude of souls enter this state, but few transcend it. I don't know whose fault that is; it certainly isn't God's. What I do know is that once his Majesty has granted a soul the blessing of attaining the Prayer of Quiet, he will not fail to give her many more favors unless she herself rejects his mercy.

It is very important for the soul to realize the immense dignity of this state. The Lord has done her an incredible favor to bring her to the Prayer of Quiet. She sees that she no longer belongs wholly to this earth because the Beloved, in his great goodness, is about to make her a citizen of heaven. That is, as long as she doesn't try to stop him.

Too bad for her if she turns back! If she does, I think she will slide all the way to the bottom. This is where I would have ended up if the Lord hadn't rescued me. Serious transgressions lead the soul into this downward spiral. Only the blindness induced by evil could cause the soul to forfeit such goodness.

So if his Majesty has favored you so highly that you have attained this state, I beg you, for the love of God, know yourself. With humble and holy confidence, hold yourself in high esteem. Otherwise, you will be tempted to return to the slave food of Egypt. But if weakness, wickedness, and misery cause you to fall as I fell, always bear in mind the good you have lost. You would be correct to lose some trust in yourself. Stand in holy awe. If you give up the practice of prayer, you will only go from bad to worse.

I consider it a real calamity when people begin to despise the path that has led them to so much good. These are the ones to whom I'm speaking. I'm not saying that they may never again forsake God or commit any transgressions. Even though there are plenty of good reasons why those who have begun to receive these blessings should be on their guard against sin, I acknowledge that we are all human. All I am saying is that they should never stop praying.

Contemplative prayer teaches us to be mindful of what we are doing. It inspires us to seek reconciliation with our God. It helps us draw the strength we need to elevate our souls. We must believe that if we abandon the path of prayer, we are flirting with grave danger. This is just my opinion. I'm not sure if I even understand what I'm saying. All I have to go on is my own experience.

The Prayer of Quiet is a little spark of True Love that the Lord begins to ignite in the soul. He wants the soul to understand the joyous nature of this love. Anyone who has experienced the Prayer of Quiet will immediately agree that this sacred spark is not something we can grasp for ourselves. Human nature tends to be greedy; we cling to any moment of delight. But no matter how desperately we may wish to kindle the blaze and bask in holy delight, all we end up doing is dousing the fire, leaving our souls cold.

The deep quietude and recollection that accompanies the Prayer of Quiet are good indicators that this little spark, no matter how small it may be, is from God and not the spirit of evil, nor is it a delight that we have fabricated for ourselves. As long as we don't extinguish it with our own imperfections, this spark will ignite the Great Fire, spreading the same flames of passionate God-love that we observe blazing in advanced souls.

This little spark is a sign of God's promise that he has chosen the soul for great things. It is her choice whether or not she will prepare herself to receive his gifts. And this state of prayer is a greater gift than I can ever express.

It makes me very sad to see how many souls attain this high state and yet how few ever go beyond it. I'm ashamed to mention it. I shouldn't say that there are only a few. There must be many, because God wouldn't sustain us for no reason. I'm only referring to what I've witnessed.

For those souls who have reached this state, I have some advice: take care not to hide your talents. It seems that God has chosen you to be of service to others. This is especially important in times like these, when strong friends of God are needed to support the weak ones. You who recognize this gift in yourself may consider yourself to be a friend of God as long as you abide by the rules that govern a good friendship even here in the world. If not, watch out! You might bring harm to yourself and, God forbid, to others as well.

All the soul needs to do during these times of quietude is be still and make no noise. What I mean by noise is rushing around with the intellect trying to rustle up reflections of gratitude and words of praise for the gift you are being given. It's that impulse of the mind to catalog your transgressions to convince yourself that you do not deserve to receive such grace. It's that commotion the faculties create, the intellect trying to conjure up images and the memory rushing to store them. These faculties wear me out. I may have a poor memory, but sometimes I seem to be incapable of subduing it.

The will needs to understand, calmly and wisely, that we cannot force God to do what we want. Any effort to do so would be like carelessly piling huge logs onto a fire and smothering it. The will ought to acknowledge its powerlessness and simply say, "Lord, what is my rightful place here? What does the devotee have to do with the Master? What is the relationship of earth to heaven?" Or it can speak any other words of love that occur to it in these moments as long as they are rooted in truth. But the will should ignore the intellect; the mind is nothing more than a grinding mill at this time.

The will may have an irresistible urge to share the joy it is experiencing with the intellect. It may strive to bring the mind into a state of recollection. Often during the Prayer of Quiet, the will is in serene union with the Divine while the mind wanders around aimlessly. It is better for the will to leave the intellect alone than to chase after it. All that the will needs to do now is remain in recollection like a wise bee and simply enjoy the gift. For if all the bees were always zipping around trying to bring the others into the hive, no bees would actually be inside the hive doing the important work of making honey.

If the soul does not take care in this matter, she risks losing a great deal. The more developed the intellect, the bigger the danger. Once the soul launches its search for concepts and starts composing little speeches, she convinces herself that she is doing something important, especially if she comes up with pretty ideas and words to express them.

The soul needs to recognize that there is absolutely no reason that God should grant us this mercy other than his great goodness. She should be aware that she is very near his Majesty and take this opportunity to ask for his continued blessing. She should also pray for the whole of the spiritual community and include those who have asked for her prayers and also those who have died. She should not use a lot of noisy words but quietly express her yearning to be heard.

More important things are enfolded in this simple prayer than in a thousand big ideas generated by the intellect. When the will spontaneously realizes its spiritual growth, it quickens with the fire of love. This inspires it to engage in loving acts toward the One to whom it owes so much. It does all this without involving the noisy intellect, which is busy searching for grand concepts. If we place a tiny twig of humility on this fire of love, we are doing far more to intensify the blaze than if we were to feed it a hundred huge logs of discursive reasoning. While we might think we are being erudite, we would only snuff the flame in less time than it takes to recite the creed.

This is especially useful advice for the learned men who ordered me to write this. Surely, through the goodness of God, you will attain this high state of prayer at some point. You might be inclined to apply biblical interpretations to spiritual experiences. Your studies may be of tremendous benefit before and afterward, but in the midst of contemplative prayer, education is irrelevant. In fact, all of your theological concepts may only serve to cool the fire of love in the will.

At times like these, I find that my intellect is so close to the light that it sees everything with incomparable clarity. And I, though I am what I am, seem to be someone else altogether. Ordinarily, I hardly understand any of the liturgy in Latin, least of all the psalms. But when I am in this state of quietude, I not only understand the prayers as if they were written in Spanish, but I even go beyond this to rejoice in the meaning that transcends all language.

I'm not talking about the occasions when learned men need to preach or teach. In that case, their studies are a good thing, because they help poor people like me who have little education of their own. It is always a good thing to offer charity and sustained compassion toward all souls, as long as the caring comes from a simple place and is dedicated to God.

When the gift of quietude comes to learned men, they should put all learning aside and simply rest in the stillness. The time will come when their knowledge will be useful to the Beloved. Then they will value their education so highly that they would not trade it for any treasure. All they will want is to use it in service of his Majesty.

Believe me, in the presence of Infinite Wisdom, a little study of humility and a few humble acts are worth more than all the knowledge in the world. In the Prayer of Quiet, there is no room for rational argument. All that is required is that we know exactly who we are. We must simply place ourselves in the presence of God. He seems to want to strip us of our reason and render us utterly foolish. Indeed, his Majesty humbles himself so radically that he allows fools to come near him!

But the intellect is still activated and moved to articulate ardent prayers of gratitude. The will, on the other hand, is very calm, and like the publican, keeps its eyes lowered. In this quiet way, the will expresses its thanks far more clearly and fully than does the intellect with all its fancy rhetoric. There is no reason in this state to renounce all forms of discursive meditation or even vocal prayer. Yet if the quietude is deep enough, the soul will find herself practically incapable of speaking anyway, at least not without a great deal of painful effort.

I believe it is possible for us to discern whether this quietude comes from the spirit of God or whether we are picking up the devotional impulse God gave us originally and trying to harness it ourselves to achieve the state we desire. Remember, if we struggle to attain the Prayer of Quiet by our own effort, it doesn't work. What little serenity we eke out dissipates quickly and leaves us feeling dry.

I also think that an experienced seeker can tell if the state of quietude comes from the spirit of evil. If that's the case, it will lack the characteristic humility and will leave the soul feeling agitated. It contributes nothing to preparing the soul to receive the effects that the genuine Prayer of Quiet, given directly by God, engenders. It neither illumines the intellect nor fortifies the will.

As long as the soul follows the directive to fix her thoughts and desires on God, directing the goodness and delight she experiences to him alone, the spirit of evil can do her little or no harm. Not only will the spirit of evil gain nothing in this way, but the joy that God arouses in the soul will be taken away from the spirit of evil in equal measure. Since the soul believes that her delight comes from God, she is filled with longing for him and motivated to seek him again and again through contemplative prayer.

If she is a humble soul and more curious about the cross than about spiritual rewards, she won't pay attention to the comforts offered by the spirit of evil. But when the consolation comes from the spirit of God, the soul will be incapable of ignoring it and will hold it in the highest esteem. Once the spirit of evil notices that the soul has humbled herself in every aspect of prayer, it will have to admit that it has lost the game and will stop coming around to bother her.

Remember when I was talking about the first water, which represented the first stage of prayer? I pointed out how important it is for beginners on the path to begin cultivating detachment from sensory gratification right from the start. They should enter a life of prayer determined to help Christ carry his cross, like faithful warriors who are dedicated to the task of serving their king with no concern about compensation, secure in the knowledge of their ultimate reward. All they need to do is keep their eyes fixed on the true and everlasting kingdom we are all striving to attain.

The same kind of concentration is required here. We always need to hold this kingdom in our minds, at least at the beginning. As we advance on the path, we will not have to strive so hard to remember that all things are impermanent, that everything is nothing, and that any refuge we find here on earth is not real refuge at all. Eventually we will discover that sometimes we need to forget these things and simply live.

Detachment, in and of itself, is a lowly goal. Spiritual adepts would consider it insulting if someone suggested that they give up the pleasures of the world simply because these things all come to an end. Even if such pleasures were to last forever, advanced souls would gladly give them up for God. In fact, the more evolved these souls have become and the more enduring the pleasures they are offering up for God, the happier they are. For souls like these, love has intensified to such a degree that it takes over everything. Love does all the work.

But for beginners, this advice about consciously cultivating detachment is of the utmost importance, and this is why I make such a point of it. Beginners should not dismiss this counsel but rather trust that following it will lead them to great good. Even souls who have already attained a high state of prayer may sometimes find themselves being tested by God to such an extent that they begin to wonder if his Majesty is giving up on them; when this happens, they will also find this teaching useful.

Don't forget, the growth of the soul is not exactly like the growth of the body. I mean, the soul does grow, but it obeys different rules. Once a child has become an adult and developed a strong body, he doesn't shrink and become small again. But the Beloved does allow this to happen to the soul. The only way I know this is that I've seen it myself. I suppose the purpose of this is to humble us for our own greater good and to remind us not to become careless in this state of exile. The higher we ascend, the more closely we must pay attention, and the less we must rely on our own devices.

The time comes when even the most radically surrendered souls must protect themselves against offending God. Their wills are so aligned with the will of God that they would rather be tortured and die a thousand deaths than commit a single imperfection. Still, they are sure to find themselves at some point or another being attacked by temptations and persecutions. When this happens, they need to pull out the first weapon of prayer and remember that everything is impermanent, that all things come to an end, and that there is life after death. In this way, they will avoid spiritual error.

Let's review what I've been saying. When we start off determined to follow the way of the cross and refuse to be lured by the craving for consolation, we build a solid foundation and protect ourselves against the tricks the spirit of evil uses to deceive us. After all, the Beloved himself pointed to this way of perfection when he said, "Take up your cross and follow me." He is our example; whoever walks in his footsteps with the sole desire of pleasing him has nothing to fear.

Such souls will begin to detect improvement in themselves and will be able to recognize that these positive effects are not the work of the spirit of evil. When these souls fall, they quickly get back up because the Lord is with them. Here are some other signs of God's presence: when it is the spirit of God that induces the deep quietude, the soul has no need for manufacturing feelings of humility and unworthiness. The Beloved himself gives this gift of prayer in such a way that it transcends anything we could achieve through our nice little rationalizations. Self-mortification is nothing compared to the true humility that springs to light when the Lord shines on us. This produces a revelation that totally undoes us.

The sudden awareness that we are nothing is a gift from God. This experience is not uncommon. And the more bountifully we are blessed, the deeper this awareness grows. God fills us with an intense desire for spiritual transformation and the determination not to give up on prayer

no matter how severely we may be tested. We are willing to suffer anything that comes our way.

While standing in humility and trepidation, we are simultaneously
certain that we will be liberated. This conviction banishes all servile fear
and replaces it with holy awe. We have matured and grown in faith. We
become conscious of the stirrings of a love for God that is free of self-
interest. We crave periods of solitude and silence so that we may more
deeply savor this grace.

I am getting tired now, so I will try to wrap this up. The Prayer of
Quiet is the beginning of all blessings. The soul clearly sees that the
flowers in her garden have been given everything they need to burst into
blossom. She is incapable of believing that the Beloved is not with her
until she turns back to see the flaws and imperfections in herself, and
then she grows afraid. This fear can be a good thing. But some souls
benefit more from the simple belief that God is with them always than
from any combination of fears that might strike them. If it is a person's
nature to be loving and grateful, then merely remembering a blessing
she has received will do more to bring her back to God than reflecting
on all the possible punishments of hell. At least this was true in my case,
wicked though I may be.

Later I will more fully describe the signs of the good spirit. For now,
it is too difficult for me to explain them adequately. I believe that by the
grace of God, I will find a way to convey what he wants me to say. While
I trust in my own experience because I have reflected on it so thoroughly
and have understood so much of what it has to teach me, I also have the
added benefit of having consulted with some very learned men. These
are holy people who are worthy of our respect. With resources like these
available, souls who have reached this stage through the goodness of
God may not have to weary themselves to the brink of death, as I did.

XVI ✠

THE STREAM OF HOLY MADNESS

L ET'S GO ON now to speak of the third water that nourishes the garden of the soul: the water that flows through a stream or a spring. This method irrigates the garden with much less labor than it takes to crank a waterwheel or pull a heavy bucket up from a deep well, though it still requires some effort to channel the flow. But the Lord is so eager to help his servant at this stage that he practically becomes the gardener himself. God is the one who does almost everything.

In this state of prayer, the faculties are lulled to sleep. They do not entirely cease to function, but they do not understand how they are functioning. The consolation, goodness, and delight the soul experiences here are incomparably more intense than what she tasted in the previous stage. The water of grace has risen up to her throat, and she is immobilized. She does not know how to move forward, and she is incapable of turning back.

All the soul wants is to rejoice in this great glory. She is like a man who is already holding the funeral candle in his hand, on the brink of dying the death he has been longing for. The delight he takes in his agony defies all description. This state of prayer seems to me nothing other than a death. It is the near total dying to all earthly things, a dying into God. And it is a joyous passing.

I don't know how else to explain this. Words fail to describe it. The soul herself doesn't know what to do. Should she speak or be silent? Should she laugh or weep? It is a glorious bewilderment, a heavenly madness. In this blessed foolishness lies all wisdom. And the soul takes great delight in her unlearning.

It has been five or six years, as I recall, since the Beloved first blessed me with this state of prayer, and he has given it to me abundantly. I have neither understood it nor have I figured out how to speak of it. And so I decided that when I came to this place in the account of my life, I would say very little about it or maybe even nothing at all. What I have understood is that the Prayer of Quiet is not yet a complete union of the soul's faculties with the Divine. I also recognized that it was a higher state of prayer than the previous one. But I confess that I could not begin to discern or describe what the difference was.

In having asked for guidance from such a simple person as myself, you have demonstrated true humility. Perhaps that is why the Lord granted me the gift of this prayer today after Communion. There I was, offering thanks to God, when his Majesty interrupted me to suggest certain spiritual metaphors and then taught me how to explain what the soul needs to do at this stage. I understood everything in a flash, and I was amazed.

How often have I been mystified and intoxicated with love but incapable of understanding what was happening to me? I knew very well that it was the work of God, but I did not know how he was working. The truth is, while the faculties in this state are almost totally united with the Divine, they are not so absorbed that they cease to function. I am so happy that today I have understood this at last. Blessed be the Lord who has given me this gift!

The only power the faculties retain is the ability to surrender themselves completely to God. Not one of them seems to dare stir. The only way that we could make them move is if we deliberately forced ourselves to shift our attention to some external thing. But frankly, I doubt that we would be able to do this successfully at such a time.

The soul utters a stream of praises here without pausing to compose them. It is the Lord who imposes order on the blessed chaos and puts words around the soul's overwhelming gratitude. The intellect is worthless here. The soul cannot contain herself. She yearns to pour out her praises. She is delightfully disquieted. Her flowers are already blooming and beginning to spread their fragrance.

The soul wishes that everyone could behold her in this state and, witnessing her glory, join her in singing God's praises. She has a profound need to share her joy; it is too great to bear alone. This reminds me of the woman in the Gospel who wanted to gather—or did gather—all her neighbors. This joy must have been what the royal prophet David felt when he played his harp and sang of the glory of God. I am deeply devoted to this glorious king. I wish everyone else would be too. David is especially good for those of us who tend to be sinners.

O God, help me! What is a soul like in this state? She wishes she were made all of tongues to do nothing but praise the Lord. She babbles a thousand words of holy madness, trying to find exactly the right way to please the One who has taken her captive.

I know a certain person who is no poet, but while taken up in this divine delirium, composed spontaneous stanzas that expressed her anguish with passionate accuracy. Her poetry was not the work of the discursive mind. She was simply complaining directly to her God about her blessed distress. And this outpouring allowed her to experience the glory that accompanied her anguish even more deeply. She wanted her whole being to shatter into pieces to demonstrate the joy she felt in such pain.

What torments would the soul in this state refuse to bear? If her Beloved offered her trials, she would gladly suffer them for his sake. In fact, it would fill her with delight to do so. I clearly see that when the martyrs suffered persecution, they were not doing this on their own. A greater power gave them the strength to endure all things. But what more terrible pain must the soul bear when she has to return to her senses and step back into the mundane world with all its petty concerns and formalities?

I honestly do not believe I have been exaggerating. There are no words potent enough to convey the exquisite joy with which the Beloved blesses the soul in this exile of hers. May you be forever blessed, my Lord! May all things praise you forever!

Even as I write this, I am not free from that holy, heavenly madness. This is the gift of your divine goodness and mercy. I have done nothing to deserve such grace. Please, my King, either make it so that everyone I speak to of your love goes crazy with love for you or else forbid me from speaking at all! Lord, either grant that I have nothing more to do with the affairs of this world or else take me out of it altogether!

This servant of yours can no longer bear the trial of seeing herself without you. If you insist on her living, please, Beloved, do not let her rest. All she wants is to be free. Sleeping tortures her. Eating poisons her. She watches herself wasting precious hours of this life on comforts. But nothing can comfort her anymore except you. Life is empty now. She no longer desires to live in herself but only to live in you.

O my true Lord and Glory! The cross you have prepared for those who have attained this state is both unbearably heavy and exceedingly light. It is light because it is so sweet. And it is heavy because there are times when the soul cannot bear to carry it another step. Yet she would never want to be free of it unless being free meant going straight to you.

When she reflects that she has done nothing so far to serve you in this life and that her only hope for serving you lies in staying alive, the soul wishes that she would never die, that her cross would grow even heavier, and that she could carry it to the end of the world. The only rest she finds is the rest that comes with doing you some small service. She doesn't know what she wants. Her only desire is for you.

O my son! (The man who ordered me to write this account is so humble that he wants me to address him this way.) These passages in which I have gotten so carried away should be for your eyes alone. Nothing could persuade me to hold myself back when the Lord transports me beyond myself. Ever since I took Communion this morning, I don't even feel like I'm the one speaking. Everything seems like a dream. If only everyone I met were stricken with this sickness I have contracted. I beg you, may we all go mad for love of the One who was called mad for love of us.

You claim to love me. Prove it. Prepare yourself to receive this blessed gift from God. Most people are too sober to let themselves go as they ought to. I may well be more guilty of this than anyone. You must not let me be that way! I call you "Father," and you are like a son to me. You are also my spiritual guide and I have entrusted my soul to you. Tell me the truth and dispel my illusions. Why is this kind of truth-telling such a rare thing?

I wish that the five of us friends who love each other in Christ could make a pact. We would gather together on a regular basis for the purpose of freeing each other from illusion. We would suggest ways in which each of us could improve our relationship with God. No one knows himself as well as someone close to him who observes him with love and concern for his spiritual growth.

These days there are groups of heretics that secretly get together just to plot wicked deeds against his Majesty. We would also have to meet in secret, because the kind of holy conversation I am proposing is not popular anymore. Even preachers are composing sermons so carefully that they will not risk displeasing anyone. Their intentions are fine. Their deeds are fine. But do they convince anyone to mend their lives? No!

Why doesn't the average sermon inspire people to renounce whatever stands between them and their God? Do you want to know what I think? I think those who preach at the pulpit are too circumspect. They are nothing like the apostles, on fire with love of God, casting aside all restraint. Their meager flames offer little warmth. I'm not suggesting that their fire should burn as intensely as the blaze in the hearts of the apostles, but it could be a little hotter than what I see.

Do you know what I think our greatest concern should be? Becoming detached from our lives and relinquishing our self-importance. All we need to do is tell the truth and hold it up for the greater glory of God. Fame and blame should be equally meaningless to us. In fact, those who risk everything for God will find that they have both lost it all and gained it all. I'm not claiming to have achieved this kind of equanimity myself, but I'm working on it.

Oh, what freedom it is to consider it captivity to live in the world and abide by its rules. This freedom is a gift from God. What slaves wouldn't risk everything to earn their ransom and return to their homeland? This is the True Path. Why linger along the roadside? The treasure we seek is so vast that unless we keep walking, we will not attain it until the end of our lives. May the Lord help us on our way!

Tear up what I have just written if you think it would be best. Consider it to be a private letter from me to you. And if I have been too bold, please forgive me.

XVII ✠

THE FRAGRANCE OF VIRTUE

I THINK I HAVE offered a reasonable account of the third water of prayer. I have told you what the soul needs to do and, more importantly, what she needs to let God do inside of her, since it is God who has taken over the job of gardener. He wants the soul to rest for a while.

The only task the will has is to yield to the delight of these blessings. It should simply submit to whatever True Wisdom wants to do to it at this point. Such surrender requires courage. The soul's joy is so intense that she feels she is about to be catapulted out of the body altogether. And what a glorious death that would be!

I think it's a good idea for the soul to abandon herself completely into the arms of God. If he brings her to heaven, then off she goes to heaven. If she is bound for hell, this does not bother her, as long as her Highest Good is with her. If her life comes to an end, so be it. And if she lives for a thousand years, that, too, is fine with her. Let his Majesty treat her as his own; she no longer belongs to herself. She has given the whole of her being to the Beloved. She has relinquished self-interest entirely.

The effects of this state of prayer are so powerful that the soul can handle anything that comes to her from God. And without any intellectual involvement, the soul fully understands the power God is giving her. She is simply amazed at what a good gardener her Beloved is and in awe of his generosity. God wants the soul to do nothing more than rest in the garden and enjoy the sublime fragrance beginning to emanate from the flowers.

The Keeper of the garden is also, of course, the Creator of the water. And in a single visit, no matter how brief, he unleashes a boundless flow.

The Heavenly Gardener accomplishes in one moment the peace the poor soul had been unable to attain in twenty years of exhausting intellectual labor. And so the fruit grows and ripens so that if it is God's will, the soul can draw her sustenance from it.

But God does not give the soul permission to share her fruits until she has eaten enough to grow strong. Otherwise, she would be distributing tastes of this sublime food to everyone else, sustaining them at her own cost. Then the soul would have offered nothing back to the One who has given her everything, and she would be starving to death herself.

Learned men will understand exactly what I'm talking about here and will be able to figure out how to apply it to their own spiritual lives. I am getting tired now, and I can't explain it any better than this.

As the Prayer of Quiet deepens, the virtues grow so strong that the soul cannot ignore them. She sees that she has changed, but she is not sure how this happened. The perfume that has begun to emanate from the flowers inspires the soul to engage in spontaneous acts of greatness. The Beloved wants the buds in the garden of the soul to open so that the soul will see the virtues that have flowered in her.

The soul remains clearly aware that she could never have acquired these virtues on her own in a million years. God knows she has tried! She understands that the Heavenly Gardener has given them to her all at once. The more profound the Prayer of Quiet, the deeper the soul's humility. She recognizes that she has done nothing to earn this divine grace except simply to submit to God's blessings and willfully embrace them.

This state of prayer strikes me as an unequivocal union of the whole soul with God. Yet it seems his Majesty has invited the individual faculties to partake of the experience so that they can understand all that he is doing for the soul and can rejoice in his great work. Sometimes— actually, quite often—the soul notices that the will seems to be thoroughly enjoy her divine captivity. This used to confuse me. That's why I'm telling you about it, so that you will be prepared when it happens to you. The will stands alone in a place of deep quiet, while the intellect and memory are free to take care of business and engage in acts of generosity.

This state may resemble the Prayer of Quiet, but it's different. In the Prayer of Quiet, the soul does not want to shift or stir; she basks in the holy repose of Mary. But in this state, the soul also becomes like Martha; she leads the active and contemplative life at the same time. She can efficiently conduct business, tend to people in need, or read a good book, but she isn't fully in charge of herself. She understands that her best part is somewhere else altogether. It feels a little like talking to a person on one side while someone on our other side is talking to us; we wouldn't fully attend to either one.

This is a deeply felt state of prayer. It brings with it a profound sense of satisfaction and joy. It is excellent preparation for the soul to attain the depths of quietude later, when she at last has the opportunity to step away from her busy life and sit in solitude and stillness.

The soul here is like a person whose appetite has been satisfied, so he doesn't crave anything. But he is not so full that he would refuse some delicious morsel if someone offered it to him. In fact, he would eat it with gusto. This soul finds the pleasures of the world to be entirely unsatisfying now, so she does not hunger for them. Everything she wants is inside of her. All she seeks is an ever-intensifying connection with God, the opportunity to enjoy him more and more, time and space just to be with him. God alone satisfies her desires.

There is another state of prayer, deeper than the second spiritual water, but not as profound as the third. It is not yet total union, but it is approaching it. The Lord may give you all three waters, if he hasn't already. When this happens, you will be happy to find them all written down here so that you can recognize what they are. It's one blessing to receive the grace of God. It's another to understand what kind of grace you're receiving. And it's a third to know how to describe and explain it. Although it may seem like the first blessing is enough, the soul who can understand the gift of grace is at a distinct advantage. Knowledge alleviates fear and confusion. Then the soul can courageously follow the path of the Lord, trampling worldly attachments underfoot.

Any one of these blessings is reason enough to praise the Lord with all your heart. Even if you have not received such grace yourself, you still have cause to glorify him. After all, if his Majesty has bestowed his gift on anyone alive, all the rest of us may benefit from it.

There is something special that happens in the advanced degree of union I'm about to describe. This seems to be particularly true for me, since God often blesses me in this way. In this state, God gathers up the will and also the intellect. Now the soul is incapable of engaging in discursive thought. All she can do is rejoice in him.

The soul here is like someone watching a spectacle; he sees so many different things that he doesn't know where to look first. Now he glances here, now there. And he ends up not really perceiving anything. The memory and the imagination in this state remain free. It is astonishing to witness the havoc these fragmented faculties wreak when they are left alone! They want to turn everything into chaos.

Sometimes I detest the memory; it exhausts me. I beg the Lord to please take mine away during these periods of prayer if it is going to insist on disturbing me so much. I say to him, "When, my God, will my soul be entirely whole in praise of you, rather than fragmented and useless?" Now I understand the harm we do to ourselves when we miss the mark. That's when we become caught by our attachments and cannot do what we truly want: to focus exclusively on God.

As I said, this happens to me frequently. In fact, it just happened to me today, so I vividly recall the nuances of the experience. My soul is torn asunder with longing to be one with that part of myself that is one with God. But this is not possible. Instead, the memory and imagination wage war on the soul, and she is powerless to defend herself. Since the other faculties are suspended, these two cannot do the soul real harm, but they cause plenty of trouble just by agitating her.

When I say that the faculties of memory and imagination are incapable of causing active harm, I mean that they are weak and easily distracted. They try to present images to the intellect, but it cannot support them. And so they flit from thing to thing, jumping from one extreme to another, and they never rest. They remind me of little nocturnal moths. This is an apt metaphor, I think, because those moths may be annoying, but they are basically harmless.

So far, God has not revealed a remedy to me, so I'm not sure what to recommend. Believe me, I would be thrilled to find a solution myself, since imagination and memory often leave me exhausted and upset. This situation equally demonstrates our profound misery and also the awesome power of God. The unleashed faculties rush around tormenting us, while the suspended faculties rest in his Majesty's loving embrace.

I have worn myself out looking for an antidote, and the closest thing I have found is to pay no more attention to the memory than you would pay to a crazy person. Just let it go its own way. Only God can stop it. When he does, it becomes his slave. Meanwhile, we must patiently endure it, as Jacob put up with Leah. After all, didn't God bless us immeasurably by allowing us to enjoy Rachel?

When I say that the memory becomes God's captive, what I mean is that no matter how hard it tries, it cannot drag the other faculties along with it. On the contrary, without any effort, the other faculties often draw the memory to them. Sometimes when God finds the memory so lost and confused, longing to be in the company of the others, he takes pity on it. Then his Majesty allows it to ignite in the flame of the same divine candle that has already burned the other faculties to ashes. Their ordinary nature has been replaced by an almost supernatural enjoyment of divine blessings.

This third spiritual water bubbles up from an internal spring and bathes the soul in peaceful glory. Her joy is so great that the body tangibly shares in the soul's delightful interlude. And the virtues flower at the taste of such grace.

It seems to me that the Beloved has helped me clearly explain the states in which the soul finds herself, at least as clearly as can possibly be understood here on earth. Feel free to discuss this with anyone who has experienced these states and has had some religious education. If a learned person pronounces my explanations valid, know that God gave them to me and please thank his Majesty very much.

Remember, even if a person has already been blessed with the delight of these deep states of prayer, he will also be grateful to comprehend what is happening to him over the course of time. If his Majesty has given you the grace to enjoy this prayer but not to understand it, this writing should help you, especially those of you who are fortunate enough to be both intelligent and well educated.

May he be praised for everything through all the ages. Amen.

XVIII ✠

THE PRAYER OF UNION

M AY THE LORD give me the right words to explain the fourth spiritual water. I need his help now more than ever.

In the previous state of prayer, the soul dies to the things of this world, yet she can tell that she is not dead altogether. She still has her senses, so she feels her profound aloneness. She makes use of external things to express what she feels, even if they are only symbolic.

In every degree of prayer I have described so far, the soul-gardener is working. In the more advanced stages, the soul receives so much comfort and delight that she would never want to abandon the cultivation of prayer. So she experiences her labor as glory rather than as toil.

In this new state, the ordinary senses are transcended. The soul rejoices without understanding what she's rejoicing in. She recognizes that she is enjoying a good thing, one that encompasses all good things within it, but the goodness defies comprehension. The senses are so occupied with this joy that they are not free to experience anything else, either exterior or interior.

In the earlier stages of prayer, the senses are allowed to give some indication of the tremendous joy they feel. But in the fourth water, the soul's joy is incomparably greater, yet she is much less capable of expressing it. Both the body and the soul are drained of the power to communicate. At a time like this, anything is perceived as a disturbance, a torment, and an obstacle to the soul's repose. The faculties are all drawn into union. Even if the soul wanted to, she would be unable to convey her delight. If she were able to describe it, she would not be in a state of union.

I don't know how to explain this prayer they call union or how it happens. Mystical theologians elucidate it, but I don't know the proper vocabulary. I don't understand what mind is or how it is different from soul or spirit. It all seems like the same thing to me. I do see that the soul sometimes shoots out of itself like a flame leaping from a blazing fire. But although the flame flies high above the fire, it is not something different from the fire. You, with all your learning, will understand how the fire and the flame are the same. I don't know how else to say it.

I want to talk about how the soul feels when she is in this divine union. We already know what union means: two separate things become one.

O my Beloved, you are so good! May you be blessed forever. May all things praise you, my God. You have loved us so much that we are truly able to speak of communion between you and our souls here in our exile. This proves your boundless generosity and magnanimity, even in the case of souls who are already good. This abundance is who you are, my Lord; you give according to your nature. O Infinite Bounty, your works are magnificent!

Even those of us who are not intellectually engaged with the things of the world find ourselves incapable of understanding divine truths. My intellect stops dead in its tracks when it ponders how you have bestowed such exalted blessings on souls who have offended you so much. I start to think about it, and I can't continue. Where could the intellect possibly go that would not be a backward motion? I cannot find the words to thank you for such precious favors. So I sometimes take comfort in uttering nonsense.

In the midst of receiving these divine favors, the soul is powerless to speak. But right after God had blessed me in this way, or else just as he was beginning, I often used to say, "Lord, look what you are doing! How quickly you seem to forget my wickedness. Obviously you have forgotten; how else could you have forgiven me? Well, I beg you now to remember it and to place some limits on your mercies. O my Creator, please don't pour such precious liquid into such a broken cup. You have already seen how I tend to spill it. Do not put a treasure like this in a place where the craving for worldly pleasures is not as deadened as it ought to be. Otherwise, you will only squander it.

"How could you entrust this fortified city and hand over its keys to such a cowardly defender? The minute the enemy attacks, she flings open the gates and lets him in! Do not let your love be so great, O Eternal King, that you would jeopardize such priceless jewels. When you place your treasure in the power of such a lowly, wretched, weak, and unworthy creature, it gives her the excuse to undervalue it. She may well strive to keep it safe—with your grace, of course—and being what she is, she requires more help than most; but she is incapable of making use of the treasure to be of service to anyone else.

"Why not? She is a woman. She is not even a good woman, but a worthless one. It seems that whatever talent you have given her is wasted by being not only hidden but actually buried deep in such vile earth. You do not generally bestow such great blessings as these on someone incapable of benefiting many other souls. I have begged you in the past, my God, and I will continue to beseech you with all my heart, to grant these blessings to someone who will make better use of them than I for the magnification of your glory. You already know that I would consider it a blessing to lose the greatest good that can be obtained on earth if it meant you would do this."

It occurred to me to say things like this, as well as other things, to God. That was until I saw how foolish I was being. What a lack of humility! The Lord knows perfectly well what is right for me. He knows that my soul would not have the strength to become liberated unless his Majesty instilled it in me through his divine blessings.

Well, then what are the effects that grace leaves in the soul? Can the soul do anything on her own to lift herself to such a high station? If so, what might that be? Let's take a look at this.

Heavenly love elevates the spirit in union. But elevation and union are two different things. To those who may not have experienced this raising of the spirit, this may seem like a false distinction. Even though the two realities are ultimately one, the Lord works a little differently in each case.

With the flight of the spirit, the soul experiences greater detachment from worldly things. In my experience, this lifting up of the spirit is a special mercy. I will admit that it looks almost exactly like union. A little fire is just as much fire as a big one. Yet it takes a long time for a bit of iron to grow red-hot in a small flame. In a big fire, the substance of even a large chunk of iron appears to be transformed quickly.

This seems to me to be an example of how these two divine favors are different from one another. Anyone who has experienced raptures will understand this perfectly. To someone who has not had such an experience, I'm sure my explanation must sound like nonsense. It is a bit ridiculous for someone like me to try and explain something that cannot possibly be put into words.

But I have to believe that the Lord is with me here. His Majesty knows that although I have been commanded to write this and am compelled by my vows to obey, my primary motivation is to draw souls into the experience of sublime grace. I would not attempt to speak of things that I have not been through. In fact, this last spiritual water is so hard to explain that when I started to write about it, I was afraid it was going to come out sounding like Greek. So I put down my quill and went to Communion.

Blessed be the Lord who bestows his mercy on the ignorant! What great things come through the simple virtue of obedience! Just as he did with the previous spiritual waters, God himself illuminated my intellect about this one, giving me just the words I need to explain this divine favor and showing me exactly how to use them. It seems that his Majesty is willing to say for me what I can neither say nor even understand myself.

I am telling the whole truth here. So whatever is good is his own teaching. What is bad comes from that sea of wickedness I call myself. There must be many souls who have attained the heights of prayer that the Lord in his mercy has granted to this miserable creature. If such souls are afraid they may have lost their way and want to consult me about it, they can rest secure in the knowledge that the Lord is helping his servant show them the true way.

The fourth heavenly water is so abundant that when it falls, it saturates the whole garden. If the Beloved were to send this rain every time the ground became a little dry, the gardener wouldn't have much to do, would she? And if there were no such thing as winter and the weather were always mild, there would be no shortage of flowers and fruit, would there? Obviously, under such circumstances, the gardener would be thrilled.

But as long as we are living on earth, this is impossible. When one water fails, we need to seek ways to obtain another. This water from heaven often comes when the gardener least expects it. Yet it is true that in the beginning stages of the spiritual path the heavenly rain almost always falls after a long period of contemplative prayer.

Between successive stages of prayer, the Lord lifts the small bird of the soul and places her in the divine nest to rest. He has watched her flying around for such a long time, striving with all her might to see God and serve him. She has strained her intellect and pushed her will. He wants to reward her for her hard work, even in this lifetime. And what a reward! A single moment of that grace is more than enough to pay the soul back for all the trials she could ever endure in this life.

While the soul is seeking God in this way, she finds herself slipping into a kind of swoon. With a rush of gentle joy, she feels everything begin to fade away. The breath and bodily powers progressively dwindle. It takes tremendous effort just to wiggle the fingers. The eyes close of their own accord. Even if a person in this state were able to keep her eyes open, she wouldn't see a thing. She cannot read or sound out words; she can barely recognize letters. If she wanted to read, the intellect would offer no help in turning the alphabet into comprehensible language. She can hear, but she does not understand what she's hearing.

The senses do not serve the soul one iota in this state. In fact, there is the danger that they will do her harm by diminishing her sublime pleasure. It is useless for her to try to speak; even if she could form a word, she lacks the energy to pronounce it. As the power of the body decreases, the strength of the soul increases, compounding the enjoyment of her glory. She experiences a vast and palpable delight.

No matter how long it lasts, this prayer causes no harm. At least, it has never caused me any. In fact, even if I had been ill before the Lord granted me this mercy, I always felt much better afterward. What harm could such a blessing possibly do? The external effects are so obvious, who could doubt that a great thing has happened to the soul? What else besides grace could rob us of our bodily strength, fill us with joy, and then revitalize our physical powers?

It is true that in the beginning this state of prayer passes so quickly (it did in my case, anyway) that the shutting down of the senses and other outward signs are almost imperceptible. But the soul has no trouble recognizing that the sun must have shone with dazzling intensity since it melted her away. It should be noted that even the longest period of time the soul remains in this suspended state is actually very short. If the faculties were suspended for half an hour, that would be a long time. I don't think it has ever lasted that long for me.

Of course, since there is no sensory awareness in this state, it's hard to know what's going on. But I do know that very soon one faculty or another recovers and the prayer passes. The will remains captive in the divine web while the other two faculties escape and revert to their mischievous ways. The quietude of the will draws them into suspension again and again, but they always come back to life very quickly.

Some people end up spending many hours of prayer in this way. Once the faculties have tasted this wine and become intoxicated, they willingly lose themselves all over again just so they can drink some more. They join the company of the will, and all three celebrate together. Remember, this absorption of the faculties is over in a flash. But their return to ordinary functioning is not abrupt. In fact, they usually linger in a state of bemusement for several hours. Every now and then, God gathers them back into himself.

We have come to the place where we need to try and say something about what the soul is feeling inside herself during this experience. Oh, if only I knew how to speak of this! We cannot understand it with our minds, let alone put it into language. I was reflecting on this after receiving Communion and being swept up into the very state of prayer I was writing about. How was I going to describe what the soul goes through at this time?

Then the Lord spoke to me. "The soul utterly dissolves, my daughter, so that it can fully unite with me," he said. "It is no longer the soul that lives, but I. Since she cannot comprehend what she understands, she understands by not understanding."

What happens in this state is so rarified that there is no way to explain it any more clearly than this. Only those who have tasted it will know anything of its flavor. All I can say is that the soul sees herself as one with God. There is an abiding sense of certainty that accompanies this encounter. The soul is incapable of doubting the truth of her union with him.

The faculties are so radically suspended here that they completely fail to function. If a person in this state has been meditating on some scriptural passage, it will vanish from his memory as if he had never been thinking of it at all. If he has been reading, he cannot concentrate or remember a thing he has just read. Nor can he recall the words to prescribed prayers.

And so the wings of the restless little moth we call the memory are singed and it cannot flutter around anymore. The will is entirely absorbed in loving, but it doesn't understand how it loves. If the intellect understands anything, it can't understand how it understands. The mind cannot understand what the soul knows. I don't think the intellect does understand because, as I've already said, it can't be understood. I really can't understand this myself!

There was something I was ignorant about in the beginning: I didn't know that God was in everything. Even though he felt so near, I thought this was impossible. But because his presence was so clear to me, I couldn't stop believing that he was there. Certain uneducated men told me that God was only present by grace. I didn't believe them. His presence was so tangible! I was confused.

A very learned man from the order of the glorious Saint Dominic liberated me from this prison of doubt. He reassured me that God was with me and told me all about how God communicates himself to the soul. This was deeply comforting to me.

Just remember, this heavenly water, this magnificent gift from God, always leaves immense blessings in the soul. This is what I'd like to talk about next.

XIX ✠

DIVINE RAIN

THE PRAYER of Union leaves the soul in a state of great tenderness. She longs to be consumed and is overcome by the urge to weep, not in sorrow but in joy. She suddenly finds herself bathed in tears without knowing when or how she shed them. She is delighted to discover that the same water that quenches the force of the fire makes it burn with even more intensity. This may sound like nonsense, but it happens.

Sometimes in the beginning of my spiritual life, when the experience passed quickly, this prayer would transport me so far beyond myself that I would wonder whether I had been dreaming or if the glory I was feeling was a reality. But when I saw that I was drenched by a water that poured so powerfully and so quickly as if from a heavenly cloud, I realized that my experience was real.

The soul is so filled with courage that she would consider it a blessing to be cut into a thousand pieces for her God. This state of prayer triggers sweeping resolutions, heroic promises, and ardent desires. The soul clearly perceives the vanity of the world and begins to develop contempt for it. This prayer refines and elevates the soul far more than any degree of prayer so far.

Her humility is deeper too, because she sees that she had absolutely nothing to do with the generous and magnificent gift she is being given and that she is equally powerless to hold on to it. Her own unworthiness becomes painfully apparent, for cobwebs cannot hide when sunlight floods into a room. She is so far from conceited at this point that she cannot imagine that she ever suffered from false pride.

Since the soul barely gave her consent for the blessed state she is in, she sees with her own eyes that she herself is capable of little or nothing. The door to the senses simply closed, and the soul was left to enjoy her Lord in private. Now that she is alone with him, what can she do but love him? It requires inordinate effort just to see and hear any external thing.

Afterward, the soul's past life and God's great glory are revealed with perfect clarity. The intellect doesn't have to scavenge for this truth. There it is, fully cooked; all the soul needs to do is eat and understand. She realizes that she deserves to be chastised and that she is being punished with glory. She dissolves in praise of God, as I would gladly melt away right now.

Blessed be you, O my Beloved! You have taken the mud that I am and transfigured me into clear water for your own table. May you be praised, O Joy of the Angels! You have willingly raised up such a vile little worm.

The soul continues to make progress. Now that she sees that the fruits are not her own, she begins to distribute them. The more she gives away, the less she seems to need. She is a soul who treasures God's gifts and also wants to share them with others. She begs God not to let her be the only wealthy one. Almost without knowing she is doing it, the soul begins to benefit her neighbors. The fragrance of her flowers has grown so sweet that other souls are attracted to her. They recognize her virtue and want to partake in the holy feast.

Few souls reach this state without having suffered innumerable misunderstandings, criticisms, and illnesses. But these trials cultivate the soil of the soul. Detachment from self-interest softens the earth, allowing the water to penetrate it so thoroughly that it almost never becomes arid again.

Yet if the ground of the soul is still hard and choked with thorns, as mine used to be, it will soon dry up. If she is not as grateful as she should be for such blessed gifts from God and if she is still inclined to miss the mark, her garden will wither. If the gardener becomes careless and the Lord in his mercy decides not to send the rain for a while, she might as well consider the garden lost.

To my great amazement, this has happened to me. If I hadn't experienced it, I would scarcely believe it. I am writing this to console weak souls like myself so that they will not despair and stop trusting in God's greatness. Even if they fall after the Lord has raised them up so high, they should not allow themselves to become so discouraged that they lose their way. Tears gain all things; one water draws down the other.

This is one of the main things that motivated me to obey the order to write this account of my miserable life and the great mercy the Lord has granted me without my deserving it. Being what I am, I have repeatedly offended him. I wish I had real authority so that people would believe what I have to say! Please, Lord, give it to me now. I repeat, let no one who has cultivated the practice of contemplative prayer grow discouraged and say, "If I end up reverting to my old ways, it would be better for me to give up prayer altogether." I believe things will get worse if the person abandons prayer and refuses to quit his bad habits. But if he stays the course, prayer will carry him into the harbor of light.

This is exactly how the spirit of evil attacked me. As I have mentioned, I wasted precious time worrying that I lacked the humility necessary to be worthy of practicing prayer. And so, for a year and a half, I did not pray at all. Well, for at least a year anyway; I don't quite remember about the other six months. All I succeeded in doing was plunging myself into hell; I didn't need any devils to drag me there.

O God, save me! What blindness! The spirit of evil is smart to lend its hand in this way, luring the soul away from prayer. The traitor knows that a soul who perseveres in prayer is lost to him. Thanks to the goodness of God, every time the spirit of evil trips such a soul and makes her fall, it is only helping her to leap up again even higher in service of the Lord. No wonder the spirit of evil is so concerned.

O my Jesus! What a sight it is to see you reach out your merciful hand and raise a soul who has fallen after she had already attained such an elevated state! Then she clearly perceives the multitude of your blessings and the depth of her own wretchedness. She acknowledges your vast power and dissolves into you.

Here she does not dare lift her eyes. Here she lifts her eyes. She recognizes her tremendous debt to you. Here she becomes devoted to the Queen of Heaven and begs her to intercede with you. Here she invokes the help of the saints who also fell after you had already called them. Here she considers herself unworthy of the very ground she walks on. She cannot believe she deserves all the blessings you have given her.

Here she approaches the sacraments with living faith in the power that God has placed in them. She praises you because you have left a healing ointment for our wounds that not only soothes them but completely eliminates them.

The soul is amazed by all this. Who wouldn't be amazed, Lord of my soul, to witness so much mercy? How could anyone fail to be moved by such a huge favor bestowed in exchange for such an ugly betrayal? I am a wicked person. I can't believe that my heart doesn't shatter as I write this.

Thank you, my Beloved, for this gift of crying. I return these small tears now as some kind of repayment for all the ways I have betrayed you. I know that the well from which I draw them is less than pure because I have so often refused your divine blessings and chosen evil instead. But please, my Lord, honor my tears. Cleanse this muddy water so that I do not tempt others to judge me as I have so often judged others.

I used to wonder why you would ignore some very holy souls who have always worked so hard to serve you, who have been deeply religious their whole lives, and instead bestow your blessings on people like me who are religious in name only. Now I see, my only Good, that you withhold their reward to give it to them all at once. They are strong enough to serve you without attachment to the fruits of their actions and so you treat them as brave souls who are free from self-interest. I, on the other hand, am weak, and I need to taste your favors here on earth.

Still, my Beloved, you know that I often called out to you to forgive the people who criticized me because they seemed justified in their judgments. This impulse arose during that time when you, in your great goodness, were helping me to learn not to offend you. I was trying to give up all the things I thought might displease you. And you responded, my beloved Lord, by beginning to open your treasure box to your servant. It seemed like you had simply been waiting for me to be ready to receive your divine jewels. Soon you were not only giving them to me but letting other people know that you had given them to me.

No matter how obvious my wickedness, some people didn't realize how wretched I was, and they began to put me on a pedestal when they found out about these divine favors. This was quickly followed by a wave of criticism and persecution from another faction. I was more inclined to agree with the second group, so I didn't blame anyone for blaming me. In fact I implored you, my God, to recognize how right they were.

Here are some of the things they were saying about me:

"She's trying to make herself out to be a saint."

"She's introducing innovations without even having managed to comply with the observance of her own monastic rule."

"She is nowhere near as good and holy as the other sisters in her house." (I must admit, I don't believe I will ever attain goodness unless God himself gives it to me from his own goodness.)

"She's actually detracting from the goodness of our community by replacing perfectly good customs with bad ones. At least, she is trying her best to convey these negative teachings, and she's capable of causing terrible damage."

I'm not saying it was only my sisters who participated in the slander. There were other people too. But those who accused me were innocent. They taught me things about myself. These must have been true things because it was you, Lord, who permitted them.

Once, in the midst of this persecution, I was reciting the Hours and I came to this verse: *You are righteous, O Lord, and your judgments are upright.* "What a great truth," I thought. For the spirit of evil has never had the power to tempt me to doubt that you, my God, embody every good thing or to question a single article of faith. Rather it seemed to me that the more my faith transcended the mundane world, the stronger it grew. This thought enkindled my devotion.

When I reflected on your omnipotence, I recognized your power to shower me with your majestic gifts. I have never doubted this power. But I still could not help wondering why you would choose to hold your blessings back from so many souls who serve you so faithfully and yet give them so generously to someone like me. Then, my Lord, you answered me. "Stop meddling," you said, "and just serve me." This was the first time I ever heard your voice and it scared me.

Later I will say more about these spiritual voices. It would only be another digression to elaborate on this topic now, and I have digressed more than enough already! I hardly know what I've said. How could it be otherwise? My readers are just going to have to put up with me. When I reflect on the patience with which God has treated me and notice my present state, I am transported all over again. I lose the thread of what I've been saying and what I meant to say next.

May I always be so foolish! May his Majesty never again grant me the power to offend him in the slightest degree! May I be consumed in the fire of prayer!

He has abundantly proven his mercy by forgiving me over and over again for the ingratitude I have shown him. When Saint Peter was ungrateful, the Lord pardoned him once, but he has pardoned me many times. No wonder the spirit of evil was able to slip in and tempt me. In public, I was pretending to be best friends with the One whom I was treating like the enemy in private.

How blind I was! Where, my Beloved, did I think I could find a remedy other than in you? What foolishness! I ran away from the light just to stumble through darkness. Such proud humility! The spirit of evil convinced me to release my hold on the pillar and the staff that supported me and kept me from falling.

I am making the sign of the cross as I write this. I don't think I ever passed through any danger as grave as the one in which the spirit of evil lured me away from prayer under the twisted pretext of humility. It made me question how someone as wicked as I could dare to approach God in this way. Wasn't it enough for me to recite the obligatory vocal prayers like everyone else? I didn't even do that well. To attempt to engage in silent communion with God, the spirit of evil suggested, was to display a severe lack of reverence and appreciation for all the favors God had shown me.

It was right to think about these things and try to understand them. But it was very wrong to use it as an excuse to give up the practice of prayer. May you be blessed, Lord, who came to my rescue.

It seems to me that this is the same way Judas was tempted, although the traitor did not tempt me quite as openly. Instead, what he did to Judas in one moment, he did to me little by little. For the love of God, let all who practice prayer be on the lookout for such deception. Know that my life was an utter mess when it didn't have prayer in it. What a fine remedy the spirit of evil offered me. What pretty humility! And what terrible agitation.

But how could my soul be calm? It was drifting further and further from its true quiet. When I remembered the blessings and mercies I had

received, the pleasures of the world looked disgusting to me. I am astonished that I could endure this. It was only hope that enabled me to go
on. I'm not sure exactly what I was thinking at this time. After all, it was
more than twenty years ago. But I do recall that I never abandoned my
determination to resume the practice of prayer eventually. I was just waiting for the day when I would be free from sin. Oh, how far astray this
hope led me! The spirit of evil would have gladly kept me hoping till
Judgment Day and then delivered me straight to hell.

The practice of prayer and spiritual reading revealed the truth about
the bad road I was following. But even though I beseeched the Lord
with copious tears, it was no use. I was too wicked. There I was, separated from prayer, amusing myself with trivial activities, exposed to a
thousand opportunities to miss the mark, and with little help in sight.
No help, actually, except for help in sinning. What else could I possibly
expect besides what happened to me as a result of these conditions?

A certain Dominican friar named Vicente Barrón deserves the credit
for waking me from this sleep. He is a learned man and worthy in the
sight of God. He made me receive Communion every two weeks, and I
began to return to my senses. I became less and less attached to my
wicked ways, although I didn't entirely stop offending God.

Since I had not lost the path altogether, however, I picked up my
progress and slowly, gradually advanced, repeatedly stumbling and
picking myself up again. Anyone who does not fail to keep walking will
eventually arrive at his destination, even if he's a little late. Giving up on
prayer is the same thing as losing your way. May God, being who he is,
liberate us!

For the love of God, pay close attention to my example and learn from
it. It should be obvious from this account that a soul may attain a state
in which God grants her indescribable blessings and she can still fall.
She needs to avoid placing herself in precarious positions. She should
not trust herself. Reflect deeply on this. It is very important.

Even though a favor definitely comes from God, the spirit of evil can
deceive the soul afterward, harvesting as much benefit from this gift for
itself as it possibly can. It uses what it steals from us to hurt us. If we have
not grown strong in the virtues and have not cultivated sufficient detachment from the world, we are vulnerable to these tricks. No matter how

powerful our resolutions are, we may be too weak to stand up to these dangers.

This is an excellent teaching. It is not mine, but God's. I would like to share it with ignorant people like myself. Even if a soul finds herself in an exalted state, she must not trust herself to enter into battle, because she may not be equipped to defend herself. We need armor to protect ourselves against the spirit of evil. Souls at this stage have not yet developed the strength they need to fight against these wicked energies and stomp them out.

The soul clearly perceives the difference between worldly and divine things. She sees herself very close to God and experiences his love for her. This love inspires confidence, and the soul is certain that she could never lose the blessing she is enjoying. The divine reward is so clear even in this lifetime that she could not imagine trading something so sublime and pure for anything as crude and impure as earthly pleasure.

This is how the spirit of evil tricks her. It uses her confidence to rob her of humility. That's when the soul gets into trouble. She believes that she has nothing left to fear in herself, and so she places herself directly in the path of danger and begins to give away her fruits with wild abandon.

This ardor does not come from pride. The soul understands perfectly that she can do nothing by herself. Her generosity springs from unconditional confidence in God. But she lacks discretion. She doesn't notice that she is still a fledgling. She can leave the nest. God can take her out. But she is not yet ready to fly. The virtues are not fully developed, and she has not had enough experience to recognize danger. She doesn't know what harm can come from too much trust in oneself. This is what destroyed me.

Because of the peril of overconfidence, we need to fall back on the counsel of a spiritual director. There are also many other reasons to engage in conversations with spiritual people. I truly believe that once God has lifted a soul to this height, he will never cease blessing her unless she totally abandons him. But when she falls, she must be extremely careful not to use this as an excuse to give up on prayer. This is how the devil tricked me, in the guise of false humility. I know I have said this already, and I would like to repeat it many more times.

The goodness of God is greater than all the evils of which we are capable. Let the soul rely exclusively on this goodness. We may be well aware of who we are and of all the favors God has bestowed on us as punishment for our wicked deeds. But the moment we wish to renew our friendship with him, God forgets our ingratitude. In fact, our transgressions make him all the more inclined to forgive us. We are, after all, members of his family. We have already eaten his bread.

Remember the word of God. Ponder what he has done for me. His Majesty began to forgive me long before I grew tired of forsaking him. He never grows weary of giving. His mercies are inexhaustible. Let us never grow tired of receiving them. May he be forever blessed. Amen. And may all things praise him.

XX ✠

PRAYER OF PAIN

I WILL NEED God's help in explaining the difference between the Prayer of Union and the experience called rapture. By the way, other terms for rapture are *flight of the spirit, elevation of the spirit, transport,* and *ecstasy.*

Rapture has a huge advantage over union. It yields a more abundant spiritual harvest. The beginning, middle, and end stages of union are undifferentiated. They resemble rapture in that they are deeply interior states. But the phenomena associated with rapture are of a much higher degree, and their benefits are of both an interior and an exterior nature.

May the Lord explain these things for me now as he has so skillfully done before! If God had not given me some understanding of how to do this, I would never have been able to say anything relevant on my own.

Let's reflect on the last spiritual water. This divine rain is so bountiful that we are almost convinced the cloud of his majestic glory is present right here in the world. If only the earth were capable of receiving it! We spontaneously express our gratitude for the gift of his awesome grace by engaging in acts of kindness.

While the soul is in the middle of thanking God, the Beloved suddenly gathers her up, the way clouds draw the morning mist, and pulls her completely out of herself. The divine cloud ascends to heaven, taking the soul along with it, and begins to reveal to her the heavenly wonders God has prepared for her. I'm not sure if this metaphor is apt, but the fact is, this is what happens.

The soul no longer seems to animate the body during these raptures. It feels like the body's temperature is dropping. A tremendous sense of ease and delight accompany this growing coldness. At this point, the rapture has become impossible to resist. In union, we are still connected to the earth, so we have the choice to surrender or fight the experience. It may be arduous, but we can fend it off if we really want to.

But in these raptures, there is no remedy. They rush upon the soul as swiftly and powerfully as a mighty eagle swooping down and bearing her aloft on its wings. Without giving us a chance to think about it or plan our escape, this cloud sends us soaring. We see that we are being carried away, but we don't know where.

Even though the experience is delightful, our nature is still weak, so it scares us at first. We need to cultivate a courageous spirit and hone our determination to risk everything and abandon ourselves into the Beloved's hands. Whether we like it or not, we have already been transported, so we might as well go willingly.

This experience has been so traumatic for me that many times I tried with all my might to resist it. I have been especially reluctant to yield to it when it has happened to me in public, and yet when I have been alone, I have been afraid I might be suffering from delusions. Sometimes I have been able to overcome it, but the struggle has left me drained, like someone who has been in a fight with a giant. At other times it has been impossible to resist. Then it has carried away my entire soul—and sometimes my head too—and I have been powerless to hold myself back. Sometimes the experience has taken up my whole body and lifted it off the ground.

I haven't levitated very often. The first time it happened I was kneeling in the choir, waiting to go up to the altar and receive Communion. I was immediately distressed because I realized how unusual the experience was and I was afraid that everyone was going to start talking about it. So I ordered the sisters who witnessed it to keep it to themselves. Since I had been appointed as their prioress, they had to do what I asked.

After that, when I felt that the Lord was about to enrapture me again, I would stretch out on the floor and ask the other nuns to hold me down. This occurred recently during a sermon on Saint Joseph's feast day. Even though we tried to hide it, some noble ladies who were visiting saw the whole thing. I implored the Lord not to give me any more favors that involved an outward show. I was getting tired of being considered special. It seems that God in his mercy acknowledged my prayer. Although that last incident was not very long ago, I have not experienced another levitation since that day.

Whenever I have tried to resist the onset of a rapture, it has felt like a powerful force was lifting me from the soles of my feet. I don't know what to compare this force to. It is far more cataclysmic than anything I've experienced in the previous stages of prayer. The struggle is so ferocious that it utterly wears me out. But in the end, fighting is futile. If this is the Beloved's desire, there is no power equal to his.

At other times, his Majesty recognizes that we are declining his favor not from fear but from true humility. He is satisfied to know we see that he wants to bless us with his grace and that we realize he is not withholding his blessing from us. In this case, the soul receives the same benefits as if she had given her complete consent.

The effects of rapture are remarkable. One is the sheer manifestation of God's great power. Another is our utter inability to hold back the body any more successfully than we can hold down the soul when his Majesty desires to raise it. We realize that we are not our own master, but that there is a Supreme Master who bestows these favors on us. When we remember that we can do absolutely nothing ourselves, deep humility is imprinted on our souls.

Still, I confess that this particular favor terrified me. If you don't resist, the same force that carries your soul away in rapture will elevate your body with equal gentleness. Yet when you see yourself lifted off the ground and remain conscious enough to witness the event, the majesty of the One who can cause such a thing is enough to make your hair stand on end. And the fear of offending such an awesome God stays with you.

This fear, however, is accompanied by a very deep love for him. And when we reflect on all he has done for such a lowly worm, the love grows even deeper. He does not seem satisfied with bringing the soul to himself. He wants the body too, even though it is made of impure clay, because it is mortal and inclined to make mistakes.

Rapture also leaves an ineffable detachment in the soul. All I can say is that this experience is of a different order than the other states of prayer. Its effects are not only spiritual. Once the spirit detaches itself from worldly things, the Lord seems to want to bring the body along.

The soul begins to suffer a new sense of estrangement from the world. Life becomes more arduous.

The pain that follows rapture is not something we can fabricate for ourselves. Nor can we simply let it go once we have felt it. Oh, I wish I could articulate this profound pain! I don't think it's possible to put into words, but I'll try.

This Prayer of Pain comes much later on the path than all the wondrous experiences of visions and voices that I will tell you about later. The time that I used to spend in prayer was filled with those delightful blessings. Now, although my prayer time is not entirely devoid of those delights, it is primarily spent in pain. Sometimes the distress is more intense, sometimes less so. I'd like to tell you about the times when it is most severe.

Later I will speak of those great loving impulses I used to experience when the Lord was on the verge of transporting me. I see now that the feelings associated with rapture were very physical compared to the purely spiritual experience of this more advanced degree of prayer. I don't think I am exaggerating when I make this distinction. I'm not suggesting that the shock that accompanies the onset of rapture is painless. But it is a pain that is shared by body and soul. This purely spiritual distress that I'm telling you about causes a terrible desolation in the soul.

We do not play an active role in the Prayer of Pain. Yet we are often overcome by an unexpected pang of desire that instantly permeates the whole of the soul. This longing wearies the soul, loosening her bonds to this earth. She rises far above herself and above all creation. God strips the soul of everything. Even if she wanted to, she could not find anything or anyone to keep her company in this desert. But she does not want companionship. She wants only to die alone here in the wilderness. She tries to speak, but she is mute. If someone speaks to her, it's pointless. No matter how much the soul may try to get away, she cannot escape this solitude.

When it seems to me that God is furthest away, he suddenly communicates his magnificence in the strangest ways imaginable! His ways are inscrutable. I don't think anyone who has not experienced this could possibly understand. God does not offer this communication as a consolation. He is trying to show the soul that she has good reason for growing weary in the absence of a blessing that encompasses all blessings.

The flame of the soul's desire is fanned by this divine communication. And it makes her solitude feel even more solitary. From the heart of this desert, the soul witnesses her delicate and penetrating pain, and she cries out as the royal prophet David cried out, "I watch, and I am like a sparrow alone on the rooftop." Maybe King David was feeling this same desolation when he wrote that. Although I suspect that, being a saint, he experienced it on a much more profound level.

This verse pops into my mind at times like these, and I think it perfectly echoes my own soul's lament. It's comforting to know that there are other beings who have experienced this radical solitude. The fact that some of these beings are as exalted as David is even more consoling. And so it seems that the soul is not connected to herself but perched high on a rooftop, removed from herself and from all created things. I think she is far above even the highest part of herself.

At other times, the soul's need is so great that she wanders around asking herself, "Where is your God?" I should mention that when that line from the psalm would come to me, I had only heard it in Latin and didn't know its translation in Spanish. Later, after I had learned its meaning, it comforted me to see that the Lord had brought it to me without my having anything to do with it.

I also used to recall how Saint Paul said that he was crucified to the world. I'm not presuming that these words apply to me; I know they don't. But it seems to me that the soul in this state experiences a kind of crucifixion. She receives no consolation from heaven, nor is she in heaven. She does not desire help from this earth, nor is she on earth. It's as if she were hanging between heaven and earth, finding no relief from either side.

Eventually the soul is given a heavenly knowledge of God. This divine understanding so far surpasses any earthly desire that it causes the soul even more anguish than before. Now she is so consumed with longing that it obliterates her sensory consciousness. But this intensity only lasts a short time. It is like the agony of death, except that it also carries with it such great joy that no comparison could adequately convey it. It is an arduous yet delightful martyrdom.

The soul totally rejects even the most alluring worldly things. She knows beyond all doubt that she wants nothing but God. She is no longer attached to any particular attributes of him but loves him as a whole. And yet she does not know what she loves! I say she does not know because the imagination is incapable of conjuring up any imagery. In fact, none of the faculties function during the time this occurs. Whereas it is joy that suspends the faculties in union and in rapture, it is pain that suspends them here.

O Jesus, if only you could help me explain this to the man who ordered me to write this account so that he could then explain it to me! This is the state my soul is in all the time now. Whenever I am not occupied with something, my soul plunges into this yearning for death. And when I feel it coming on, I am afraid that I will never die. Yet as the pain engulfs me, I long to suffer like this for the rest of my life, even though the pain is so great that no one could possibly endure it.

The sisters who have witnessed me in this state say that sometimes my pulse seems to stop. My arms become rigid, and my hands are so stiff that I cannot even clasp them in prayer. The next day my wrists ache and my whole body hurts, as if all my joints were dislocated.

Sometimes I really think that if this Prayer of Pain continues, it must be the Lord's will to end it by ending my life. This suffering feels like more than enough to kill me. But I know that I don't deserve death. When I am in this agony, all I want is to die. I don't think about purgatory. I don't think about how my sins merit hell. I am oblivious to everything but my passionate longing to see God. This solitude in the desert of my soul feels better to me than any earthly companionship. The only possible comfort for a soul in this anguish would be to talk with someone else who has experienced it.

But no matter how much the soul complains of her torment, no one seems to believe her. Her suffering is so acute that she no longer desires solitude, but she can't tolerate company either, unless it is someone to whom she can complain. The soul is like a person with a rope pulled tight around her neck. She is suffocating, desperate for relief. Her distress puts her in danger of death, and her desire for companionship seems like a sign of cowardice.

Believe me, I know what it feels like to be close to death. My illnesses have brought me to death's door more than once. This spiritual distress is as serious as any fever I have ever endured.

There arises an overwhelming desire for the soul and the body not to be separated, and so the soul calls out for help. She begs for relief. By expressing her pain and distracting herself, the soul seeks a remedy to help her survive. On the other hand, the spirit, which is the higher part of the soul, does not want to turn away from the grace of the pain.

I don't know if I'm managing to make any sense here, but I strongly believe this is what happens. Do you see what little rest the soul can find in this life? The Lord used to comfort me and relieve my soul through prayer and solitude. Now these things only bring torment. Yet this torment pleases the soul so deeply and she sees it as so valuable that she desires this suffering beyond all the holy favors she used to receive. And she believes that this is the safer path because it is the way of the cross.

This state of prayer carries a very special blessing with it. Even though the body experiences only pain, the soul both suffers and rejoices. The soul somehow derives exquisite joy from this acute pain. I don't know how this happens, but it does. I, for one, wouldn't trade this gift the Lord gives me for any of the others I will tell you about later. Remember, this Prayer of Pain comes after all the other blessings I am writing about. This is the favor the Beloved is granting me now.

In the beginning, I was afraid. It almost always frightens me when the Lord gives me a new gift. Eventually, as I make progress, his Majesty reassures me. When I first started to experience the Prayer of Pain, God told me not to fear but to treasure this gift above all the others he had given me. The soul is purified by this pain. It is refined and polished, like gold in a crucible. God dips our souls in the enamel of his grace so that we radiate his blessings. The Prayer of Pain purges our souls of whatever would otherwise have to be purged in purgatory.

I always knew this was a great favor, but after God reassured me, I felt much better about it. My spiritual guide tells me that this is a good thing. Since I am so wretched, I always have something to fear, but I could never believe that this Prayer of Pain was bad. On the contrary, I was in awe of such a generous blessing, especially when I reflected on how little I deserved it. Blessed be the Lord who is so good! Amen.

I seem to have wandered off the subject again. I started by talking about raptures, but this other state I've been describing transcends rapture. It has a transformative impact on the soul.

Let's get back to raptures and enumerate their most common features. They often seemed to drain the weight from my body and leave me exceedingly light. Sometimes I couldn't remember how to touch my feet to the floor. When the body is in rapture, it's like a corpse; it doesn't have the power to do anything for itself. It is frozen into whatever position it was in when the rapture came on—sitting, perhaps, with open hands.

It's rare to faint, although I have sometimes lost consciousness altogether. If the senses shut down, it's usually only for a short time. Rapture is supremely disorienting. While the body is powerless to perform any outward action, the soul is still able to see and hear things, even though they feel like they are coming from far away.

At the height of the rapture, the faculties are left behind in the wake of the soul's intense union with God. In those moments, I believe the soul fails to see or hear or feel anything but him. But as with the Prayer of Union, the soul's total transformation in God only lasts a short time. While it endures, the faculties feel nothing and the soul understands nothing. Maybe the soul doesn't understand what's happening because God doesn't want her to know such things while she is still here on earth. He knows we are incapable of containing this knowledge. I have discovered this for myself.

How is it, you may ask, that the raptures sometimes last for such a long time? And why do they happen so often? In my case, the rapture is not always continuous; rather, I experience it at intervals. It's true that the Beloved often enfolds my soul and suspends my faculties for a while. But then he releases my senses and keeps only my will in captivity. The other two faculties behave like the small pointer on a sundial; they never stop moving. Unless, of course, the Sun of Justice wants them to, and then he simply brings their activity to a halt.

Complete rapture may only last for a moment, but the surge of power that propels this flight of the spirit is so intense that the will remains absorbed for a while. Even when the other faculties begin to stir again, the will rules the body. Nothing the restless faculties do to try and vanquish the will has any effect. If the Lord wishes to suspend the faculties again, the will sweeps them back up into union with it. Whether or not

Santiago

ESPAÑA

CORREOS 0,78€

5-7-07

Dear Sr. mercy, - Happy Birthday -!
we arrived in Santiago today
A Beautiful city with a very interesting history
of people who make Pilgrimages here.
We will tour the cathedral tomorrow
& other points of interest.
We have enjoyed to travelling
& touring Northwestern
Spain. We will spend
a few more days in spain
then travel to Sicily.
may God Bless you always -
You are in our thoughts &
prayers. With love

Sr. mercyLeporno OCD
Carmelite Monastery
89 Hiddenbrooke Dr.

Beacon N.Y. 12508   USA

we want to close our eyes, they close of their own accord. If our eyes stay open, we don't notice anything or register what we see.

There isn't much a person in this condition can do. When the other faculties join the union, there is even less to do. Anyone who experiences rapture should not be alarmed if the body feels constricted for a few hours and the mind and memory are distracted. True, the faculties are busy praising God and trying to figure out exactly what just happened to them. But they are not even fully awake for this task. They are like people who have been asleep and dreaming for a long time and are having some trouble waking up.

I've gone to such great lengths to describe this experience because I know of some people here in Ávila to whom the Lord has been granting these favors. To an unlearned spiritual guide who has not gone through this himself, the enraptured person might appear dead. It's a shame what these people have to suffer when their guides don't understand them!

Maybe I don't know what I'm talking about. Since the Lord has already given you tastes of this rapture, you will know whether or not I have successfully explained myself. Although since it's been quite a while since you've had an episode, you might not have observed its effects as much as I have.

So then, no matter how hard I try to stir after a flight of the spirit, it takes a long time until my body is able to cooperate. The soul has carried away its strength. But if a person is ill and suffering from racking pain before a rapture, he often returns to himself healthy and strong afterward. There is a mysterious medicine available to a person in such a state of prayer.

Rapture teaches the body to obey the soul. So when the Lord wishes the body to share in the blessing, healing happens. If the rapture has been particularly intense, the person may go around for a day or two (or even three) with the faculties so absorbed that she seems to be in a kind of stupor. She is still more outside herself than in.

When she has to go back to everyday life, she feels despair. Here the fledgling soul has shed its down and sprouted wings to carry her high. Here Christ's banner is fully unfurled. It truly seems like the guardian of the fortress has climbed (or been lifted) to the highest tower to proclaim the name of God. She looks down on the people below with the perspective of someone who is out of harm's way. Like someone who has been reassured of victory, she no longer fears danger; she almost craves it. Here the soul clearly sees that everything below is trivial and does not matter as much as she thought it did.

Anyone who attains this height perceives many things. The soul doesn't want to want anything anymore. She is not interested in free will. She gives the keys of her will back to the Lord. This is exactly the way I feel right now. "Take it," I beg him.

Behold. Now the gardener is promoted to the position of steward. Her only desire is to do God's will. She doesn't want to be the ruler of herself or of anything else, not even of a single pear tree in God's orchard. If there is anything good here, she wants his Majesty to give it away. From now on, the soul desires nothing for herself. She wants to be in total harmony with his will and his greater glory.

The truth is, if the rapture is authentic, all of these things I'm telling you about happen. If the benefits and the other effects I mentioned are not sustained, then I sincerely doubt that the experience came from God. I would suspect that they were the product of the kind of seizure Saint Vincent warned us about. I have clearly observed that an hour or so after the rapture has passed, the soul is left with such a sense of freedom and mastery over all things that she doesn't recognize herself. She doesn't understand how she could be the recipient of such goodness. She clearly sees that it has nothing to do with her. But she also understands the tremendous value that each of these raptures carries with it.

No one would believe this unless he had experienced it, so people don't believe the poor soul who reports on God's gift to her. After all, she used to be such a wretched creature. Now here she is suddenly striving for things that demand the utmost courage. The soul is no longer content with serving her Beloved in insignificant ways but becomes intent on serving him to the fullest extent of her ability. Observers judge this as nothing more than temptation and foolishness. If only they could understand that these desires don't come from the soul but from the One to whom she has handed over the keys to her will. Then they wouldn't be so surprised.

In my opinion, the soul who has attained this state does not speak or act for herself anymore. Her sovereign Lord is taking care of everything. O God, help me! The psalmist was so right. And we will all be correct when we cry out with longing for the wings of a dove. He was clearly talking about the flight of the spirit in that psalm. When the spirit takes flight, it rises above all creatures and above itself first of all. It is a gentle journey, a delightful odyssey, a flight that makes no noise.

What power a soul has when the Lord brings her to this place! She sees everything without being caught up in it. How ashamed she feels of the time when she used to be enmeshed. She is shocked by how blind she was. What sorrow she feels for those who are still blind, especially if they are people of prayer who are already blessed by God. She wants to cry out and let them know how deluded they are. Sometimes she even does cry out. And then a thousand persecutions rain down on her head.

People judge such a soul to be seriously lacking in humility, particularly if she is a woman. They point out that she is trying to teach the people from whom she should be learning. So they condemn her. And they have ample reason to do so. They can't possibly know the loving impulse that motivates her. There are times when the soul simply can't help herself. She is overwhelmed by the need to disillusion the people she loves and the desire to be liberated from the prison of this life. She recognizes that the life she used to live is nothing but the life of a captive.

It wearies the soul to reflect on the time when she was so concerned about her reputation. She resents having been led to believe that what the world calls honor is honor. She sees that this is just a big lie and that we are all beguiled by it. She understands that true honor has nothing to do with illusion and everything to do with reality. True honor lies in discriminating between what is of value and what is worthless. It's a matter of judging something to be something and nothing to be nothing. Everything that comes to an end is nothing and less than nothing and is not pleasing to God.

The soul laughs at herself when she remembers having been so attached to money. Actually, I don't think I personally ever had cause to confess coveting money. But it was enough of a fault to have at least been attracted to it. If I could have purchased the good I now see in myself with mere money, I would have valued it more highly. But I see that I have only won this goodness by giving up everything.

What can we buy with this money we want so badly? Is it anything of value? Is it something that lasts? If not, why do we want it so much? That which provides such empty relief costs us dearly. Often the only thing we buy with money is a ticket to the everlasting fires of hell. Oh, if only everyone would see money as worthless dirt! How harmonious the world would be then. How many lawsuits would be avoided. If self-interest and pride of money were eliminated, what friendships would form among all peoples. I think this would solve almost all of society's problems.

The soul sees how blind people grow in the face of pleasure and how all it gets us is worry and strife. What restlessness! What discontent! What a waste of energy! In this state of prayer, the sunlight is so bright that not only does the soul become aware of the cobwebs that shroud her, but she perceives even the tiniest speck of dust. And so, no matter how hard the soul tries to be perfect, once this Sun truly shines on her, she will see herself as impure. The soul is like water in a glass. It looks very clear when it's in shadow, but the minute the light strikes, you can see many particles floating in it.

This is an apt metaphor. Before the soul's experience of ecstasy, she thinks she is doing absolutely everything in her power to please God and not to forsake him. But when she attains this height of prayer, the Sun of Justice strikes her eyes and opens them. When she sees so many motes of dust, she wants to shut them again. She has not yet become fully a child of the mighty eagle who can gaze directly at the sun. In the short time that she can keep her eyes open, the soul sees herself as very muddy. She recalls that line in the psalm that says, "Who shall be just in your presence?"

When the soul looks into this divine Sun, its brightness dazzles her. When she looks into herself, the dust clouds her eyes and the little dove is blinded. So the soul is often left bedazzled, absorbed, and frightened. The wonders revealed to her make her swoon.

This is where the soul gains true humility. She doesn't care if others say bad things about her. She has no need to say good things about herself. Now the Lord, not the soul, distributes the fruits of the garden. Nothing sticks to her hand. All the good in the soul is directed toward

God. If she says anything about herself, it is only for his glory. She knows that nothing in the garden is her own. Even if she wanted to ignore this truth, she could not avoid seeing it. In spite of herself, the soul sees with her own eyes how God closes her eyes to the things of the world only to open them to the truth.

XXI ✠

Advice to World Leaders

To wrap up what I've been discussing, I will remind you that the soul does not need to give her permission to be transported in this way. She has already surrendered herself completely to God. She has willingly delivered herself into his hands, and she knows that there is nothing she can do to fool him because he knows everything.

Things are different here on earth. There is so much deception and duplicity here. A certain person persuades you that he is your friend, and then you find out that it was all a lie. Who can live in a world so rife with deceit and betrayal? The more you care about worldly things, the more difficult it is.

Blessed be the soul the Lord brings to an understanding of the truth! If only world leaders could enter this exalted consciousness. It would be so much more worthwhile for them to strive for this state of prayer than for all the power in the world. What righteousness would prevail in a nation like this. What atrocities would be avoided.

Any man who reaches this stage has such unshakable love of God that any fear of risking his honor or his life falls away. This is an especially great blessing for someone who has the obligation to lead his community. Such a king would be willing to lose a thousand kingdoms if God would increase his faith by a fraction of a degree and give him the opportunity to shine a little light of faith into the hearts of the doubters. And rightly so. The benefits would be so much greater than worldly dominion: a kingdom without end. One drop of water from that place makes everything here on earth seem vulgar. Imagine if the soul were totally immersed in that water.

O Lord, even if you were to give me the authority to proclaim these truths publicly, no one would believe me. No one believed those who expressed themselves better than I have. But at least it would satisfy me to have a real voice. I would count my life as nothing if it meant that I could clearly communicate even one of these sacred teachings to the world. Who knows what I would do after that? I am not to be trusted.

In spite of what I am, I keep having these irresistible impulses to speak the truth to political leaders. But since I do not have access to these men, I turn to you, my Lord, and beg you to make all things right. You well know that I would gladly forfeit all the blessings you have given me and transfer them to these rulers, as long as I could remain in a state where I would never offend you. If they could experience what I have experienced, I know that it would be impossible for them to allow the violations they have been condoning.

O my God! Please help world leaders understand the magnitude of their responsibilities. You have singled them out. I have heard it said that when a powerful ruler dies, there are signs of his death in the heavens, as there was a sign in heaven when Jesus died. My heart quickens with devotion, my King, when I realize that you have provided these signs to show world leaders how important it is to walk in the footsteps of the Lord.

I certainly am growing bold, aren't I? Please tear this up if it sounds bad to you. Believe me, I could say this a lot better in person, if only they would listen to me. I sincerely pray for our leaders, and I would like to be of some help to them. Such an urge makes a soul reckless. I would gladly risk my life to gain what I believe in. Living is empty once we have seen the grand illusion with our own eyes and realized what suffering comes from walking in blindness.

Once a soul has attained this level of prayer, she does not merely desire to serve God; his Majesty gives her the strength to manifest the desire. The soul would not hesitate to try anything that might be of service to him. Any sacrifice for his sake feels like nothing, because she knows that anything other than pleasing him means nothing. The trouble is that people as worthless as I am don't find many opportunities to do something useful.

May it please you, my God, that the time may come when I will be able to repay you a speck of all I owe you. May it be your will, O Lord, that this servant of yours actually serve you in some way. Other women have done heroic things for love of you. I'm no good for anything but talk. This must be why you don't put me to work, my God. Everything with me adds up to nothing more than a bunch of wishes and words about how much I should be doing for you. The best of my intentions give me no relief, since they are always coupled with fear of failing you.

Before you do anything else, Good of all good, my Jesus, fortify my soul. Then help me to help you. Who could bear receiving so much and giving so little? I don't care what it costs, my Beloved. Please don't let me come into your presence empty-handed anymore. Shouldn't our reward be in proportion to our deeds?

Here is my life. Here is my honor. Here is my will. I give them all to you. I am yours. Use me as you will. I know all too well, my Beloved, how little I am capable of. But now I have reached you. Now I have climbed the watchtower, and I can see truths I could not see before. Now I can accomplish anything, as long as you don't leave me. If you leave, even if only for a brief time, I will go back to where I was, which was hell.

It's excruciating for a soul who has found herself in this place to return to the mundane world. This life looks like a farce. It feels like a complete waste of time to have to deal with physical needs like eating and sleeping. Everything wearies the soul, and she can't figure out how to escape. She sees herself as a prisoner in chains. Now she understands why Saint Paul beseeched God to free him from the body. Her cries join his, and she begs God to liberate her.

This condition is so intense that it seems as if the soul were straining to break free of the body and go off in search of this freedom. No one else seems to be willing to deliver her. The soul wanders around like a slave sold into captivity in a foreign land. What distresses her most is that she rarely encounters anyone else to join in her complaints and prayers for freedom. Everyone seems to want only to live. Oh, if only we could be more detached. If only we didn't derive our satisfaction from any worldly thing. Then the pain of living without the One we love and the yearning to live a true life would mitigate any fear of death!

If a woman like me is so often brokenhearted in the face of my exile, I wonder sometimes what the saints must have felt like. The charity I have given has been tepid, and my deeds have not assured me of true rest. What did Saint Paul and the Magdalene and others like them go through? The fire of love was blazing in them. It must have been a state of perpetual martyrdom for them.

The only people who bring me any comfort are the ones I encounter who have the same desires as I have and accompany them with actions. I mention action because there are people who consider themselves detached and broadcast this fact. Long years of spiritual practice and conformity with religious dogma would suggest that they have attained some degree of perfection. But even from a distance, the soul can tell the difference between those who have nothing but words and those who have confirmed these words through action. She understands what little good the first group does and how much work the second group gets done.

I have already told you about the fruits of the raptures that come from the spirit of God. The truth is, some of these effects may be more and some less. What I mean by "less" is that in the beginning some of the effects of rapture may not be proven with actions. This makes it impossible to prove their authenticity.

Raptures cause the soul to grow in perfection. They banish every last trace of cobwebs. This takes time. As love and humility flourish in the soul, the flowers of virtue spread their perfume for the enjoyment of this soul and of others. Actually, the Beloved can work such wonders in a rapture that the soul is left with almost no work to achieve a state of perfection. Only those who have tasted this experience will be able to believe what the Lord himself gives to the soul at this stage.

In my opinion, nothing we can do will bring us to this place. I am not denying that a person who makes a concerted effort on the spiritual path will, with the help of God, achieve some degree of detachment and transformation. There are many benefits to be gained by diligently implementing some of the methods taught by authors who have written about prayer. But it will be a laborious process and will take much longer. In rapture, without our doing anything, the Lord lifts up the soul and transports her from this earth. Even if such a soul deserves these favors no more than I did, God gives her mastery of all earthly things. I cannot overemphasize my own lack of merit; I had almost none at all.

Why does his Majesty do this? Because he wants to. And he does it the way he wants to. It doesn't matter whether or not the soul considers herself to be ready. His Majesty will prepare her to receive his blessing. Just because a soul has cultivated her garden well does not necessarily mean that she has earned rapture. Although it is absolutely true that anyone who takes good care of the garden and strives to be detached will be blessed. But sometimes it is God's will to display his great glory in meager soil. He so thoroughly prepares the ground of a wretched soul that she is incapable of turning back to her former life of offending him.

The mind has grown so accustomed to dwelling on the real truth that anything less feels like a game of make-believe. Sometimes the soul laughs to herself when she sees serious men, men of prayer and religion, making a big deal about some minor point of dignity or honor that she has long since trampled underfoot. They claim that it is a matter of discretion and that the more prestigious their status, the more good they can do. The soul understands they would do far more good in one day than in ten years if they thought a lot less about their authority and simply loved God.

Thus, the soul walks a troubled path, bearing many crosses, but she experiences rapid growth. Her companions think she has reached the summit, but then God grants her new favors and she ascends even higher. The soul is his soul. He is in charge. He illuminates her. It seems that he is guarding her against offending him. He helps her to wake up in service of him.

When my soul reached this sublime state, all the evil in me disappeared and the Lord gave me the strength to walk away from my bad habits. It no longer bothered me to be exposed to temptation and to spend time with the people who used to distract me. It was as if these occasions for error were not excuses for missing the mark at all. In fact, what used to do me harm was helping me. Everything was an opportunity to know and love God better. Everything reminded me of what I owed him, and this prevented me from going back to the way I was.

It all happened so quickly, I knew that I had nothing to do with my dramatic spiritual progress. His Majesty, in his great goodness, had blessed me with his favors and given me the strength to handle them. From the day the Beloved gave me my first ecstasy to the present moment, he has been increasing my strength. In his kindness, he has held my hand so that I would not turn back. It seems to me that I don't do anything now. And it's true. He does it all.

I believe that a soul in this state could be in the company of any kind of people and not be thrown off course. As long as she receives God's favors with humility and gratitude, always bearing in mind that the Beloved gives them and that she herself does almost nothing, she will retain her equanimity. Even if people are unconscious and corrupt, the soul will not be disturbed or enticed. On the contrary, the experience will help her to grow. These souls have grown so strong that God has chosen them to serve others. As the soul comes nearer to God in this place, he communicates very deep secrets to her.

With ecstasy come true revelations. With ecstasy come great favors and visions. All these phenomena humble the soul and fortify her. They dilute her attraction to the things of this life. They give her glimpses into the magnificent life the Lord has prepared for those who devote themselves to him.

May it please his Majesty that the boundless generosity he has heaped on such an ungrateful wretch serve as an inspiration to those who read this to give up everything for God. If the rewards his Majesty bestows on us even in this lifetime are so radical, imagine what he has in store for us in the next.

XXII ✠

SACRED HUMANITY

IF YOU WILL permit me, there is one more thing I'd like to say. I think it's very important, and if you think so too, you can draw on it whenever you need to give some advice on this subject. That could happen.

Books on prayer suggest that the soul is ultimately capable of lifting her own spirit with tender humility and raising it above all created things. The authors acknowledge that this can only happen after the soul has spent years purifying herself (the purgative stage) and has begun to receive God's light (the illuminative stage). They admit that the flight of the spirit is a totally supernatural phenomenon that God works on the soul, but they recommend ways in which the soul can contribute to her evolution in prayer.

Here is what they say: get rid of all physical images and contemplate pure divinity. Even the thought of Christ's humanity, they say, is an impediment to perfect contemplation. They use what Christ said to his disciples at the time of his Ascension to support their theory. It seems to me, by the way, that if the disciples had faith that he was both God and man, as they did after the Holy Spirit came to them, his form would not have been an obstacle. After all, he had no need to speak these words to his Blessed Mother, did he? And she loved him more than all of them!

The theologians I am referring to think that since contemplative prayer is entirely spiritual work, any corporeal thing can hinder it. Contemplatives, they advise, should try to think of God in a general way. He is everywhere, they say. We are immersed in him.

This is good—sometimes. But I cannot bear that we should withdraw completely from Christ or place his divine body on the same level with all created things and our own earthly miseries. May his Majesty give me the ability to explain what I mean by this.

I don't mean to contradict this theory about contemplative prayer. These authors are learned and spiritual men, and they know what they're talking about. God leads souls by many different paths. It is not my place to meddle. I can only speak about the way God has led me and the danger in which I placed myself by trying to put some of the things I was reading into practice.

I do believe, however, that people who have not passed beyond the stage of visions and raptures are inclined to think that formlessness is the best path. This is what I used to think. But there is a level of prayer that transcends union. If I had adhered to the practice of formless contemplation, I never would have arrived where I am now. In my opinion, this practice is a mistake. Maybe I am the one who is mistaken, but I will tell you what happened to me.

I didn't have a spiritual director when I was reading those books on prayer, and I thought I was getting somewhere on my own. Later, of course, it became painfully apparent to me that unless his Majesty gave me some understanding through experience, books were not very helpful, since I didn't know what I was doing. So when I began to experience the Prayer of Quiet, I tried to banish all corporeal associations from my mind. I still felt too wretched even to dare to elevate my own spirit. I thought that would be presumptuous of me.

I believed, though, that I felt the presence of God. And I did feel it. So I endeavored to recollect myself in his presence. The Prayer of Quiet is a lovely prayer. If God lends his assistance, it brings unspeakable delight. Since the fruits I derived from this prayer were so delectable, no one could possibly have convinced me to return to meditating on the humanity of Christ. I would have considered this only an impediment.

O Lord of my soul and my highest Good! O crucified Christ! I cannot look back on this opinion of mine without terrible pain. What was I thinking? I feel like I became a traitor. But it was a matter of sheer ignorance.

I had been deeply devoted to Christ all my life. This effort to transcend his humanity came fairly recently—just before the Lord began to grant me all those raptures and visions—and I didn't keep it up for very long. I easily returned to my customary practice of praising the Lord, especially when I received Communion. I wished I could keep a painting or statue of him with me at all times, since his image was not as deeply etched in my soul as I would have liked.

Is it really possible, my Lord, that it entered my mind for even an hour that you could be an obstacle to my greatest good? Where have all my blessings come from, if not from you? I cannot bear to think that I was at fault in this matter. It makes me so sad! I was only a victim of ignorance.

And so you in your goodness decided to remedy the situation by sending me someone to correct this error. Later you allowed me to see you so many times that I couldn't help but understand how severe my mistake had been. This moved me to convey this truth to everyone I could and to write it down here.

In my opinion, this rejection of sacred imagery prevents souls who have already tasted the Prayer of Union from evolving beyond that experience and attaining radical spiritual liberation. I have a couple of reasons for thinking this. Maybe I'm not saying anything at all. But I learned this from experience. My soul was in terrible shape before the Lord flooded it with his light. His blessings were coming in small packages. Once I had opened them, it was over. I didn't have the companionship of Christ to sustain me through the trials and temptations that inevitably came up.

The first reason I think it's a mistake to dismiss all images is that it shows a lack of humility. It's such a subtle lack and so well concealed that it could easily go unnoticed. Who could possibly be so proud and miserable that after he had spent a lifetime engaged in ardent prayers, penances, and persecutions, he would fail to feel anything other than joyous gratitude when the Lord allowed him to remain at the foot of the cross with Saint John? I was that proud. I was that miserable. Only stupid people like me would be anything other than deeply grateful for this honor. When everything should have been going right for me, I made it all go wrong.

Sometimes our health or our temperament keeps us from being able to dwell on the Passion of Christ. It is excruciating. But what stops us from being with him in his risen state? We have him so near to us when we participate in the Blessed Sacrament. He is already glorified here. We don't have to gaze upon him when he is weary, broken, and bleeding;

Teresa of Ávila: The Book of My Life
By Mirabai Starr
Audiobook read by Tessa Bielecki

With this fresh, contemporary translation of *The Book of My Life*, Mirabai Starr brings the beloved Spanish mystic to life for a new generation. And in the audio edition, Tessa Bielecki delivers such an engaging reading of *The Book of My Life* that it seems as if we are listening to Teresa of Ávila herself.

The audiobook also includes Teresa of Ávila's "bookmark" prayer, sung in English and Spanish. This moving prayer was found in Teresa's prayer book after her death, and it is another lingering display of her deep connection to the Divine.

Tessa Bielecki is the cofoundress of the Spiritual Life Institute, a modern Carmelite community with retreat centers in Colorado and Ireland. She is the author of *Holy Daring* and *Teresa of Ávila*.

Visit www.newseedsbooks.com to hear an audio sample of the reading.

New Seeds Books
An imprint of
Shambhala Publications

Book and audiobook available at your favorite bookseller, or at www.newseedsbooks.com.

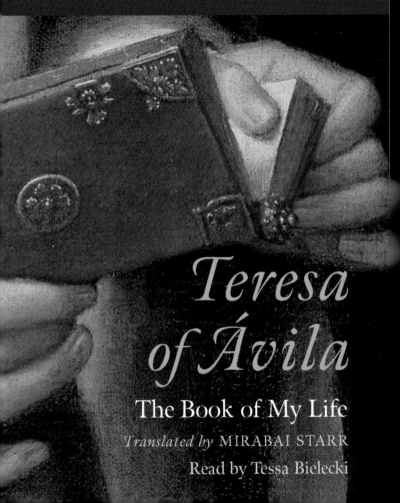

*Teresa
of Ávila*

The Book of My Life

Translated by MIRABAI STARR

Read by Tessa Bielecki

exhausted by the side of the road, persecuted by the people for whom he did so much good; doubted by his own apostles. Who could bear to think about his suffering all the time? Behold him free of suffering here, full of glory, about to ascend to heaven. As our companion in the most Blessed Sacrament, he strengthens us and gives us courage. It does not seem possible for him to leave us, even for a moment, ever.

Under the pretext of serving you, my Beloved, I abandoned you. I did not know you when I was offending you. But once I came to know you, how could I have thought it was a good thing to reject you so persistently? What a bad path I was walking! I realize now that I was not on any path at all until you brought me back home to you. When I saw you beside me, I saw all blessings. Once I looked at you as you really were, standing before the judges, there was no trial I was not willing to suffer.

Whoever lives in the presence of such a good friend and excellent master, one who stepped forward to be the first to suffer, can endure all things. The Lord helps us; he gives us strength and never fails us. He is a true friend. After my encounter with Christ, I clearly saw that God wanted me to receive his blessings through the sacred humanity of Christ, in whom his Majesty is well pleased. I have learned this truth over and over again through experience. The Lord has told it to me. I have definitely seen that this is the gate I must pass through if I want his sovereign Majesty to reveal great secrets to me.

And so, even if you have reached the summit of contemplation, you can trust that if you take this path, you will walk safely. All the blessings we seek are available through this Lord of ours. He will teach us everything. All we have to do is look at the example of his life. Unlike worldly friends, this friend will never abandon us in our labors and our troubles. What more could we want than to have such a companion by our side? Blessed is the soul who perpetually keeps him near her.

Think of the glorious Saint Paul. It seemed that the name of Jesus was always on his lips. That's how close he held his Lord in his heart. Ever since I had this realization, I've been carefully considering the lives of some of the great contemplatives and saints. I see that they also took this path: Saint Francis through the stigmata; Saint Anthony of Padua with the Infant. Saint Bernard rejoiced in the sacred humanity, as did Saint Catherine of Siena and many others. You would know this list better than I do.

Of course, the path of turning away from forms must be a good one if so many spiritual teachers advise it. But in my opinion, it's only appropriate when a soul is very advanced. Until then, it is best to seek the Creator through his creatures. The ability to transcend the physical depends on the particular blessing God grants each soul. I'm not talking about that. I'm talking about the most sacred humanity of Christ, which should not be equated with ordinary corporeal things. I wish I knew how to explain this clearly.

Once God decides to suspend the faculties, this presence is taken from us. Even if we desire to hold on to Christ's form, all forms fall away. We accept this. Blessed be such a loss that enables us to fully enjoy what we seem to be losing! Only then is the soul completely engaged with loving the One the intellect labored in vain to know. Then she loves what she did not understand. Then she rests in a joy she never could have experienced unless she had lost herself to gain herself.

But I don't think it's right to give up the wholehearted effort to keep his sacred humanity present with us at all times. May the Lord grant us this blessed presence! Otherwise, the soul is left floating around in the air. No matter how filled with the Divine she may think she is, she is completely ungrounded.

Living human beings need human support. Remember, lack of support can lead to lack of humility. That's when people try to elevate the soul before God elevates it. They are not content to meditate on something as precious as Christ's sacred humanity. They long to be Mary before they have worked with Martha. When the Lord wants to raise up the soul, even if it's the very first time she has ever practiced prayer, she has no reason to be afraid. But let's cultivate our consciousness. This miniscule lack of humility may seem to be nothing, but it does a great deal of harm if you are trying to advance in contemplation.

10 –Bear in mind that we are not angels. We have these bodies. It's crazy to desire to be angels while we are still on earth, especially if we are as earthbound as I was. Our thoughts generally need something to anchor them. It's rare for a soul to become so transported and so filled with God that she doesn't need any forms to hold her.

During those times when it's difficult to maintain our equanimity, such as when we are negotiating business or enduring persecution or experiencing spiritual aridity, Christ is a very good friend to have. We can picture him as a man and identify with his weakness and his troubles. He keeps us company. Once we have begun to develop this habit, it's easy to find him beside us when we look for him.

There will be times, though, when we are neither capable of finding Christ nor of transcending form. When this happens, it's a good idea to cultivate the detachment I've been talking about and not go rushing around in search of spiritual consolations. Embrace the cross. Unconditionally. This is the best thing. Christ was deprived of all consolation and abandoned in his suffering. Let's not abandon him again. He can support us far better than we can support ourselves. In his hands, we will ascend to great heights. When Christ determines that it's appropriate to remove himself, he will remove himself and allow his Majesty to draw the soul beyond herself and beyond all forms.

God is very pleased to see a soul humbly accept his son as mediator. He appreciates it when a soul loves his son so much that even when his Majesty desires to elevate the soul to the highest level of contemplation, she questions her own worthiness. "Depart from me, Lord," says the soul with Saint Peter, "for I am a sinner."

I am a living example of this; it is the way God has led my soul. Other souls find a shorter route. I have discovered that humility is the ground of prayer, and the deeper the soul bows down in prayer, the higher the Beloved will lift her up. I do not remember a single time when he bestowed his favors on me that I had not first been overwhelmed by my nothingness. His Majesty has revealed truths to me that I could never have imagined, truths that helped me to know myself.

I believe that when a soul meddles in the Prayer of Union in hopes of furthering her own progress, she will quickly trip and fall. Unless her foundation is solid, she may think that she's doing something useful, but she's actually hindering her progress. I'm afraid such a soul will not achieve true poverty of spirit. True spiritual nakedness means putting down our tools and resting in aridity. Having already given up looking for earthly comforts, we now give up our search for consolation in prayer. The only solace we seek is participation in the trials of the One who lived a life of trials.

The consolation this gives us should not cause us pain and agitation.

This is what certain souls suffer when they become overly attached to their efforts to find devotion through their intellect. They think if they are not always striving and laboring with the mind, they are failing. As if they had any control over God's blessings. I'm not saying they should not make every effort to be in God's presence, but if they can't even conjure up a decent thought, they shouldn't kill themselves trying. Who do we think we are? We are only his servants. Powerless.

But this is what the Lord wants. He wants us to acknowledge our powerlessness and behave like those little donkeys some people employ to propel the waterwheel. Even though they are wearing blinders and have no idea what they're doing, they draw more water than the gardener can with all his busy labor. Our job is simply to place ourselves in God's hand. Then we can walk our path in freedom.

If his Majesty calls us to his secret chamber, we should joyfully go to him. If he doesn't, we should be content to serve him through humbler tasks and not always try to sit down in the best seat. God cares more about us than we care about ourselves. He knows the best fit for each of us. Once we have delivered the whole of our will into the hands of God, why would we presume to direct our own life? In my opinion, our interference does more harm here than in the earlier stages of prayer. These blessings are supernatural. If a person has a bad voice, forcing herself to sing is not going to make it better. But if God gives her a good voice, she doesn't even need to practice; she just opens her mouth and makes music.

Let the soul surrender to his will and trust in his great goodness. Let her always ask him to grant us his grace. Once she has received permission to sit at Christ's feet, she shouldn't budge. Let her stay there as long as she likes, emulating the Magdalene. If she is strong, God will lead her into the wilderness.

This explanation should be enough to satisfy you, at least until you find someone with more experience and more knowledge than I have. If you encounter seekers who are beginning to receive tastes of the Divine and think they are the architects of their own spiritual growth and gratification, don't believe them. How gloriously God reveals himself when he chooses to, entirely independent of our petty little efforts!

No matter how much we may try to elevate ourselves, when God decides to carry away our spirits, it is like a giant lifting a piece of straw. We are incapable of resisting. Wouldn't it be strange if a toad believed it could fly of its own volition whenever it wanted to? It seems to me even more difficult and arduous for our spirit to lift itself up to God unless he chooses to raise us to himself. The desire to fly does us no good as long as we are weighed down with a thousand earthly burdens. It is true that flying is more natural to us than it is to a toad, but we have become mired in the muck and have lost our ability to soar.

14. I'd like to conclude by saying this: whenever we think of Christ, we should think of his love. It is with love that he has bestowed so many gifts on us. It is with love that God has given us such a sign and promise of his great love. Love gives rise to more love. Even if we are just beginning on the path and are still very wretched, let us strive to carry this divine love with us wherever we go and to increasingly awaken ourselves in love. If the Beloved decides to bless us by pressing the seal of his love into our hearts, everything will be easy for us. Heavy tasks will become light, and we will finish them quickly.

God knows how much we need his love. In the name of the great love he revealed to us through his glorious Son and in the name of the love Christ demonstrated for us at such a high cost to himself, let his Majesty give us his love again and again. Amen.

I just need to ask you one question. When the Lord begins to grant such sublime favors to the soul—when he places her in a state of perfect contemplation, for instance—shouldn't she become immediately and irrevocably perfect? Simply by virtue of the fact that someone who tastes such a blessing by definition loses all craving for earthly consolations, it seems like this should be the case. Why is it such a gradual awakening? The more raptures and other divine favors the soul receives, the more sublime are their effects and the more detached the soul becomes from the things of this world. The same Lord that blesses the soul with these experiences could sanctify her in an instant. Instead, he perfects her virtues little by little over time. Why?

This is what I'd like to know, since I have no idea what the answer is. I do know there is a big difference between the degree of fortitude God leaves in the soul in the beginning, when the rapture is over in the twinkling of an eye and its effects are almost imperceptible, and the power instilled later on when the transport lasts much longer. I often think this must be because we are incapable of preparing ourselves all at once.

The Lord steadily fosters the young soul until she has developed the resolution and strength of a mature being, capable of trampling all worldly things under her feet. What he did in a short time for the Magdalene he does more slowly for the rest of us, in proportion to the effort we make to allow him to do his work in us. Let us not stop believing for a minute that God will reward us a hundredfold, even in this lifetime!

Here's another metaphor that occurred to me. Since the divine favors more advanced practitioners receive are the same as those given to beginners, we could compare these favors to some common food that everyone eats. People who eat just a little are left with a good taste in their mouths for a short time. Those who eat more derive some nourishment from it. And the ones who eat abundantly draw life and strength.

In fact, this last group eats the food of life so often and is so filled by it that no other food could possibly satisfy them. It is obvious to them how much good it is doing them. Their palates have so completely adapted to its sweetness that they would rather starve than eat anything else. Ordinary foods only detract from the exquisite taste this good food leaves in their mouths.

Encounters with holy people are like this too. Such exchanges are far more beneficial when they occur over many days than when they last only one day. If our conversations are prolonged, we take on the qualities of our saintly companions, God willing. It all depends on what his Majesty wants and who he chooses to bless in what ways. The important thing is that anyone who begins to receive divine favors needs to make up her mind to detach herself from the world and cherish these blessings as they should be cherished.

It seems to me that his Majesty is testing us to see if we truly love him. First he challenges this one, then that one. If our faith has faltered, he may reveal himself with such sublime joy that it quickens our faith by offering us a glimpse of what is to come. "Look," he says, "this is only a drop in a vast sea of blessings." He leaves nothing undone for those he loves. Once he sees that they have accepted his gifts, he gives of himself without end. He loves all who love him.

What a good Beloved we have! What a good friend! O Lord of my soul, who has the language to explain what you give those who surrender to you? Who could ever express the terrible loss of the ones who attain this state only to lose it by holding on to themselves? I know that this is not your will, Lord. You prove this by visiting a dwelling as meager as mine. May you be blessed forever and ever.

If you decide to share these teachings on prayer with other spiritual people, please, I beg you again, make sure that they really are spiritual people. If they are only familiar with one road or have gotten stuck halfway, they will not be able to understand what I'm saying.

God leads some people along a very exalted path right from the beginning. Then they think that everybody else should walk the same way: quieting the intellect, avoiding all forms and images. But by following these practices, some people end up as dessicated as dried-out husks. There are others who experience a taste of quietude and jump to the conclusion that they have achieved this on their own and can do it again whenever they want. Instead of evolving, these souls slide back. So experience and discernment are always important. May the Beloved in his goodness grant us these qualities.

XXIII ✠

A New Life

I'D LIKE TO RETURN now to where I left off in the story of my life. I suppose I have digressed more than I should have. But that was only so that you would be able to grasp more easily what I am about to reveal.

From now on, this is another book of my life, a new one, because this is a new life. The life I wrote about up to this point was my own. The one I have been living since I began to share the teachings on prayer is the life God has been living in me. This is how it seems to me, anyway. Otherwise, how could it be possible for so many bad habits and negative actions to have fallen away in such a short period of time? Praise the Lord who freed me from myself!

Thus, when I finally became determined to avoid opportunities for error and devote myself to prayer, the Lord began to grant me his favors. It was as if all he wanted was for me to be willing to receive his gifts. His Majesty blessed me with the Prayer of Quiet on a regular basis and quite often gave me the Prayer of Union, which absorbed me for long periods of time.

During those years, there was a movement spreading throughout Spain in which the devil was preying on certain women called Illuminists, causing them to fall into serious spiritual delusions. I was terrified of this happening to me. But it's not as if I had any power to fend off the wondrous sweetness and delight I experienced in prayer. Besides, I was always left with this unshakable certainty that it came from God. When I observed that I emerged from these states strengthened and improved, it only confirmed my faith that they were real.

But as soon as I became distracted, I grew afraid again. I wondered whether the spirit of evil was making me think that the experience was good. Maybe he wanted to suspend my intellect and deprive me of mental prayer precisely so that I would stop thinking about the Passion of Christ or making use of my mind for spiritual purposes. I worried that I was losing instead of gaining. I did not understand contemplation at all.

The more his Majesty shed his light on my soul, the greater grew my desire not to offend him. My fear increased in proportion to my awareness of my vast debt to him. This anxiety intensified to such a degree that I was finally compelled to search for spiritual guidance to help me sort things out.

I had heard about some Jesuits who had recently come to Ávila, and I had always been very attracted to the Society of Jesus. I didn't know any of the members personally, but I was impressed by what I had been told about their way of life and the method of prayer they practiced. I did not consider myself worthy of speaking to them, however, or strong enough to follow their guidance. This made me even more anxious. Being who I was, how could I have a conversation with them?

So I stalled for a while, struggling mightily within myself, shedding copious tears. I longed to consult a spiritual person and ask him to help me identify the states of prayer I was experiencing and to clarify things in case I was going astray. I resolved (again) to do all I could to avoid offending my God. I knew how weak I was, and my lack of fortitude scared me. I could not shake this fear. I procrastinated in reaching out to the Jesuits.

God, help me! What a terrible mistake it is to withdraw from good in the effort to become good. The spirit of evil seems to make himself especially troublesome when the virtues are just beginning to ripen. He knows that a sure cure for a troubled soul lies in consulting the friends of God, and he undermined my resolve to do this. I convinced myself that I was waiting until I had mended my ways, just as I had during that period when I abandoned prayer. I was so caught up in all my little bad habits that I didn't even see how bad they were. I may have spent the rest of my life finding ways to avoid reaching for a hand to pull me out of this quagmire if the Lord had not finally stretched out his own hand to me first. May he be blessed!

When I noticed that my fear was escalating in proportion to the progress I was making in prayer, I couldn't figure out if my experience was very bad or very good. I understood that there was something supernatural about my prayer because I was not always capable of resisting these states, nor could I conjure them up whenever I wanted to. I thought to myself, "All I can do is try to keep my conscience clean and avoid opportunities for missing the mark, even in small ways."

I came to the conclusion that if the prayer came from the spirit of God, I could only gain from the practice of purifying my conscience. Whereas if the spirit of evil was responsible, my effort to make myself right with God certainly couldn't do me any harm; in fact, the spirit of evil would be the loser. And so, that's what I decided to do. But after a few days of striving and beseeching God to help me on my way, I realized that my soul lacked the strength to attain such perfection on my own. I still had some attachments. They were not so terrible in and of themselves, but they were enough to spoil everything.

People were talking about a learned priest named Gaspar Daza in Ávila. The Lord had begun to reveal this man's life of goodness and holiness to the world. I tried to make a connection with him through a mutual acquaintance, a saintly gentleman named Francisco de Salcedo, another citizen of our city. Don Francisco is a householder but lives such an exemplary and virtuous life and has such a prayerful and generous heart that his integrity radiates throughout the community.

There is ample cause for don Francisco's reputation for perfection. He has done many souls a tremendous amount of good. He has so many gifts that even his status as a married man cannot prevent him from using them. He is extremely intelligent and exceedingly kind to everyone. His conversation is never tedious but always gentle and gracious, as well as honest and insightful. Everyone who talks with him feels delighted by the exchange. He directs all things toward the greater good of every single soul with whom he comes in contact. He seems to be entirely focused on doing whatever he possibly can to soothe and serve everyone he meets.

It was through the diligent intervention of this blessed man that my soul was saved. I was in awe of his humility. I think he has been practicing prayer for almost forty years—maybe two or three years less than that, I'm not sure. He lives as perfect a life as his family state will allow. His wife is a great servant of God, charitable and angelic, so she does not hold him back in any way. In fact, God seems to have chosen her to be the companion of a man he knew would also be a great servant of his. Don Francisco and I happen to be distantly related.

So don Francisco arranged for that learned priest to come visit me. The two men were close friends. I was hoping to take this priest as my guide and confessor. When don Francisco brought Father Daza in to speak with me, I was intimidated in the presence of such a holy man. I tried to tell him about my soul and my experiences in prayer, but he didn't want to hear my confession because he was too busy.

Not long after that, Father Daza began to guide my soul with holy determination. He treated me as if I were much stronger than I was. And indeed, after the heights of prayer he knew I had experienced, I should have been strong enough to avoid offending God in any way whatsoever. When I saw how determined he was to get me to give up all those little flaws I was still caught by, I became deeply distressed. I did not have the courage or fortitude to transcend these things so immediately and so perfectly. I began to realize that his insistence that I die to all my soul's attachments at once might be dangerous, and I decided to exercise more caution in our relationship.

I guess what I'm trying to say is that I came to the conclusion that this priest's methods were not best suited to my soul. I could not make use of what he gave me because his gifts were appropriate for a more perfected soul. As for me, I may have been advanced in terms of the favors I had received from God, but I was a total beginner when it came to virtue and mortification. The truth is, if I had only had access to this one guide, my soul would never have flourished. When I saw that I could not do what he told me to do, I became so distressed that I nearly lost hope and gave up on everything.

It amazes me sometimes to reflect that even though this priest had a special gift for beginning to lead souls on their path to God, it was not God's will for him to understand my soul and direct it accordingly.

I'm starting to see that what happened was for my greater good, because it propelled me to get to know the holy Jesuits and call upon their wisdom.

Around this time, I arranged with don Francisco to come to the Incarnation and talk to me sometimes. His willingness to spend time with someone as wretched as I only confirmed his tremendous humility. He began to visit me and encourage me on my path. He told me that I shouldn't think I could give up all of my imperfections in one day. Little by little, he assured me, God would do his work in me. He confided in me that he himself had been plagued for many years by all kinds of petty habits that he simply couldn't break.

O humility! What blessings you bring to those who possess you and also to those who come into contact with those who possess you! I truly believe I am right in referring to don Francisco as a saint. Thus, for my benefit, this saint told me about his weaknesses, or at least what his humility made him believe were weaknesses. In light of his station in life, these things were not imperfections at all. Because of my monastic vows, on the other hand, the same things would have constituted serious faults in me.

I am not telling you all this for nothing. It may seem like I am making a big deal of trivial things, but these things are of vital importance to a fledgling soul when she is first learning to fly. As they say, her feathers have not yet grown in and she needs all the help she can get. Still, I know that no one will believe what I'm saying unless he has been through it himself. It is only because I hope to God that you will help many souls that I even bother to mention it here.

This holy man was my salvation. He seemed to know exactly what would heal me, and he had the charity, the humility, and the patience to stay with me, even when he saw that I was not thoroughly rectifying my life. Gradually and with discretion, he showed me ways to conquer the spirit of evil. My love for him grew so strong that I looked forward to the days I saw him more than anything else, even though he did not come very often. When he went a long time without visiting me, I would worry that he was staying away because I was so wretched.

As don Francisco became more familiar with my extensive transgressions, he noticed a dramatic inconsistency between the favors God was bestowing on me and the imperfections in my character, even though I began to make some real improvement as our relationship unfolded. I told him about the experiences I had been having, hoping he could shed some light on them.

"These are states generally attained only by very advanced souls," he remarked, "and you have convinced me that you are still impure. I am concerned that the only explanation for this discrepancy is that a bad spirit is responsible for some of your experiences, although I cannot draw a definite conclusion about this. Still," he mused, "everything you have told me about your prayer sounds very good."

Our main problem, I think, was that I didn't know how to explain what I had been going through, because God was only just beginning to give me some understanding of these states, and I couldn't quite articulate it yet.

Don Francisco's fears blended with the fear I was already feeling, and I became extremely distressed. I cried and cried. All I had ever wanted was to please my God! I could not persuade myself that the devil had anything to do with my sublime experiences. On the other hand, maybe my sins had made me so blind that I couldn't see the true source of these states.

I started looking through books to see if I could learn some language to help me explain myself better. I found one called *Ascent of the Mount*. It gave a detailed description of the soul's union with the Divine and matched my own experience perfectly. It said that in the midst of this state of prayer, all thinking ceases. That's just what I had been trying to say. When I enter into that place, I can no longer think of a thing.

I marked the relevant passage and gave the book to don Francisco.

"Please, Father," I asked him, "share this with Father Daza. Maybe between the two of you, you might be able to look it over and tell me what I should do. I will give up prayer altogether if that's what you think would be best."

Why would I want to keep placing myself in harm's way? If I had made no progress after almost twenty years of practicing prayer and had only succeeded in getting myself ensnared by the devil, I might as well quit practicing. Yet the thought of giving it up made my heart unbearably heavy. I had already experienced what happened to my soul when I stopped practicing prayer.

No matter which way I looked, I saw tribulation. I felt like a person caught in the middle of a river trying desperately to get back to the shore. Wherever he turns, he faces greater danger. He is on the brink of drowning. This is a terrible trial, and I have suffered many like it, as you will soon see. Maybe it doesn't seem like an important issue to you, but it might be helpful in understanding how the spirit is tested.

Spiritual directors need to be especially careful when they are dealing with women. We are more sensitive, and it can damage us to be told directly that the spirit of evil is the cause of our inner states. This can create terrible suffering. Yet women should seriously consider this opinion and turn away from any danger they may be facing. Also, they should be counseled to keep certain experiences secret. Their spiritual guides should guard these women's secrets too.

I am speaking from the perspective of one who has suffered a bitter trial in this respect. There are men with whom I have discussed my inner life who have not kept it secret. By checking my experiences with this one and the other one, they have done me great harm. They have spread private things about me that should have been kept private. These matters are not for everybody. And then they made it look as if I were the one who had broadcast these things!

I believe it was not really their fault. I believe the Lord allowed this to happen to test me. I'm not saying, by the way, that they disclosed things I had shared with them during confession. But these were men to whom I gave a full account of myself because I thought they might enlighten me, and instead they betrayed me. They should have kept quiet! I never dared to conceal anything from these men.

All I'm saying is that men should use more discretion in counseling women like me. They should encourage us, waiting patiently for the Lord to give them the help they need to help us. My excessive fear made me particularly vulnerable. If the Lord had not helped me, I would have been in big trouble. Given my weak heart, I'm astounded that more damage wasn't done to me.

And so I handed don Francisco a written account of my experiences in prayer and accompanied this with a verbal explanation. Since he was a layman, this was not a confession, of course. I simply made it clear how very wretched I was. Don Francisco shared all this with Father Daza, and the two men pondered with great charity and love what would be best for my soul.

I waited for their answer with intense trepidation. I asked everyone I knew to pray for me during this time, and I prayed a lot for myself. Finally, one of the two men came to me and, with heart-wrenching anguish in his voice, informed me that they had come to the mutual conclusion that the source of my experiences was the devil.

They advised me to consult the Jesuits. If I told them I was in trouble and asked them to come, they would certainly come. I was instructed to tell the Jesuits everything, all about my life and the states of prayer I had experienced. "Offer a very frank confession," they said, "so that the power of the Sacrament may enlighten the confessor and he will be able to guide you correctly." They assured me that this order was very experienced in spiritual matters. "Do whatever they tell you," they warned me, "because your soul is in serious danger."

This hurt me and alarmed me so severely that I didn't know what to do. All I could do was cry. I was sitting in the oratory in deep pain, wondering what would become of me, when I opened a book. The Lord must have placed it in my hands. I read the words of Saint Paul, who assures us that God is very faithful, that he would never let those who love him be deceived by the devil. I found this profoundly consoling.

I began to prepare for my general confession, writing down all the good things and the bad ones. I was trying to present the clearest account of my life I possibly could. I was determined not to leave out a single pertinent detail.

I remember that after I had finished my account and read it over, I was struck by how much evil there was in it and how little good. I felt miserable. I was also deeply distressed that the members of my household would notice that such holy people as the Jesuits were coming to speak with me. By now, my own wickedness was a cause of terror, and I was afraid that unless I made a concerted effort to avoid any possible opportunity for error, things were only going to get worse for me.

I made arrangements with both the gatekeeper and the sacristan of the Incarnation not to tell anyone about my special visitor. But it was no use. It turned out that when the Jesuit came to call for me, there was someone standing near the door, and she spread the news throughout the house. What fears and obstacles the spirit of evil places in the path of a soul who wants only to get to God!

Father Diego de Cetina was a true servant of God and very wise. I knew he knew the language of the soul. After I had told him all about my states of prayer, he explained to me exactly what I was experiencing. He was very encouraging.

"These experiences definitely come from the spirit of God," he assured me. "But your prayer does not yet have a solid foundation. You need to return to your practice. You do not yet understand mortification." This was true. I wasn't even sure what the word meant. "You should never give up prayer but rather work very hard at it, since God is granting you such special favors."

Father de Cetina suggested that maybe God wanted to do good for many souls through me. He said other things like this, as if he had foreknowledge of all that God was going to do with me later. He pointed out that it would be a terrible mistake for me not to respond to the favors God was bestowing on me. His words impressed themselves into my heart. All in all, it felt to me like the Holy Spirit was speaking through him to heal me.

His guidance was very humbling to me and seemed to transform me completely. What a marvelous thing it is to have your soul be understood by another soul!

"You should devote your daily meditations to a phase of the Passion," Father de Cetina told me. "For now, dwell exclusively on Christ's humanity, and try to resist the experiences of recollection and bliss. Do not to make any room for these altered states until I direct you otherwise."

Father de Cetina left me comforted and reassured. The Lord helped us both to understand my situation and figure out the best path for me to take. I was determined not to stray from his guidance in the slightest degree, and I have maintained my resolve to this day. Praise be to the Lord who has given me the grace to obey my spiritual directors, even if I do not always do so perfectly! The Jesuits have always been my best guides.

At this point, my soul turned a corner and began to make noticeable progress, as you will see.

XXIV ✛

RESISTING THE GIFTS

MY CONFESSION to Father de Cetina soothed my soul. I felt prepared to do whatever it might take to reach God. Although my confessor did not pressure me in the slightest, I felt compelled to change many subtle habits. Father de Cetina did not seem to take these matters very seriously; he was far less concerned with technical details than he was with the love of God. But his emphasis on loving God inspired me all the more, because he gave me tremendous freedom and never coerced me.

I spent almost two months trying with all my might to resist God's favors and gifts. The changes inside me began to show on the outside. The Lord was giving me the courage to endure things that people who knew me considered to be extreme. Even the sisters in my own house wondered if I was taking renunciation a little too far. Compared to the way I used to be, I can see why they were concerned. But compared to what I think my monastic vows truly require, these austerities fell short.

By resisting God's gifts and favors, I gained something even better: direct knowledge of God himself. I used to think that I had to be in solitude to receive the blessing of his presence in prayer. I would seclude myself and hardly dare to stir. Then I found out that solitude has nothing to do with it. The more I tried to distract myself, the more the Lord enfolded me in his sweetness. His glory seemed to surround me everywhere I went; there was nowhere to hide from his grace.

My intense effort to repress these states was painful. But the Lord's desire to bless me and reveal himself to me overpowered my best intentions to resist. During those two months, he made his gifts and favors more dramatic than ever before, eradicating any last shred of doubt that

I had the power to resist them. I renewed my love for Christ's sacred humanity. The foundation of my practice began to take shape, and the edifice of prayer settled into place. The austerities that my illnesses had prevented now became irresistible to me.

The holy man who heard my confession speculated that maybe the reason God gave me such poor health was because I had not done enough penance and so his Majesty had created some for me. Father de Cetina ordered me to do some austerities that made me exceedingly uncomfortable, but he assured me that they could do me no harm.

I did everything he told me. It felt as if the Lord himself were telling me what to do. God gave this man the ability to direct my soul and gave me the ability to obey him. I became so sensitive that every time I began to offend God, even in the smallest way, I felt it in my soul. If I was holding on to some petty luxury or comfort, I could not recollect myself in prayer until I had given it up. I fervently prayed for the Lord to hold me in his hands. Now that he had connected me with his servants, I beseeched him not to allow me to turn back. I felt that if I were to fall, it could damage the reputations of my spiritual guides.

Around this time, Father Francis Borgia, who had once been Duke of Gandia, came to Ávila. He had given up all his worldly wealth and status to enter the Society of Jesus. Father de Cetina and the holy gentleman I've told you about, don Francisco, arranged for me to speak with him. Father Borgia was renowned as a very advanced soul who had been given great gifts from God. He had sacrificed many things for God, and God had already repaid him, even in this lifetime. Since I was making such dramatic progress in prayer, they thought it would be helpful for me to discuss these things with him.

Well, after Father Borgia had listened to my account, he told me that my experiences definitely came from the spirit of God. "I see no reason for you to continue trying to push these gifts away," he said. "I can see how this resistance has been an appropriate practice up to now, but it would be a mistake to continue it. The time has come to embrace all blessings. You should still begin each period of silent prayer by meditating on a phase of the Passion, but then if the Lord transports your spirit, you must let him take it. But you shouldn't try to make this flight of the spirit happen on your own either."

Since Father Borgia was so evolved, he knew the right medicine to give me and the advice that would be most useful. His counsel deeply consoled me. My friend don Francisco was also very relieved to hear that my experiences came from God. This helped him to help me in many different areas.

Right around this time, my confessor, Father de Cetina, was transferred away from Ávila. I was heartbroken. I was convinced that I would never find another guide like him and that I was bound to slide right back into my wicked ways. It felt like my soul had been banished to the desert. I was inconsolable and filled with anxiety. I didn't know what to do with myself.

A relative of mine arranged for me to go and stay with her for a while, which indirectly led to my finding a new Jesuit spiritual director. First, the Lord brought me into friendship with a young widow of noble family, named doña Guiomar de Ulloa. Doña Guiomar was a devout practitioner of contemplative prayer and a very close friend of the Jesuits. I stayed at her house for many days, and she had me speak to her own confessor. Simply listening to the holiness of their conversation uplifted my soul.

My new spiritual director, Father Juan de Prádenos, began to guide me toward greater perfection. "Hold nothing back from God," he told me. Father Juan led me with great gentleness and skill. My soul was still very fragile. I was not strong enough to give up some of my friendships voluntarily. I didn't believe that I was offending God through these connections, but I was inordinately attached to them. It felt like it would be ungrateful of me to walk away from them.

"Pray about these relationships," Father Juan said. "If you recite the Veni Creator, God will enlighten you about the best thing to do."

One day, after I had spent a long time in prayer begging the Beloved to help me please him in every way, something happened that changed my life. I was just beginning the hymn when a rapture came upon me so suddenly that it almost carried me out of myself. It was the first time God had ever given me the gift of rapture, and it was so powerful that I could not possibly doubt what was happening.

In the midst of it, I heard these words: "From now on I no longer want you to speak with human beings but with angels." I was terrified. The transport was so intense and the words resonated so deeply that I couldn't help but be afraid. Yet once I adjusted to the novelty of the experience, the fear faded and I was filled with a sense of deep consolation.

These words have been fulfilled. Since that day, the only people I have been able to form close bonds of friendship with are those I believe are loving God and trying to serve him. If they're not, it's difficult for me to feel much affection for them or find any comfort in their presence. This has been something that is beyond my control. And it doesn't matter whether these people are old friends or even relatives. If the person does not seem willing to love and serve God or isn't interested in discussing the spiritual path, it is a painful cross for me to deal with them.

Ever since then, I have had the courage to give everything up to God. It seems to me now that all he ever wanted was my utter transformation. Commands were pointless. My spiritual director saw how attached I was to certain friendships, but he did not dare say that I should give them up. He had to wait until the Lord did it for me. I couldn't give them up on my own either. I had tried, and the distress it caused me was so severe—especially in light of how innocent and good these relationships were—that I abandoned the effort.

But now the Beloved himself set me free and gave me the strength to do his work. I told my spiritual director what had happened, and I let everything go, just as I had been told. It did my guides a lot of good to witness the determination in me.

May God be forever blessed! In an instant, he gave me the freedom that I could never attain through all my hard work over so many years. I had often jeopardized my health by trying to force myself to give up things I was not ready for. But since he who is the all-powerful and true Lord of all did it for me, I felt no pain.

XXV

SPIRITUAL VOICES

A<small>T THIS JUNCTURE</small>, it would be a good idea to explain what happens when the soul hears spiritual voices and how they make her feel. Ever since the Lord first granted me this favor, it has become a very common experience for me.

Although we do not hear the words with our physical ears, they are so distinct that we understand them with absolute clarity. In fact, we could not resist hearing and understanding them even if we tried with all our might to shut them out. Here on earth, if we do not want to listen to something, we can stick our fingers in our ears or focus our attention on something else so that even if we hear the words, we do not understand them. But when God speaks directly to the soul, she has no choice.

Even if I wanted to avoid what God has to say, he makes me listen to him. And he sharpens my mind so that I clearly understand what he wants me to understand. It doesn't matter whether I'm trying to understand or not. God wants us to realize that he is all-powerful. God is our supreme Lord. I have a lot of experience with this matter, because I struggled for two years to resist these experiences and I couldn't do it. I still try sometimes, and I still can't do it.

There is a danger of becoming deluded here. Only a very experienced spiritual practitioner is safe from delusions. In general, there are three different sources of spiritual voices: the spirit of God, the spirit of evil, and our own minds. Then there is another kind of voice, which is the spirit speaking to itself. I'm not sure how this last experience works, but it occurs to me today that it would be possible. I have a great deal of experience with the voices that come from God. Many of the things he said to me came true after two or three years. So far, nothing I have heard has turned out to be a lie.

Sometimes when a person approaches God with great love and lays a certain request at his feet, the intensity of her feeling might lead her to imagine that she hears his response to her prayer. And it is quite possible that she is correct. But anyone who has experienced genuine spiritual voices will easily be able to hear the difference between words that come from her own mind and those that come from the spirit of God. If the message is something the intellect has fabricated, no matter how subtle it may be, an experienced person will know that the mind is composing and conveying it.

The main difference is that in one case the words are contrived and in the other they are simply heard. The intellect will recognize that it's not really listening because it's too busy making things up. The words it puts together sound muffled and vague. They do not carry the clarity and authority of a true spiritual voice. In this case, we have just as much power to shift our attention away from the content of our own minds as we do to keep quiet when we no longer want to hear the sound of ourselves talking. When the words come from God, it is impossible to divert our attention.

A more obvious sign that the voice is coming from our own minds is that the words have no lasting effect. The voices that come from God are both words and works. What I mean is that even if the words are critical rather than devotional, they cultivate the soul and make her grow. They bless her and give her light. They move the soul to a place of deep tenderness and quietude. If the soul has been suffering from agitation and aridity, it feels like God is liberating her from all her worries with a wave of his hand. He seems to be proving to her that he is all-powerful and that his words are works.

It seems to me that the difference between a true spiritual voice and an intellectual one is no more and no less than the difference between listening and speaking. When I'm talking, I am arranging what I'm going to say in my mind. But when someone else is talking to me, all I have to do is listen without any effort. With an intellectual voice, we can't be sure if the words were really spoken. We hear them the way someone who is half asleep will hear the conversation in a room where she is lying down. When the voice comes from God, it is so clear that we don't miss a single syllable.

We often hear true spiritual voices when our souls and our minds are so agitated and distracted that we couldn't succeed in stringing together a coherent sentence if we tried. Yet here are these elaborate discourses fully prepared and handed to us, speeches we could not possibly have written even in our clearest state of consciousness. And at the sound of the first word, the soul is utterly transformed.

How could the soul suddenly understand things that had never even crossed her mind before, especially when she is enraptured? How can she apprehend these things when the faculties are suspended and the imagination is dazed?

I'd like to make something clear: the soul does not see visions or hear spiritual voices when she is actually in the midst of a rapture. During rapture, all the faculties are completely lost, and in my opinion, we can't see or hear or even understand a thing. The soul is completely under the power of Another. The Beloved gives her no freedom at all.

This state of total absorption doesn't last long, however. It is after the intensity of the rapture has passed, but while the soul is still transported, that the voices come. Even though the faculties are starting to come back, they are barely functional. They certainly aren't capable of putting sentences together.

There are so many ways to tell the difference between a voice that comes from God and one conjured up by our own intellect that we have no reason to be fooled more than once. I mean, if a soul is experienced and vigilant, she will easily be able to distinguish between them. Not only do the voices that come from the intellect fail to produce any lasting effects, but the discerning soul has trouble believing them. They sound like nonsense to her. She doesn't take them any more seriously than she would take the ravings of a lunatic. When the voices come from God, on the other hand, they have lasting effects, whether the soul consciously acquiesces to them or not.

When we hear a true spiritual voice, we experience it as though we were listening to the teachings of a very holy person or a great sage who would never lie to us. The voice bears absolute authority. This analogy is still inadequate. For the words carry such majesty that even if we do not know who is speaking them, we tremble if they are words of reproach and we melt if they are words of love. The sentences are so complex and are spoken so quickly that we never would have had time to compose them ourselves. There's no reason for me to dwell on this any longer. Suffice it to say that an experienced person is not likely to be deceived unless she wants to be deceived.

It is impossible to doubt a spiritual voice when it is happening. It is only afterward that I have sometimes wondered if I made it up. But then later I discover that what I heard has turned out to be true. The Lord imprints the words on our memory so that we cannot forget what he said. However, the voices that come from our own minds are like the first stirrings of a thought; they pass before they are fully formed.

A divine voice may fade over a long period of time but never so completely that we lose the substance of what we heard. When the voice conveys a particular teaching or bestows a favor, we may not retain the details, but if it takes the form of prophecy, in my opinion, it is impossible to forget. At least this is the case for me, and I have a terrible memory.

It would be extremely wicked for someone to claim that she has heard a divine voice when she has not. But it would be impossible for the soul not to realize whether a voice is an artifact of her own mind and does not originate from the spirit of God. Otherwise, she might spend her whole life laboring under the illusion that she knows something that she does not know. How could she? Either a soul wants to understand or she doesn't.

Say the soul tries to push away what she's hearing because it scares her. Or maybe she has convinced herself that silent prayer is the only valid spiritual practice, so she rejects all language and all concepts. Then how could the intellect possibly have the freedom to make up these sacred speeches? Such things take much more time than the soul has allowed herself. The voices that come from God instruct us in a flash. We instantaneously realize things that would take us a month to put into words. The intellect and the soul herself are amazed at what they understand.

This is the way it is. Anyone who has experienced it will know that

what I am saying is literally true. I praise God for giving me the ability
to describe it this way. I'll just wrap this up by saying that I think we
can create intellectual voices whenever we want. Every time we sit in
prayer we might talk ourselves into believing that we are hearing the
words of God.

But we cannot make God speak to us. Sometimes I spend many days
hoping to hear the voice of God and nothing comes. Then at other times,
when I don't want to hear a spiritual voice, I am suddenly given direct
knowledge of divine things.

It seems to me that someone who has not had this experience might
try to mislead others into thinking that he understands something that
he could not possibly understand. The big clue that it is not a true spiritual voice is that, if pressed, the person will report that he heard it with
his physical ears. I never knew there was any other way to hear things
either, until I experienced it myself. And hearing in this other way has
created severe trials for me.

When the voices come from the spirit of evil, not only do they fail to
create any positive results, but they leave negative effects in their wake.
I have only experienced these voices two or three times, and on each
occasion God gave me ample warning ahead of time. Not only do these
diabolical voices dry out the soul, but they also leave her terribly disquieted. I have experienced aridity and disquiet many times after the Lord
has given me severe temptations and spiritual trials. This kind of inner
turmoil still plagues me on a regular basis. But I understand where it
comes from.

The agitation that accompanies a voice from the spirit of evil is different. The soul intuitively resists it. She feels troubled and upset without knowing why. But I'll tell you why: it's because what the spirit of
evil says to her is bad, not good. I wonder if one spirit doesn't detect the
presence of the other. The sense of consolation and delight the spirit of
evil gives to the soul is very different from what she receives from the
voice of God, but if someone had not experienced an authentic spiritual
voice, she might easily be deluded by these false messages.

The consolations that come from God are deeply pleasurable. They
are gentle and refreshing, simultaneously intense and quiet. Little bursts

of religious emotion, sometimes accompanied by tears, are evidence of a good beginning, but they do not constitute true devotion. At the first mild breeze of persecution, these blessings drop their tiny blossoms. They don't do much to help the soul distinguish between the effects of a good spirit and a bad one.

So it's important to stay conscious. Beginners on the spiritual path are easily deceived when they start having visions and revelations. Personally, I did not experience visions and voices until God, in his great goodness, had already brought me to the Prayer of Union. Except, that is, for the time I saw Christ many years ago. Oh, if only his Majesty had allowed me to understand then, as I understand now, that this was a true vision! It would have done me so much good.

When visions and revelations come from the spirit of evil, they do not leave tender effects in the soul. Instead, she feels frightened and agitated afterward. I am absolutely certain that the spirit of evil could never deceive a soul who really questions herself. Nor would God allow a soul who is fortified in the faith, a soul who would suffer a thousand deaths for one of its sacred teachings, to be deluded by false phenomena.

With this love of the faith, a living faith that God himself pours into the soul, she strives to act in harmony with the doctrines of the Church. Grounded in her commitment, she checks her experiences and beliefs with this person and that person. Even if the heavens themselves were to open to her, the soul would not be tempted to deviate in the slightest degree from what the Church holds to be sacred.

Say the soul sometimes wavers in her thoughts about the faith. Say she hears a voice or sees a vision that conflicts with it in some way. Then she should not consider the revelation safe. The same would be true if the soul were to find herself saying, "If God is telling me this, it must be true, just as what he said to the saints was true." I don't mean that the soul actually believes this, but this is the way the spirit of evil first tries to tempt the soul. Even to linger over these thoughts for more than a moment is very risky.

But I really feel that if the soul is strong in the faith, she will not be tempted by this kind of pride. The same Lord who grants the soul these divine gifts gives her the power to resist delusions. Fortified in this way, the soul is inclined to defend even the most minor teaching of the Church. I mean, if a soul is not strong in the faith and she has a vision that does not strengthen it, she should not trust the revelation. She may not immediately notice the harmful effects, but they accumulate over time.

Here is what I see and know through experience: the proof that a spiritual voice has a divine origin is that it conforms to holy scripture. Even if I think that the experience comes from the spirit of God, the slightest deviation from scripture would assure me that the spirit of evil is its true source. In such cases, there is no need to go searching for signs or to wonder what spirit is responsible for the revelation. The discrepancy is the only sign I need to convince me that it comes from the spirit of evil. If the whole world were to conspire to persuade me that it comes from the spirit of God, I would not believe it.

Here's another sign. When we hear voices that come from the spirit of evil, all blessings seem to run away and hide. This leaves the soul feeling restless and touchy. She gleans nothing but negative effects from the experience. Even though she may think she is inspired to do good things, her desires quickly wither. These false voices give the soul false humility. What she considers humble is only anxious and confused. I think anyone who has heard the voice of the good spirit will understand this distinction.

Still, the devil's tricks can be subtle. The best way to protect yourself is to question each experience and seek wise counsel. Make sure you have a spiritual director who is learned. Hide nothing from him. No harm can come to you in this way. Well, I have to amend that statement: quite a bit of harm has come to me because of the excessive fears of certain men.

At one time, a group of men I deeply trusted got together and had a long discussion about me in hopes of coming up with a remedy for my soul. I had good reason to trust these men. They loved me and only wanted the best for me. They were concerned that I might be deceived by the devil. When I was not in prayer, I shared their fears. But as soon as I prayed, God always granted me some favor and reassured me.

At first, I only had direct contact with one of the men, but after he gave me permission to contact the others, I spoke to all of them. I think there were five or six of them. They were all faithful servants of God.

"We have unanimously concluded that your experiences came from the devil," my confessor reported. "We decided that it is not good for you to receive Communion so often and that you should stop spending so much time alone."

I was terrified. And my heart trouble only made matters worse. I didn't dare be by myself in a room during the day in case I slipped into an ecstasy or started hearing voices. All these men were convinced that my experiences came from the spirit of evil when I could not believe this myself, and I became deeply conflicted. I was afraid that my inability to agree with them was the result of a sinful lack of humility on my part. Look at who they were. They all led incomparably better lives than mine, and they were learned men besides. How could I not believe them? I tried to force myself to agree with their conclusions. I focused my thoughts on my wretched life and decided that because of this, what they were saying about me must be true.

In deep distress, I walked out of the church and into an oratory. I had not received Communion for many days, and I had been avoiding solitude, both of which were major sources of comfort for me. I had no one to talk to. Everyone was against me. Whenever I tried to share my experiences with them, it seemed like they were ridiculing me, implying that I was making it all up. Some people warned my confessor to watch out for me. Others insisted that the voices I was hearing came from the devil. Only my confessor consoled me. Although he took their side, I found out later that he did that just to test me.

My confessor had told me that even if my experiences came from Satan, he couldn't hurt me as long as I did nothing to offend God. He said I should pray earnestly, and if the voices were truly diabolical, God would take them away. Many people started praying for me: my confessor, his brothers, and other servants of God who knew of my troubles. I joined my prayers with theirs. For nearly two years, we spent a large portion of our prayer time beseeching his Majesty to lead me by some other path.

But when I reflected that the voices I had heard so often might come

from the spirit of evil, I became inconsolable. Since I was no longer setting aside special hours for solitary prayer, the Lord took it upon himself to bring me into a state of recollection in the middle of an ordinary
conversation. Then he would say whatever he pleased, and there was
absolutely nothing I could do about it. Even though I did not want to
listen, I had to.

I was terribly alone. There was no one I could confide in, no one to support me. I could not pray out loud. I could not read. I was confounded by
unrelenting strife and in constant fear that the spirit of evil was going to
deceive me. I was totally agitated and thoroughly exhausted. I didn't
know what to do with myself. I have experienced intense distress many
times in my life, but never as extreme as this. I would burn with this pain
for four or five hours at a time. There was no solace for me from heaven or
from earth. The Lord left me to suffer and to fear a thousand invisible
dangers.

O my Lord, you are a true friend! How powerful you are! You can do
everything it is in your will to do, and as long as we never stop loving,
you never stop willing. All things praise you, Lord of the universe. Oh,
who will be the voice to cry out for you, proclaiming throughout the
world how faithful you are to your friends? All things pass away. You,
Lord of all, endure forever. The suffering you allow those who love you
to endure is miniscule. You treat us so tenderly, Lord, so delicately and
delightfully. If only none of us would ever pause for a moment to love
anyone but you. It seems, Lord, that you vigorously challenge the one
who loves you so that in the depths of his trial he will discover the depths
of your love for him.

O my God! If only I had the intelligence, the education, and an
entirely new language to express your wonders as my soul understands
them. Words fail me, my Lord. Everything fails me. But as long as you
do not abandon me, I will not fail you. Let all learned men rise up against
me. Let all created things persecute me. Let all the spirits of evil torment
me. Do not fail me, Lord. I have already tasted the blessings and refuge
you give to those who trust in you alone.

As I sat in the oratory, weary to my core, I suddenly heard a voice say,
"Have no fear, my daughter, for *I AM,* and I will never leave you. Have
no fear."

Although I had not yet begun to have visions, these words alone were enough to lift my burden completely. Even if there had been a human being alive who could have soothed my soul (and there wasn't), it would have taken many hours, and still no one would ever have been able to persuade me to be at peace. And behold! In a single moment, this voice brought me calm, courage, strength, security, deep quietude, and radiant light. I watched my soul transform before my own eyes.

I think at the time I would have denied to the whole world that I had heard the voice of God. Oh, what a good God! Oh, how good the Lord is and how powerful! He not only writes the prescription but delivers the cure. His words are works. O God, help me! Look how he bolsters our faith and intensifies our love.

And so, as I had done so many times before, I pondered the day when Christ commanded the winds to be quiet during a storm at sea. "Who is this," I asked myself, "whose words all my faculties instantly obey? Who pours out his light and banishes the densest darkness in a single moment? Who melts this heart of stone? Who gives the water of holy tears when it seemed like the drought would last forever? Who inspires these desires and bestows this courage?"

This made me wonder, "What am I afraid of? What is this? All I want is to serve this Lord. I have no other goal than to please my Beloved. It's not my own happiness I want, or relief, or any other benefit. The only blessing I seek is to do his will." In that moment, I felt so confident of this truth that it was effortless to affirm it.

"If this Lord is powerful," I reminded myself, "as I see that he is and know that he is, and if evil spirits are his slaves, as I have no doubt that they are since this is an article of faith, and if I am a servant of this Master, then what harm can they do me? Why shouldn't this love give me the strength to battle all of hell?"

I picked up a cross, and it really did feel like God was infusing me with courage. Within a short time, I found myself so radically transformed that I would have been perfectly comfortable wrestling with demons. With that cross in my hand, I felt like I could easily vanquish any evil. "Come on now, all of you," I said. "I am a servant of the Lord, and I'd like to see what you can do to me!"

It became obvious to me that I was intimidating to the little devils, because I grew very calm. All my fears drained away and never came back. I still encountered spirits of evil from time to time, but I wasn't afraid of them anymore. In fact, it seemed like they were afraid of me. The Lord of all gave me authority over them, and now I pay no more attention to them than I do to buzzing flies. They are such cowards that when someone doesn't care about them, they lose all their strength. The only times they have any power is when they see people giving in to their attacks or when it is God's will to let them tempt his servants and put them through trials for their own good.

May we always be in awe of the One who deserves our awe. And may we understand that sometimes one small transgression can cause more trouble than all the sins of hell.

These demons frighten us because we set ourselves up to be frightened. We are overly attached to our reputations, possessions, and pleasures. When we love and desire what we should be rejecting, we are in conflict with our true selves. That's when the negative energies catch us and use our own weapons against us. Instead of taking up what we have to defend ourselves, we put our swords into the hands of our enemies and make them attack us. What a shame!

But if we embrace the cross, reject everything but God, and devote ourselves to serving him, the devil will avoid us like the plague. He is a friend of lies. He is the lie itself. He will have nothing to do with anyone who walks in truth. When he sees that a person's inner sight is darkening, he will rush in to put out the light altogether. If he sees that a person has put her trust in worldly things as a child puts her trust in toys, he will treat that person like a child and attack her over and over again.

May it please God that I not be so blind! May his Majesty help me find refuge in the true source of refuge. By true honor may I know what honor is and delight by true delight. I thumb my nose at all the spirits of evil. They shall be afraid of me.

I don't understand these fears. Why do we run around crying, "The devil! The devil!" when we can be saying, "God! God!" and make the devils tremble? We know perfectly well that the spirit of evil cannot move a muscle unless the Lord lets him. What is this? Without a doubt, I fear those who fear the devil more than I fear the devil himself. He can't do anything to me. But these men, especially if they are confessors, can wreak terrible havoc. They tormented me so badly for so many years that I can't believe I was able to endure it. Blessed be the Lord, who truly helped me!

XXVI

A LIVING BOOK

ONE OF THE GREATEST gifts the Lord ever gave me was the courage to fight against the spirits of evil. The only thing the soul should ever be afraid of is offending God. Our Lord and King is all-powerful. There is nothing he cannot do. He rules over all created things. All we have to do is walk in truth, walk with a pure conscience, walk in the presence of his Majesty, and we will have nothing to fear.

That's why I wanted to live in a state of perpetual awe. I did not want to risk for an instant offending the One who could annihilate us in an instant. If his Majesty is pleased with us, then anyone who is against us will end up clapping his hands to his head in despair.

We can accept this truth at face value and move on, or we can inquire more deeply. Who is this soul who lives such an upright life that she pleases God completely and can rightfully conclude she has nothing to fear? Not my soul! My soul is wretched, worthless, and overflowing with a thousand miseries. But the ways of God are different than the ways of human beings. He understands our weaknesses.

Through deep inner examination, the soul discovers that she truly loves God. Once a soul reaches an advanced state of prayer, love doesn't hide as it did in the beginning. It is driven by a powerful impulse and accompanied by such an intense yearning to see God that everything else wearies the soul and wears her out. I have already said this, and I will say it again. Anything other than God is a torment to the soul who is in love with him. If she is not resting in him, she is restless. This love does not come in disguise; it is completely revealed.

There was a time when I was suffering from a continuous stream of criticism from the people of Ávila and from the Carmelite order. I had countless opportunities to be grief-stricken. That was when the Lord said to me, "Why are you afraid? Don't you know that I am all-powerful? I will fulfill my promises to you."

And he has! This voice so thoroughly strengthened me that I felt I could embark on any new venture in service of the One I love, even if it caused me even more severe trials. I would gladly take on more suffering for his sake.

This has happened to me more times than I can count. Sometimes he would scold me. Sometimes he still scolds me when I make mistakes. These divine criticisms are enough to dissolve my soul, but at least they motivate me to change, because his Majesty's words are both counsel and cure.

At other times, especially when his Majesty wants to grant me some exceptional favor, he reminds me of my past transgressions. Then I feel as if it is Judgment Day and I have to account for my whole life. These spiritual voices present the truth with such penetrating clarity that I have nowhere to hide.

Sometimes the Lord warns me of imminent danger to myself or to others. He has often told me about things that were going to happen three or four years in the future. All these things have come true; I can give you concrete examples. There are so many signs showing that these spiritual voices come from God that we have no excuse for doubting them.

The Lord has often told me the safest course to follow: make sure my spiritual director is a learned man and then tell him everything. Explain the whole state of my soul to him and describe in detail the favors the Lord grants me. Obey him. When I don't take this path, I am not at peace. Of course, since women have no learning, how can we expect to have peace?

I had a confessor who badly humiliated me. He seemed to purposely disquiet my mind by presenting me with constant challenges and utterly distressing me. Looking back, I think he is the spiritual director who did me the most good. Although I was very fond of him, I was often tempted to leave him because his methods interfered with my prayer.

But every time I considered ending the relationship, I would hear a voice telling me not to. This divine rebuke upset me more than anything my confessor did. I had questions on the one hand and reproofs on the other. The process exhausted me, but I was so stubborn that my will would never bend unless it was worn out.

The Lord once told me that if I wasn't resolved to suffer, then I was not truly submitting. He said that if I would simply fix my eyes on what he had suffered, everything would be easy.

After it was determined that the spiritual voices I was hearing indeed came from the Good Spirit, a man who heard my confession advised me that it would be best if I kept quiet and didn't mention them to anyone. "Such things should not be talked about," he said. This did not strike me as wrong. Whenever I told my spiritual director about the voices, I felt so abashed that my shame was worse than when I had serious sins to confess. I expected that my confessors would not believe me and would make fun of me, especially when the divine favors were dramatic.

My resistance to talking about the voices was so intense because it felt like revealing these things was disrespectful to the wonders of God, so it was best to remain silent. But I came to understand that this confessor had advised me badly and that I should not keep anything from my spiritual director. There is great security in telling him everything and great danger in keeping secrets.

Whenever the Lord told me to do something in prayer and my confessor told me something else, the Lord would speak again and tell me to obey him. Then he would change my confessor's mind so that he would agree with what the Lord had said. When the Inquisition banned many books written in Spanish, I was bereft. Reading was such a joy for me. The only sanctioned books were in Latin, which I could not understand.

Then the Lord spoke to me. "Don't be sad," he said, "for I shall give you a Living Book."

Since I had not yet experienced any visions, I couldn't understand why God would say this to me. A few days later, I understood this perfectly. The Lord gathered me into his presence, showed me his love by teaching me in so many ways, and gave me so much to think about that I have had almost no need for books ever since. His Majesty himself has become the Living Book in which all truths are available. Blessed be such a book that indelibly imprints on our minds everything we need to understand and do!

Who could possibly see Christ persecuted and covered with wounds without embracing, loving, and longing for those wounds? Who could witness the glory God gives those who serve him without recognizing that anything we do and suffer is nothing in light of such a reward? Who could imagine the torment of those who are condemned to the fire without realizing that the trials of this life are sheer delights by comparison and appreciating how much she owes the Lord for so often freeing her from that place?

With God's help, I will say more about these things later. For now, I'd like to get on with the account of my life. May it please the Lord that I have been clear in what I have said so far. I'm sure that anyone with experience will understand me and see that I have been successful. I wouldn't be surprised, however, if it all sounded like nonsense to someone without experience. Since I am the one telling the story, I wouldn't blame anyone who might dismiss it as nonsense; he would have a good excuse! May the Lord help me to do his will.

XXVII ✠

The Perils of Temperance

I't's time to return to the story of my life. Well, there I was, enduring terrible affliction. I had many people praying on my behalf, beseeching the Lord to lead me by a more secure path, since the one I was on, they told me, was dubious.

The truth of the matter is that although I wanted to want to change, I couldn't truly bring myself to want it. This is because I could see how much my soul was flowering since the raptures and spiritual voices had begun. Except, that is, for when I wilted under the criticism I received and the fears it instilled in me.

I noticed that I was a completely different person than I had been before. How could I desire a different path than the one that had transformed me? So I placed myself in God's hands and trusted that he would carry out his will in me. He alone knew what was best for my soul. I saw that the road I was on led to heaven and that I had been on my way to hell before. I tried with all my might to convince myself that the devil was deceiving me and to make myself desire another path, but I was powerless.

I offered up all my actions, in case there might be a good deed among them, in service of this intention. I invoked my favorite saints to free me from the spirit of evil. I dedicated several novenas to the effort. I entrusted myself to Saint Hilarion and devoted myself to Saint Michael the Archangel. I begged many other saints to petition the Lord to show me the way. Maybe the holy ones of God would be able to obtain the truth from his Majesty and pass it along to me.

This went on for two years. I prayed; they prayed. But no matter how much we all prayed for God either to lead me on some other path or to reveal the truth about the one I was on, the spiritual voices continued. At the end of two years, I had the following experience.

It was the feast day of the glorious Saint Peter, and I was sitting in prayer, when I saw Christ sitting next to me. Actually, to put it a better way, I was aware that Christ was beside me. I didn't see anything with my bodily eyes or even with the eyes of my soul, but I felt him there at my side. I realized that he was speaking to me. I had no idea that a vision like this was possible, and at first I was very much afraid. All I could do was weep.

With one word, however, Christ reassured me. He restored my customary calm. I felt quiet and blessed and fearless. This was not an imaginary vision. I knew that Jesus Christ was at my side, but I did not perceive his form. I simply felt him at my right side and recognized that he had always been there and always would be there, witnessing everything I did. Each time I drew my attention within, there he was. Unless I let myself become totally distracted, it was impossible to ignore that he was with me.

I rushed to my confessor and anxiously told him everything. "In what form did you see him?" he asked me.

"I didn't see him," I answered.

"Then how did you know it was Christ?"

"I don't know how, but I cannot *not* be aware that he is beside me. I saw him, I mean I *felt* him, very clearly. My soul has been more easily and more deeply recollected ever since. In fact, the Prayer of Quiet is almost continuous now. It is an exceedingly clear state. Besides, the effects are very different from what I used to experience."

All I could do was offer metaphors and analogies to try and explain myself. But there is no adequate comparison for this vision. A very holy and spiritual man named Father Pedro de Alcantará told me that this vision is one of the most sublime we can receive and also the most difficult for the spirit of evil to interfere with. Other learned men have confirmed this. Women like me, who know very little, are incapable of describing this state. Maybe men of learning can explain it better.

For instance, if I say, "Well, I do not see it with the eyes of the body, nor do I see it with the eyes of the soul, because it is not an imaginative vision," you will rightfully wonder how I can be more certain he is at my side than I would be if I actually saw him.

You must not think of this experience as being like a blind person or someone in a dark room who cannot see the person next to him. It's a little bit like that but not very much. In the case of blindness or darkness, the person perceives things through his other senses. He will hear the other person stir or speak. He can touch him.

In this kind of vision, it is not dark, and there are no other senses operating. Yet the vision reveals knowledge to the soul that is more radiant than the clearest sunlight. I don't mean that you directly perceive the sun or its brightness. But there *is* light, even though you don't *see* light, and it lights up everything. It illuminates the mind so that the soul can enjoy the great blessings the vision brings with it.

4. A sense of connectedness to God is not uncommon. Seasoned practitioners of silent prayer, particularly if they have experienced the Prayer of Quiet and the Prayer of Union, sometimes find that as soon as they sit down with the intention to pray, the One they are praying to seems to be there listening. They become aware of feelings of tender love and faith and a deepening of their most cherished resolutions.

This is a blessing from God, and anyone who experiences it should be grateful. It is a sublime prayer, but it is not a vision. In the Prayer of Quiet and the Prayer of Union, his Majesty makes himself known through the effects he leaves in the soul. But this vision I'm talking about is different. The soul sees very clearly that Jesus Christ, son of the Virgin, is present. In the other states of prayer, the soul feels divine influences. In this vision, however, she not only experience these holy feelings, but she knows that the most sacred humanity has become her companion and that he wants to grant her favors.

5. "Who said it was Jesus Christ?" the confessor asked me next.

"He told me himself," I answered. "Many times."

Before Christ told me who he was, he impressed himself so firmly into my consciousness that I knew he was there, even though I didn't see him. And before he did that, he told me he was coming. If a person I had never met but only heard of came to speak to me while I was in a dark room or blind and told me who he was, I would probably believe him.

But I wouldn't be able to assert the fact with as much confidence as I would if I had seen him with my own eyes.

With this vision, without being able to see him, I could confidently claim that Christ was with me. He carves such deep knowledge into the soul that I could no more doubt it than if I had seen the Lord with my own eyes. Even less. Sometimes our eyes play tricks on us, and we suspect that we might have imagined what we saw. In a vision like this, we might experience a flicker of skepticism, but it is quickly replaced by unshakable certitude.

It's the same kind of knowing the soul has when God speaks to her without words. He uses the language of heaven, and it's difficult to translate to mortals. No matter how much we may want to understand, we won't really get it until the Lord teaches it to us through experience. He places what he wants the soul to know deep inside her, without images or words.

It is worth deeply pondering the manner in which God gives the soul a clear understanding of his desires and truths and mysteries. God often explains the visions he gives to me in this ineffable way. There are a number of reasons why I think that the spirit of evil is least able to interfere in an experience of this nature. If these reasons turn out to be bad ones, then I must be mistaken about the whole thing.

The kind of vision that comes without seeing and the kind of language that comes without hearing are so spiritual that the faculties of sense and reason are completely quieted. The spirit of evil has nothing to react against. Sometimes the faculties are momentarily suspended, but usually, I think, they are fully engaged. These visions and voices do not generally occur in the midst of contemplation. In fact, they almost never do.

Yet when they happen, I don't believe we have anything to do with it. It all seems to be the work of the Lord. It's as if food had been put into our stomachs without our eating it or even knowing how it got there. We know very well that it is there, but we have no idea what kind of food it is or how it entered our bodies. In the case of this sublime prayer, the soul doesn't know how it got there. She didn't see anything or feel anything. She didn't even want anything. The intellect never knew that such a thing was possible.

In the kind of spiritual voices I was talking about before, God brings awareness of the message to our minds whether we want to hear it or not. We grasp exactly what is being said. It's as if the soul hears with other ears, and God makes her listen. She cannot be distracted. It's like this: someone speaks in a loud voice to a person with good hearing, and the listener does not stop up his ears. He may not be interested in what he's hearing, but he participates by paying attention so that he will understand it.

In the kind of spiritual voice I am talking about now, the soul does not play any part. She is relieved of even the minor responsibility of listening. She finds everything already prepared and eaten for her. She has nothing to do but savor it. She is like a person who never bothered to learn how to read or engage in the work of learning and yet finds that she possesses all knowledge within herself. She has no idea how the knowledge got there. She never studied. She doesn't even know her ABCs!

This feels to me like an apt metaphor for this heavenly gift. The soul sees that she has become wise in an instant. Such profound secrets as the mystery of the three divine persons are so clearly understood that the soul would boldly defend these wondrous truths against the arguments of any theologian on earth.

She is utterly amazed. She sees that one favor from God is enough to change her completely. A single one of his blessings frees her from attachment to things and replaces it with love for the One who carves out the vessel of the soul so that she can receive such grace. She does nothing of her own volition to deserve this. She is filled with love for the Friend who treats her with such sublime loving-kindness that she could never describe it in words.

Some of God's favors are so wonderful that people may become suspicious when they see them being showered on a person who has done nothing to merit them. Someone who does not possess a living faith will be incapable of believing in them. So unless my superiors command me to elaborate on them, I intend to say as little as possible about the blessings God has bestowed on me.

The only favors I will dwell on are certain visions that might do others some good—or at least prevent souls from being shocked and doubting the validity of their own experience when such things happen to them. If I can help people by explaining the path and the way that the Lord has led me, I will be fulfilling my obligations in writing this account.

Back to our discussion of the special kind of understanding the Lord instills in the soul. It seems to me that he wants to convey some knowledge of what happens in heaven. I never knew this until God in his goodness allowed me to see it when he showed himself to me in a rapture. Just as in heaven souls understand one another without language, so it is in this kind of vision.

God and the soul understand each other perfectly because this is his Majesty's will. No other device is required for these two friends to manifest their love. Two people on this earth who love each other deeply and understand one another well do not require signs or techniques. The mere exchange of a glance is enough to communicate everything that matters.

That must be the kind of love unfolding between the soul and her Beloved in this kind of vision. Without the soul knowing how, the two lovers gaze directly at one another's face. It reminds me of the way the bridegroom speaks to the bride in the Song of Songs. At least, I think that's where I have heard about this kind of seeing.

Oh, how wondrous is God's loving-kindness! He allows me to gaze upon him with eyes as impure as the eyes of my soul. May this vision teach us, Beloved, no longer to look at vile things. Let nothing other than you ever satisfy us again.

Oh, how ungrateful mortals can be! What extremes you go to on our behalf, O Lord! I know from experience that what I'm saying is true. I know that whatever I say about you is only a tiny fraction of what you do for the soul you transport to such exalted states.

Oh, you souls who have begun to practice prayer and have true faith in your hearts, what good things can you still seek in this life that could compare with the least of these divine blessings? How, indeed, could any worldly pleasure measure up to the treasures of eternity?

Reflect on this. God gives himself wholly to anyone who gives up everything for him. He loves everyone with no exceptions. I am living proof that God leaves no one out. Look how wretched I was, and look at the heights to which he has lifted me. Please note that this account is the abridged version of what has actually happened to me. I am telling you just enough to place the visions and other blessings God gives the soul into a meaningful context.

I could never describe how the soul actually feels when the Beloved gives her knowledge of his secrets and wonders. This joy surpasses all understanding. It so far transcends any pleasure we experience here on earth that once we have tasted it, we can't help but disdain mundane things. All the sweetest earthly delights put together resemble a pile of garbage. I would find it unbearable even to attempt to compare these two kinds of happiness. Even if we were offered worldly pleasure without end, it would not come close to a single drop from the vast, overflowing river God has prepared for us.

It's a shame. And I am certainly ashamed. If it were possible to be embarrassed in heaven, my embarrassment would be most acute there. Why do we crave all these blessings and delights and eternal glory at the expense of the good Jesus? Since we do not help him carry his cross with the Cyrenian, shall we not at least weep with the daughters of Jerusalem?

How can we enjoy all the pleasures and distractions of this life when we know what it cost him in blood? It's impossible! Do we really believe that our petty aspirations for honor could possibly repay him for the persecution he endured, for the suffering he took on to allow us to prevail forever? Such a path goes nowhere. It's the wrong, wrong road. We will never arrive anywhere if we take it.

You should shout these truths from the rooftops. God has taken the freedom to proclaim them away from me. I wish I could broadcast these teachings with every breath. As it is, I have been so slow in hearing and understanding God that it is embarrassing even to mention these things. You'll see what I mean. I'd rather remain silent. Instead, I will simply share what comes to my mind from time to time. May it please the Lord to bring me to the place where I might rejoice in the blessings I am writing about.

What unexpected glory the blessed ones will enjoy! What happiness they will feel when they discover that in the end, finally and at last, they held nothing back from God. According to their strength and state, they did everything they possibly could for him. The more they had, the more they gave. He who has rejected all riches for Christ will find himself abundantly wealthy. He who has not sought honor for himself but instead has cultivated humility will find himself deeply honored. He who was thrilled to be considered crazy, since that's what they called Wisdom herself, will find himself exceedingly wise.

How few holy madmen are alive today! Our sins preclude this blessed madness. Such fools for God seem to be extinct. Where are the ones who would risk everything and perform heroic feats for love of Christ? O World! O World! How much of your honor is won by the small handful of those who truly know you?

We think we serve God better by being wise and discreet. Maybe so, but I doubt it. We jump to the conclusion that we are failing to set a good example unless we act with somber dignity and carry out our duties with cool authority. We think it's weird if a monk wears old, patched robes, and we fear a scandal if a nun slips into ecstatic states. That's the way the world is today. We have forgotten the perfect love and the sublime raptures the saints experienced.

In these troubled times we live in, I think this sober mentality causes far more harm than the discomfort created by spiritual teachers who counsel us to reject the things of the world and back up these teachings with action. The Lord converts such sacrifices into great blessings. If some people are scandalized by holy foolishness, it brings other people to their senses. Now more than ever before, we need living examples of what Christ and his apostles suffered for love.

What a great example of a Christ-like life God has recently taken from us in the form of the blessed Pedro de Alcantará. The world is not yet ready to bear so much perfection. They say that times are changing and that our health is weaker than it used to be. This holy man lived in the present age, yet he carried the expansive spirit of the old days. He thoroughly trampled this world underfoot. Maybe there are not many people who are capable of performing such radical austerities as Father Pedro, but there are many ways to practice detachment. When the Lord detects sufficient courage in us, he teaches us the right way. And what exquisite courage God gave to this great saint I'm talking about. As we all know, Father Pedro performed rigorous penances for forty-seven years.

I'd like to say something about his practices, because I know it's all true. He told the holy Maria Daza and me about these things because he hid nothing from us. The reason Father Pedro confided in me was because he loved me so much. As I have said before and will say again, the Lord desired to forge such love between this holy man and myself so that Father Pedro would always come when I needed him most, to encourage me and defend me.

I think Father Pedro told me that for forty years he slept only an hour and a half each night, and that at the beginning, conquering sleep was his most severe trial. He practiced staying awake by always standing or being on his knees. When he did sleep, he did so sitting up, with his head propped against a piece of wood he had nailed to the wall. It is well known that he could not have stretched out even if he had wanted to. His cell was only four and a half feet long!

No matter how hot the sun or how rainy the weather was during all those years, Father Pedro never pulled up his hood or put on sandals. The only clothing he had was a coarse serge robe that he wore tight against his body with a short cloak made of the same material. He told me that he came up with a technique for fooling his body into thinking it was warm enough. When the weather was very cold, he would take off the cloak and leave the door and the small window of his cell open for a few minutes. Then he would close them and put his cloak back on; the contrast made him feel warm again.

He often ate only every three days. When I expressed my surprise, he said that these things were easy for anyone once you got used to them. One of his companions told me that Father Pedro once went without food for eight days. He must have remained in a state of prayer the whole time. Father Pedro was known for his frequent transports of ecstatic love for God, one of which I witnessed personally.

During his youth, Father Pedro engaged in extremes of poverty and renunciation. He told me he lived in a monastery for three years, and the only way he recognized any of the other monks was by the sound of their voices because he never raised his eyes. He had no idea where anything was in the house; when he needed to go somewhere, he just followed the other brothers' feet. He used the same method when he traveled. For many years, he never looked at a woman.

By the time I met Father Pedro, he said it did not matter whether he looked or did not look. All was one to him. But he was very old by this time. He was so frail that he resembled the knotted roots of a tree. Yet with all his holiness, he was very amiable. Unless someone asked him a direct question, he did not say much, but he had a very lively mind, and he was delightful to talk to.

There are so many more things I could say about this man, but I'm afraid that you will ask me what all this has to do with anything. I will conclude by saying that Father Pedro ended his life as he lived it: teaching and enlightening his followers. When he saw that he was dying, he recited this psalm: "I rejoiced when they said to me, ?Let us go to the house of the Lord.'" Then he fell to his knees and died.

After Father Pedro's death, the Lord was pleased for him to guide me even more effectively than he had during his life. Father Pedro's teachings continue to show me the way. I have often seen him in radiant glory. The first time he appeared to me, he told me that the penance that earned him this glory was a blessed thing.

A year before he died, when I was traveling many miles away from here, he appeared before me. I knew that his death was near and told him so. Then as he was dying, he came to me and told me that he was going to his rest. I did not believe it but mentioned it to a few people. A week later, the news came that Father Pedro had died. Or to put it a better way, he had begun to live forever.

Look how a life of harsh austerities ended in such great glory! I think he comforts me more now than when he was still on this earth. The Lord once told me that he would grant me anything I asked him in Father Pedro's name. And many of the prayers I have offered up in his name have been fulfilled. May the Lord be forever blessed. Amen.

I certainly have gone on and on, haven't I? May what I have said serve to inspire you to let go of the things of this world. As if you did not already know about this and weren't already determined to abandon all attachment and hadn't, in fact, already begun to put this renunciation into practice.

I see such spiritual decline in this world that even if this writing accomplishes nothing more than tiring out the hand that wields the pen, I find it consoling. Everything I am saying is directed against myself.

May the Lord forgive me for offending him in this and any other matter. And may you pardon me too. I do not mean to weary you. It's as if I were asking you to do penance for my sins by making you read all this.

XXVIII ✠

HIS HANDS

LET'S GET BACK to our subject. I lingered for quite a few days with this vision of Christ continually before me. It was doing me so much good that I was reluctant to come out of it for even a moment, and so I remained in a state of perpetual prayer. I took care of whatever business I had to attend to in such a way that it would not displease the One I love, who I now knew was witnessing everything I did. Although the barrage of warnings I received from others sometimes scared me, I could not sustain this fear in light of the tender assurances that came from my Lord.

One day while I was in prayer, the Lord decided to show me just his hands. I could never begin to describe such beauty! The vision shocked me. I am always frightened when God gives me a new supernatural favor. A few days after this, he showed me his divine face, and I was completely absorbed.

Since the Lord would ultimately grant me the favor of seeing him whole, I wondered why he chose to reveal himself to me little by little. Later I understood that his Majesty was giving me exactly as much as my delicate nature could handle. May he be forever blessed! Such a crude and lowly vessel as I was could never have contained such glory. The Lord in his mercy was preparing me to receive him fully.

Why, you may ask, does it require such strength to see some hands and a face? Glorified bodies are so exquisite that a mere glimpse of such supernatural beauty leaves a soul dazzled and confused. At first, this vision stirred intense fear in me. But the agitation soon melted into a sense of calm certainty and peace.

Then one day, his most sacred humanity appeared to me in his risen form, whole and radiant. It was the Feast of Saint Paul, and I was at Mass. He looked like he does in the paintings, beautiful and majestic. Even though this was an imaginative vision, I did not see it with the eyes of my body but only with the eyes of my soul.

I recall that you insisted I write about this when it happened and I obeyed, but it is very difficult to put into words without ruining it. I made the best description I could at that time, and I see no need to repeat it here.

I will only say that if there were nothing in heaven to delight our sight other than the exalted beauty of glorified bodies, this would be enough. Especially the vision of the humanity of our Lord Jesus Christ. And if he sometimes reveals himself to us here on earth, in proportion to our ability to bear such glory, can you imagine what it will be like when we are given that blessing to enjoy infinitely and for all eternity?

Those who know more about theology than I do say that an intellectual vision is more perfect than an imaginative vision like this one, and an imaginative vision is more perfect than the kind of vision we see with the eyes of the body. This last kind, the corporeal vision, is the kind in which the spirit of evil can most easily meddle and delude us.

I did not understand these distinctions at the time Christ revealed himself to me in an imaginative form. I wanted to see him with my body's eyes so that my confessor would believe that I hadn't invented the whole thing. As soon as the vision passed, I wondered if I had imagined it. I was so concerned that I might have inadvertently deceived my confessor that it made me cry. I wished I had never mentioned it to him!

So I went to him and tried to explain.

"Have you intentionally deceived me?" he asked. "Or have you, in fact, simply described the vision as you saw it?"

I told him the truth. "I would never knowingly lie to you, not for anything in the world!"

He tried to calm me down. "I know this very well."

After that, I started to worry about having come to him with these speculations about deception. I don't know how the spirit of evil drove me to torment myself with the thought that I had made up the vision.

But then the Lord bestowed the gift of this vision again and made it abundantly clear to me that it was real. This truth quickly dispelled any doubts about my having imagined it. In fact, afterward I could hardly believe I had ever wondered about it. How foolish of me! If I had spent a thousand years trying, I would never even know how to begin, let alone succeed in imagining and conveying something so beautiful. In its luminous whiteness alone it surpasses anything we can perceive here on earth.

It isn't a dazzling radiance. It's a soft whiteness, an infused glow. It delights the eyes and never strains them. The brilliant vision of divine beauty does not weary the eyes either. The brightness of the sun seems tarnished in comparison with this light. It makes you never want to open your eyes again after it has passed. It's like the difference between sparkling, clear water flowing over a pristine crystal that shimmers in the sun and muddy, cloudy water oozing along the ground. This doesn't mean you perceive the sun or that the light resembles sunshine. In fact, the light of the vision seems like natural light and sunshine seems artificial. It is a light that never gives way to darkness. Nothing disturbs it.

Ultimately, it's ineffable. No matter how fine a mind a person may have, he could never come close to imagining the nature of this light, even if he tried all his life to understand it. God gives us this light so suddenly that we don't even have time to open our eyes. It doesn't even matter if our eyes are open or closed. When God chooses to give us this vision, we see it whether we want to or not. No distraction or resistance can fend it off. No effort or intention can make it happen. I have learned this through experience.

I would like to say something about the way the Lord reveals himself in these visions. I will not presume to explain how it is that such a powerful light is put into the deepest part of the soul or how such a vivid image is imprinted on the mind. This is a matter for men of learning to explicate. The Lord has not given me knowledge of how such things work.

I am so ignorant and dull-witted anyway that no matter how hard these men try to explain the theological mechanisms behind the visions, I have trouble grasping them. It may appear to you that I have a sharp intellect, but I don't. Again and again, I have discovered that I cannot understand a thing unless I am spoon-fed, as they say. Sometimes my spiritual directors have been astonished by my ignorance. To tell you the truth, I haven't really bothered to try understanding how God causes visions like this, even though I have had a great deal of contact with men of learning over the years and countless opportunities to ask questions about these things.

If I had a concern about whether or not something qualified as a sin, I would certainly bring it up. But I didn't feel compelled to analyze the rest. All I needed to know was that God is in charge of everything. I saw that there was no reason to be afraid of this vision and that my only task was to give him thanks for it. Challenges only seem to increase my devotion. In fact, the more intense the difficulty is, the more my devotion flowers.

All I can do is share what I have come to see through experience. You will be able to explain how the Lord works much more precisely than I can. You can clarify whatever remains obscure in my writing and articulate the things I didn't know how to say. What I know is that sometimes I would see an image, but in many other instances I did not. Instead, I perceived Christ himself. He identified himself with absolute clarity.

Other times, the vision was vague, like a painting rather than a living presence. But even this is a poor comparison, for paintings like this do not exist on earth, no matter how perfectly rendered they may be, and I have seen some excellent religious art. It's ridiculous to believe that this vision is any more like a painted image than a portrait can be equated with the man it represents. No matter how skillfully it is painted, a portrait will never look so lifelike that it can be mistaken for anything other than dead matter. As nicely as this metaphor functions, it's time to leave it behind.

Actually, the example I just used is more than a comparison, since comparisons are never completely accurate. This is the literal truth. The difference between the vision of Christ and a painting of him is neither more nor less than the difference between a living man and his portrait. What we see in this vision may be an image, but it is a living image. It is not a dead man we are seeing but the living Christ. He makes it clear that he is both man and God. He does not appear as he was in the tomb but in his resurrected form after he left the tomb.

Sometimes he comes with such majesty that no one could doubt that it is the Lord himself. Especially after receiving Communion, since our faith teaches us that he is truly present in this Blessed Sacrament. Then he reveals himself so clearly as the Master of this dwelling that the soul seems to be utterly consumed in him.

O my Jesus! Who could ever describe the magnificence with which you reveal yourself? O Lord of the entire world and of the heavens! O Lord of a thousand other worlds, of numberless worlds! O Lord of the heavens that you might yet create! Through the majesty with which you reveal yourself, the soul understands perfectly that it is nothing for you to rule supreme over this earth.

In this vision, I clearly see your power, my Jesus. All the spirits of evil are powerless by comparison. Whoever truly loves you easily tramples all hell underfoot. I suddenly understand why the devils were afraid of you when you descended into limbo. They must have wished they had a thousand lower levels of hell into which to flee from such awesome splendor.

I see that you want the soul to know how vast this glory is and to grasp the power that this most sacred humanity has when it is joined with absolute Divinity. In this vision, the soul is given a glimpse of what it will be like on Judgment Day when she beholds the sovereignty of this king and witnesses the righteousness with which he disciplines the wicked. Once she has had such a vision, the soul can no longer ignore her own wretchedness, and she is left with true humility. It triggers deep self-examination and inspires her to genuinely repent her transgressions. Even though the soul sees that this God is the God of love, she feels so naked and exposed that she doesn't know where to hide. She is completely consumed.

I would go so far as to claim that when the Lord chooses to reveal himself in all his grandeur and majesty, the vision has such intense power that it would be impossible for any soul to bear it unless he gave her supernatural assistance. He puts her into an ecstatic rapture, and the vision of him dissolves into a pure enjoyment of his presence.

Could it be true that the soul forgets the vision once it has passed? No, the majesty and beauty remain so deeply imprinted on the soul that they are unforgettable. Sometimes, however, the Lord wants the soul to endure a period of aridity and solitude during which she even seems to forget God.

Other than these divinely ordained dry spells, the soul is fully transformed from this vision and lives in a permanent state of absorption. She
enters into a higher love, a new and living love for God. While an intellectual vision—that is, a vision in which the soul perceives God without
form—is more perfect than an imaginative vision, a wondrous thing
happens when the Divine represents himself in our imagination. In proportion to our ability to withstand such glory, his presence lingers in our
memory and perpetually occupies our thoughts.

These two kinds of vision almost always come hand in hand. In an
imaginative vision, we perceive the excellence, beauty, and glory of the
most sacred humanity with the eyes of the soul. In an intellectual vision,
we are given an understanding that God is God, that he is all-powerful
and can do everything, that he commands all and governs all, that his
love permeates all things.

Such a vision should be cherished. In my opinion, it is immune from
any contamination. From the effects of this vision, it is clear that the
spirit of evil has no power here. I think the spirit of evil tried three or
four times in the beginning of my spiritual path to masquerade as the
Lord of Love, but I didn't believe it. He takes the form of flesh, but he
cannot even come close to representing the true glory of God. He tries
to invalidate the true vision the soul has seen, but the soul spontaneously
resists his efforts. She feels defensive, restless, and nervous. She loses the
devotion and delight she experienced when the vision came from God.
She can't concentrate on prayer.

The few times this happened to me early on, I knew something was
wrong. Even if a person has only experienced the Prayer of Quiet, I
think she will be able to deduce the difference between a false vision
and a divine favor by their effects alone. It's obvious. I don't think the
spirit of evil can deceive a soul who doesn't want to be deceived. If she
walks in humility and simplicity, she will walk safely.

Anyone who has had a true vision will almost immediately be able to
discern a false one. Although the false one may begin with similar feelings of consolation and sweetness, the soul is repelled by it and has the
urge to push it away. Even the sense of consolation is different. It isn't
pure. It doesn't feel like sacred love. The spirit of evil is quickly un-
masked. So in my opinion, he can do no real harm to an experienced soul.

Could such a vision be the work of the imagination? This is the most impossible of impossible things. It's utterly ridiculous to think it! The perfect beauty and pure luminescence of a single one of the Beloved's hands completely transcends the imagination. How could we instantaneously see things that we have never even thought about, things so far beyond anything we can comprehend here on earth that we could never have begun to invent them with our imagination?

Even if we could create these things in our minds, they would never carry the lasting effects of a true divine vision. In fact, they would have no effect at all. The soul would be left exhausted by the effort. Say we want to fall asleep but sleep won't come, so we lie awake. Sometimes we need to sleep. We feel that heaviness in our head and the urge to doze off, so we lie down. When we can't fall asleep, we think that we must be doing ourselves some good by just resting in bed. But if it is not true sleep, it will not sustain us or refresh our head. Instead, we will be even more tired than we were before we lay down.

That's how a self-generated vision would make us feel. The soul would be left exhausted. Instead of being fortified and nourished, she would find herself drained and unsatisfied. I cannot overemphasize the richness of a true vision. It can even restore health and comfort to the body.

When I was repeatedly accused of inventing my vision or being deceived by the devil, I offered this analogy as evidence of the validity of my experience. The Lord gave me other comparisons as well, but it was pointless. These men were very pious. Compared to them, I was a lost soul. And because God was not leading them on this same path, my experience frightened them. Their own fear convinced them that what I was seeing must be the result of my sins. I hardly spoke to anyone except my confessor and a few people he ordered me to tell about my experiences, but somehow my confidentiality was violated and my secrets were spread around.

"Look, " I said to them once. "If you were to tell me that a person I knew well and had just finished talking to was not who I thought he was and that I had only imagined that it was he, you can be assured that I would believe what you said and not what I saw. But," I went on, "if this person left some jewels in my hand as tokens of his great love, I would not believe you even if I wanted to. Because where I was poor before, now I would find myself rich."

I was trying to show them that these visions left jewels in my soul that changed me completely. Even my confessor admitted that I was transformed. The difference in me extended to every area of my life. I could not fake it; everyone saw that it was real.

"Remember how wretched I was?" I asked them. "If the devil did this to deceive me and carry me off to hell, why would he do it by such uncharacteristic means as wiping away my vices and replacing them with virtues? Why would he fortify my spirit instead of weakening it? Why would he change me for the better?"

I found out that my confessor used this same argument to defend me. Father Baltazar Alvarez was, as I said, a very holy Jesuit. He was a discreet man and exceedingly humble. As it turned out, his humility brought me great trials. Even though he was extremely learned and deeply prayerful, God did not lead him along the path I was on, so he didn't trust himself to guide me.

Father Baltazar also suffered terrible trials on my behalf. People warned him to beware of me and not to let the devil deceive him into believing anything I told him. They brought up examples of other people who had been deceived in this way. All of this worried me. It seemed like I was chasing everyone away and that there would be no one left to hear my confession. All I could do was weep.

Thanks to divine providence, Father Baltazar chose to continue hearing my confession. He was such a great servant of God that he would have been willing to put up with anything for God's sake. He assured me that as long as I followed his advice and did not offend God, he would not give up on me. He always encouraged me and soothed my anxiety. He insisted that I not withhold anything from him, and I never did. Even if my vision did come from the spirit of evil, Father Baltazar reminded me, I would be safe as long as I told him everything. Then, not only could the devil do me no harm, but the Lord would draw good out of the evil.

This priest did his very best to perfect my soul. Since I lived with such trepidation, I strove to obey him, even though I did not always succeed. During the three years or so that Father Baltazar was my confessor, my trials caused him great suffering. I was persecuted terribly. The Lord allowed people to make very harsh judgments about me. They went to Father Baltazar with all of these issues, and he was often blamed for them. But he was innocent!

If he had not been such a holy man and the Lord had not supported him so much, he could never have endured such suffering. On the one hand, he had to deal with people who did not believe in him, people who were convinced that I was going to hell. On the other hand, he had to calm me down. Whenever God gave me a vision, the new experience would frighten me. Father Baltazar was determined to reassure me. But although he did what he could to dispel my fears, he sometimes accidentally intensified them.

All these trials came to me because I was and still am a sinner. This priest was deeply compassionate and comforted me. If only he had trusted himself more, I would have suffered less. God showed him the truth in all things. I believe the simple sanctity of his office enlightened him.

I had many conversations with the religious men who were having doubts about me. I guess I must have spoken carelessly, because they completely misinterpreted my intentions. When I simply said exactly what was on my mind, they thought I was lacking in humility. This was particularly painful to me in the case of one of them, a man I loved very much. He was a profoundly holy person, and I was spiritually indebted to him. When I saw that even he did not understand me, I was crushed. I knew that he sincerely wished the Lord to light my path so that I would make real progress.

Well, as I was saying, I spoke without reflecting on how it might come across, and this was interpreted as arrogance. Whenever they detected the slightest fault in me—and they saw many—they would condemn everything else out of hand. They would ask me things, and I would answer directly, without analyzing myself. They thought I considered myself wiser than they were and that I was presuming to teach them. They truly thought they were doing what was best for me; they went to my confessor to inform him of my transgressions, and he would have to reprimand me again.

This went on for quite some time. I felt like I was being attacked from every side. Only the favors the Lord was granting me enabled me to bear these trials. I'm telling you this so that you will realize what a terrible hardship it is not to have a guide who is familiar with this particular spiritual path. If the Beloved had not been blessing me as he was, I don't know what would have become of me. These troubles were enough to drive me out of my mind. Sometimes I found myself so beset by tribulations that all I could do was lift my eyes to the Lord. The notion of a group of powerful men against one little woman as weak and wicked as I was may not sound like such a problem when I describe it here, but believe me, this was one of the most severe trials I ever suffered in a life of severe trials!

May it please the Lord that I have been of some service to his Majesty by going through all this. I am totally convinced that the people who condemned me were serving God the best they knew how and that all of this was ultimately for my greater good.

XXIX ✠

The Beautiful Wound

ONCE AGAIN, I've wandered far from my topic. I was about to tell you the signs for discerning whether or not a vision is the product of the imagination. How could we create a picture of Christ's humanity in all its detail and conjure his great beauty out of thin air? If the image were to represent him at all, it would take a very long time to generate. We are certainly capable of doing this. We could visualize him, gaze upon his form and radiance, gradually refine the image, and commit it to memory. Since this is the work of the intellect, who can stop us?

But there is no way we could create the kind of vision I'm talking about here. We see what the Lord shows us when he wants us to see it and in the form in which he wants to show it to us. No matter how hard we try, we cannot produce it or remove it, add to it or subtract from it. We look at it whenever we want to see it or look away when we don't feel like seeing it anymore. And if we try to focus on one particular feature, Christ disappears.

God granted me this blessing frequently over the course of two and a half years. A little over three years ago, he replaced the vision with a more sublime favor, one that he has been giving me almost continually ever since.

When I first began to receive visions of Christ, I was aware that he was speaking to me. I gazed at his great beauty and felt the sweetness of the words that came from his divine mouth, even when they were stern. I desperately wanted to know the color of his eyes and how tall he was so that I could accurately describe them later. But I was never worthy enough to see these things, and striving to do so produced no results. In fact, the effort only made the vision vanish.

Sometimes I see him looking at me with heartbreaking compassion. In general, the vision is so powerful that my soul cannot bear it and slips into a sublime rapture. I lose the vision so that I can more fully enjoy the vision. So it's not a matter of being willing or unwilling. It is clear that all the Beloved wants of us is humility and holy bewilderment. He wants us to accept what we are given and praise the One who gives it.

This is true for all visions, without exception. There is nothing we can do about it. Nor can we undo anything. We can't see more and we can't see less than we are offered. The Lord wants us to be clearly aware that this is not our work but his Majesty's. That way, we avoid spiritual pride. Instead, we are humbled and awestruck when we realize that just as the Lord takes away our power to see whatever we want to see whenever we want to see it, so he may remove any of his other favors and gifts and we will be left utterly lost. As long as we live in this exile, we should always walk with trepidation.

Our Lord almost always appeared to me in his risen form. It was the same when I saw him in the host during Communion. If I were suffering some tribulation, he would occasionally show me his wounds to give me encouragement. Sometimes he appeared on the cross or in the garden. A few times I saw him wearing the crown of thorns. Sometimes he would be carrying his cross, depending on what I or other people needed. But his body was always glorified.

I was persecuted terribly for speaking about these visions. I weathered innumerable insults and trials. The men who were observing me were so convinced that I was possessed by an evil spirit that some of them wanted to arrange an exorcism. This did not bother me much. What really upset me was when I saw that my confessors were afraid to hear my confession because of things that people were saying about me.

In spite of the fears they filled me with, I could never manage to regret having seen these heavenly visions. I would not trade a single one of them for all the blessings and delights in the world. I have always considered a vision an offering of great mercy from the Lord. The Lord himself has assured me many times that visions are priceless treasures.

I found my love for God growing stronger and stronger. Whenever I went to the Lord to lament my trials, I came away from my prayer feeling consoled and strengthened. I still didn't dare contradict my critics though, because I could see that they would only interpret this as evidence of a serious lack of humility, and this would make things worse. I did discuss everything with my confessor. Whenever he saw that I was troubled, he made a sincere effort to comfort me.

My visions began to increase in frequency and intensity. One of the members of the group of men who were scrutinizing me insisted that I was being deceived by the devil. This priest had sometimes heard my confession when my regular confessor wasn't available.

"Since you seem incapable of resisting these diabolical intrusions," he said, "you must make the sign of the cross and thumb your nose whenever you feel a vision coming on. If you do this with conviction," he continued, "the devil will leave you and never come back." He must have misread the distress on my face. "Don't be afraid," he said magnanimously. "God will protect you."

But I didn't believe the visions came from anything other than God in the first place! It was excruciating for me to obey the command and make this rude gesture at my Beloved. Nor could I possibly desire that these visions go away. But in the end, I did what I was told.

With many tears, I persistently begged God to free me from any deception. I begged Saint Peter and I begged Saint Paul, both of whom were dear to me, since it was on their feast day that the Lord first appeared to me. Christ himself had told me that they would guard me against being deceived. I often clearly perceived them on my left. This was not an imaginative vision. These two saints were powerful protectors of mine.

Thumbing my nose in the Lord's face caused me unbearable anguish. When I saw him there with me, I would not have been able to believe this had anything to do with the devil if they broke me into a thousand pieces. This mandate was a severe penance for me. I couldn't bear to make such a disrespectful gesture while I was having a vision of Christ. Since obeying it would have required my crossing myself and thumbing my nose every five seconds anyway, I started holding a cross in my hand instead.

The situation reminded me of the way Christ was persecuted by his own people. I begged the Lord to forgive me. Whenever I thumbed my nose at him, I was only obeying the ministers he had placed in his

Church to represent him. He told me not to worry and reassured me that I did the right thing to obey them. He also said that he himself would show them the truth. When they prohibited me from practicing prayer, the Lord seemed to become annoyed. He told me to tell them that they were now crossing over into tyranny. He gave me clear signs for determining that a vision did not come from the spirit of evil. I'll say more about this later.

The cross I carried was attached to a rosary. One day as I was holding it, Christ took it from me with his own hands. When he gave it back to me, it was completely changed. Now the cross was composed of four large stones. They were incomparably more valuable than diamonds. Nothing can be compared to supernatural things. A diamond seems imperfect and fake next to the precious stones Christ handed to me.

Christ's five wounds were inscribed on the jewels with the most intricate skill. He told me that from now on I would behold the cross in this new way. And this is exactly what happened. I was never again able to see the wood from which the crucifix was fashioned. But no one else seemed to be able to see these precious stones.

As soon as I tried to obey the command to reject these favors from God, they began to happen more frequently. My very effort to resist them seemed to propel me into a state of unceasing prayer. I even seemed to be praying in my sleep. My love for my Lord grew so intense that I complained to him that I could not bear it. But no matter how much I tried, I could not stop thinking about him.

Although I strove to obey my superiors when I could, there was almost nothing I could do about it. And the Lord was no help! He kept me in a constant state of prayer. On the one hand, he told me to do what they said. On the other, he reassured me and taught me what to say to them. And he still does. The arguments he gave me to offer my critics were so sound that I have felt perfectly secure ever since.

His Majesty soon followed through on his promise to make it abundantly clear to me that my visions came from him. He began to increase my love for God to such a degree that I didn't know where it came from or how to obtain it. This love was supernatural. I was dying with desire to see God. I didn't know where to seek the life I was longing for except through death. Such powerful impulses of love coursed through me that

I didn't know what to do with myself. Nothing satisfied me. I couldn't stand to be with myself. It truly seemed like my soul was being torn away from me.

O Lord, you Supreme Trickster! What subtle artfulness you use to do your work with this miserable slave of yours. You hide yourself from me and afflict me with your love. You deliver such a delicious death that my soul would never dream of trying to avoid it.

These impulses are so intense that it would be impossible for anyone who has not experienced them to imagine what they feel like. They do not disquiet the heart. They are not the same as those bursts of devotional emotion that commonly overwhelm the spirit. They are of a much higher order of prayer than these. I have found that the best way to handle impetuous spiritual stirrings is to gather them gently within myself and quiet my soul.

This lower condition should be treated the same way you might deal with children who are having a tantrum. You know when they cry so hard that it seems like they are about to choke to death? The minute you hand them something to drink, the sobbing ceases. That's what this is like. Natural weakness is sometimes confused with true religious emotion. Reason needs to step in and take command of the situation. When we reflect on the rush of feeling more deeply, we may be surprised to see that it does not have a totally perfect source but rather comes from the sensory part of the soul.

Let this child be comforted with a gentle caress. Let us not bludgeon the child but draw out his love with our love. Let us contain this love and not spill it like a pot that heats up too fast and boils over because we've fed the fire too much wood. Let us moderate the source of the flame. Gentle tears regulate the fire. Passionate tears put the fire out. Their source is emotional, and they can do us harm.

In the beginning, I used to experience this kind of crying, and it always left my spirit so exhausted and my mind so confused that it took me a few days before I was fit to pray again. It's really important to cultivate discrimination during the early stages of the spiritual path. That way, everything will unfold smoothly, and the spirit learns to work on the inner planes. We need to strive consciously to avoid getting caught by external feelings.

These higher impulses I am talking about are very different. We ourselves do not put wood on the fire. It is already burning, and we are suddenly thrown into it to be consumed. We are ablaze with anguished longing for God. We do not try to feel the pain of this wound caused by our separation from him; we are overcome by it.

Sometimes an arrow of love pierces the heart and penetrates the deepest core of the soul so that she doesn't know what has happened or what she wants, except that all she wants is God. It feels like the arrow has been dipped in a poisonous herb that makes her reject herself for love of him. She would gladly give up her life for him. It's impossible to explain the way God wounds the soul or to exaggerate the agony this causes. It makes the soul forget herself entirely. Yet this pain carries such exquisite pleasure that no other pleasure in life can compare to that happiness. The soul longs to die of this beautiful wound.

The blending of pain and glory was very confusing to me at first. I couldn't understand how they could coexist. Oh, what a gift it is to behold a wounded soul! We need to understand her condition as a sacred one and recognize that she has been wounded for a sublime purpose. The soul did not make this love happen. Rather, it seems that a spark of the boundless love the Lord has for the soul has leapt out of the flame and landed on her, setting her on fire. Oh, how many times do I remember the words of David when I am in this state: "As the deer longs for streams of water, so my soul longs for you, O God." I seem to embody this passage literally.

When these love longings are not quite as intense, they can be somewhat subdued. The soul tries to find some relief through certain penances, because she does not know what else to do. But she no more feels the pain of these sacrifices than a dead body would feel its blood being shed. She is desperately seeking ways and means for dealing with the love of God that consumes her, but no self-inflicted bodily pain can mitigate this soul pain. Such low remedies as physical penances make poor medicine for such a high disease. They can alleviate the condition a little, and the soul can make do in this way while she begs God to give her a more permanent cure for her suffering. But she sees no real way out except by dying. Death feels like the only way the soul can fully enjoy her Beloved.

Sometimes, however, this pain is so severe that the soul is incapable of doing penances or anything else. The body becomes paralyzed. She cannot move her hands or feet. If she is standing, she drops into a sitting position. She is like a person being transported by others. She cannot even draw a breath on her own. She may utter a few sighs, but they are inaudible. She doesn't even make a sound; the sighing happens on the inside.

While I was in this state, the Lord chose to give me the following vision. I saw an angel in bodily form standing very close to me on my left side. Although angels have appeared to me many times, I have rarely seen them in bodily form. Usually I see them without my eyes, like in those intellectual visions I was telling you about before.

This time, however, God wanted me to see the vision like this. The angel was not large; he was quite small and very beautiful. His face was so lit up by flame brilliantly lit that I thought he must belong to that highest order of angels who are made entirely of fire. He didn't tell me his name, but I know there is a big difference between various angelic realms. I wouldn't know how to explain such things.

I saw that he held a great golden spear. The end of the iron tip seemed to be on fire. Then the angel plunged the flaming spear through my heart again and again until it penetrated my innermost core. When he withdrew it, it felt like he was carrying the deepest part of me away with him. He left me utterly consumed with love of God. The pain was so intense that it made me moan. The sweetness this anguish carries with it is so bountiful that I could never wish for it to cease. The soul will not be content with anything less than God.

The pain is spiritual, not physical. Still, the body does not fail to share some of it, maybe even a lot of it. The love exchanged between the soul and her God is so sweet that I beg him in his goodness to give a taste of it to anyone who thinks I might be lying.

On the days when this vision appeared to me, I wandered around in a kind of stupor for many hours. I didn't want to look at anything or say anything. All I wanted was to embrace my pain and hold it close. This was greater glory than any created thing could ever offer me.

Sometimes it was the Lord's will for these raptures to be so intense that I could not resist them, even if I was among other people. To my great dismay, people started talking about them. As time went on, the suffering that accompanied the visions grew softer. But in the beginning, the pain could be so excruciating that the Lord lifted my soul and carried her into ecstasy. In that place, there is no room for suffering. It is pure joy.

May he be forever blessed. He has granted so many favors to one who has so poorly responded to his great gifts.

XXX ✠

FIRE AND WATER

WHEN I REALIZED that there was little or nothing I could do to fend off these powerful visionary impulses, I grew afraid. I didn't understand how suffering and joy could go together. I already knew that physical pain and spiritual delight were compatible, but this intense combination of profound inner pain and exalted joy confounded me.

I kept trying to resist my visions as I was ordered to do, but the effort was futile; it only exhausted me. I would pick up my cross to defend myself against the One who is the defender of us all. It was perfectly clear that no one understood me. But I didn't mention this to anyone except my spiritual director, since it only would have been interpreted as further proof of my lack of humility.

The Lord was pleased to relieve the bulk of my trial by bringing the blessed Father Pedro de Alcantará to the city of Ávila. As you may recall, I mentioned him earlier and said something about his unusual self-sacrifice. Someone verified to me that he did, in fact, wear a shirt made of tin shavings for more than twenty years. Father Pedro wrote several books in Spanish about the practice of prayer. His work has become very popular. Since he lived what he writes about, his words are very helpful to people who are inclined to walk a spiritual path. He also rigorously followed the first rule of the blessed Saint Francis.

Remember the wealthy widow I told you about, doña Guiomar de Ulloa? Well, not only was she a good friend of mine, but she was a good friend to God. Guiomar knew all about my predicament. She had witnessed my great suffering and had been a tremendous source of comfort to me. Her faith was so strong that she was incapable of believing that my experiences were anything other than God-given. She did not agree at all with the men who insisted that my visions came from the spirit of evil.

Guiomar was a very intelligent person and totally trustworthy. God gave her many favors in prayer. He also chose to enlighten her about matters of which learned men were ignorant. My spiritual directors allowed me to confide in her because she was extremely perceptive about certain things. Sometimes the Lord shared some of the favors he granted to me with Guiomar and accompanied them with words of wisdom that contributed to the growth of her own soul.

When Guiomar heard that Father Pedro was in town, she obtained permission from my superiors to have me stay at her house for a week so that I could talk more easily with the holy man. She made these arrangements without even telling me about it, so that all I had to do was show up and unburden my soul. During this time, Father Pedro came to Guiomar's house to meet with me, and I also spoke with him at some churches. Over the years, I spent a great deal of time with him on many different occasions.

I gave Father Pedro as clear and honest a summary of my life and my spiritual path as I possibly could. Whenever I shared with anyone about my soul, I always tried to speak with transparency and truthfulness. I wanted them to know about my very first spiritual stirrings, and if there was anything I considered dubious, I would openly accuse myself. So I laid my soul bare to Father Pedro without duplicity or cover-up.

Right from the beginning, I saw that Father Pedro understood me through experience. That was all I needed. I didn't even understand myself at that time. I didn't know how to put words around my experiences the way I do now. Later God allowed me both to understand and describe the favors that his Majesty granted me. But back then I needed someone who had been through it himself so that he could explain the nature of my experiences.

Father Pedro's teachings about imaginative visions were especially enlightening to me. I had been having a great deal of difficulty understanding what I saw with the eyes of the soul. I thought that the only worthy visions were those we see with our bodily eyes, and I didn't experience any of those.

This holy man explained everything to me. "Don't worry," he said. "Just praise God." He reassured me that my experiences were the work of the Spirit. "Nothing could be truer or more reliable than these divine favors," he said, "except for the teachings of our faith."

I seemed to provide Father Pedro with some comfort as well. He was incredibly kind and helpful to me. From the time we met, he took an active interest in me and confided his own concerns and business matters. Father Pedro saw that the Lord had given me powerful desires for the things he had already obtained, as well as the courage to bring these longings to fulfillment. He genuinely enjoyed talking with me. For there is no greater pleasure for anyone God has brought to this state than meeting someone else in whom the Lord has begun to light the fire of love-longing. It was only just beginning for me then. God grant that I may be further along that path now.

Father Pedro showed me the most touching compassion. "You have already suffered one of the worst trials on earth," he said, when I told him how those good men had opposed me. "But you still have a long way to go. You are very needy, and there is no one in this city who is capable of understanding you."

He told me he would speak to my spiritual director and also to don Francisco, who had caused me the most grief. It was only because of his great love for me that don Francisco waged this war against me. He is a pious man, and since he saw that my soul had so recently been very wretched, he couldn't reconcile it with the divine favors I had suddenly begun to receive.

The holy Father Pedro assured these men that my experience was valid. He gave them many good reasons that they should feel safe and asked them not to bother me anymore. It didn't take much to placate my confessor, but don Francisco wasn't quite convinced. It was enough, however, at least to stop him from terrorizing me so much.

Father Pedro and I agreed that from then on I would document each of my experiences in writing. We promised to pray for one another. He was so humble that he valued the prayers of someone as lowly as I! This embarrassed me. He filled me with comfort and joy and infused my practice of prayer with new confidence.

"Try not to doubt that your prayer comes from God," he told me. "But if doubts do arise, or if you want to be absolutely sure, check your experiences with your confessor. That should keep you safe."

I appreciated his assurances, but I couldn't fully take them in. Mine was a path of fear. If people told me my experiences came from the spirit of evil, I was inclined to believe them. But there was no man on earth who could either frighten me enough or reassure me enough for me to believe him over the feelings that God himself had planted in my soul. So although Father Pedro's words soothed and calmed me, they didn't entirely banish my anxiety, especially when the Lord plunged me into the soul suffering I'm about to recount.

Overall, however, Father Pedro did console me. I couldn't thank God enough for the gift of friendship with this holy man. I had often prayed to my glorious father, Saint Joseph, as well as to our Lady. Since Father Pedro was the primary representative of an order of Saint Joseph, I believed the glorious saint had brought him to me, so I thanked him too.

Sometimes I would suffer so many bitter spiritual trials, compounded by such severe bodily pain and sickness, that I was left utterly helpless. This still happens even now, although to a lesser degree. At other times I grew seriously ill, but since I was not experiencing that soul suffering, I bore it with great joy. It was only when all my afflictions were combined that I was reduced to such a miserable state.

Then I forgot all the favors the Lord had granted me. They were like a dream. The only thing I could remember was pain. My mind was dulled, and I was plagued by a thousand doubts and suspicions. It seemed as if I had never understood the spiritual life and had imagined everything that had happened to me. Not only had I been deluded myself, I concluded, but I had deluded good men. I considered myself so thoroughly wicked that all the evil that had ever befallen the world must have been my fault.

This was a case of false humility. The spirit of evil invented all this to try and disquiet me and push my soul into despair. Since then, I have had a great deal of experience with the spirit of evil. He realizes that I see through him, so he doesn't torment me the way he used to. It's easy enough to recognize him through the effect he has on the soul. He begins by disturbing her, continues to agitate her throughout the time he is working on her, plants darkness and distress inside her, and leaves her so dried out that she has no inclination toward prayer or any other positive act.

The spirit of evil seems to smother the soul and constrict the body, rendering them both powerless. It makes us feel so wretched that we hate ourselves. But these exaggerated thoughts of our own wickedness have nothing to do with true humility. True humility does not cause inner turmoil and spiritual unrest. True humility creates the opposite effect. It consoles the soul. It fills her with quietude, serenity, and light.

True humility may carry an element of pain, but the soul experiences her suffering as a gift from God and hopes that her suffering serves him in some way. It grieves the soul to see how she has offended her Beloved, but at the same time, her spirit is relieved by his great mercy. She is enlightened enough to feel shame about her shameful behavior, but she is thrilled to see that God hasn't given up on her, and she praises him.

When the spirit of evil creates a state of false humility, it banishes the light and obliterates all that is good in the soul. It seems as if God has wiped everything out with a flaming sword. The soul dwells on God's righteousness but has trouble remembering his mercy. The spirit of evil is not powerful enough to make the soul lose her faith, but that faith no longer brings any consolation. Instead, when the soul does consider God's mercy, it only makes her feel worse because she thinks she should have done more to earn it.

This kind of self-loathing is one of the spirit of evil's most insidious, painful, and deceptive tricks. I'm warning you about this so that if he tries to tempt you in this way, you will have the foresight to recognize it. Don't think it's a matter of academic learning or theological knowledge. Even though I am impoverished in these areas, the minute I escape from his clutches, it is obvious to me that I have been deceived and that my negative feelings were groundless. I have come to understand that the Lord allows the spirit of evil to test us in this way just as he permitted the devil to tempt Job, although less severely because we are less saintly.

Now I'm going to tell you about another way the spirit of evil tempted me. It happened the day before the Feast of Corpus Christi, to which I am deeply devoted, though not as much as I should be. Sometimes I struggle with this temptation for as many as fifteen days or even three weeks (maybe longer), but this time it only lasted until the feast day. It especially comes up during Holy Week, when prayer is my refuge.

My mind is suddenly caught up in a stream of trivial thoughts. These things are so ridiculous that at other times they would make me laugh. The spirit of evil invades the intellect, ties it up, and does whatever he wants with it. The soul is no longer master of herself, and all she can do is think absurd thoughts. These thoughts have absolutely no purpose; they neither engage her nor release her. They serve only to oppress the soul so that she feels as if she no longer fits inside herself.

Sometimes it feels as if the devils are playing ball with my soul and she can't break free of their grasp. The soul's suffering during these times is beyond description. She seeks relief, but God will not allow her to find any. The light of reason remains, which overrides free will, but it is unclear, as if the eyes were covered with a film.

The soul in this state is like a person who has so often taken a certain path that his feet remember the way even when it's dark out. He knows the places where he might stumble because he has seen them in the day-time, so he's on his guard for those spots. The soul, too, moves by acquired feel and so avoids offending God. Of course, this analogy does not take into account the fact that the Lord always holds the soul in his hands, which is what really matters.

During these times, faith and all the other virtues are put to sleep. But they are not lost. The soul never stops believing in the teachings of the Church, but all she can do is pay lip service to them. She is miserable and numb. She knows God the way a person hears something far away in the distance. Her love grows lukewarm. When she listens to someone talking about God, she believes him only because the Church tells her to, not because of any real memory of God's presence. Entering into solitude and prayer only increases the soul's anguish. She cannot bear the inner torment, yet she cannot identify its source.

In my opinion, this experience is a mirror of hell. Actually, the Lord confirmed this for me in a vision. The soul is burning inside herself, and she has no idea who started the fire or where it came from or how to get away from it or what to put it out with. When she tries to soothe herself with a good book, she feels as if she has forgotten how to read. I remember one time when I tried to read the life of a saint. I was hoping it would

absorb me and that seeing the way he suffered might offer me some solace. After I read the same few lines four or five times, I understood even
less than I had at the beginning, so I put the book down. This happened
to me often, although for some reason this particular instance stands out
in my mind.

It's even worse trying to carry on a conversation with someone. The
spirit of evil puts me in such a foul temper that they all think I'm going
to bite their heads off. I can't help it. I consider it an accomplishment
just to be able to control myself. Actually, I know it's the Lord who keeps
me under control. He holds me in his hands during times like this and
prevents me from doing anything that might cause harm to my neighbors or offend God.

It's absolutely useless to seek spiritual guidance when the soul is in
this condition. This has been my experience, anyway. Even though the
confessors I had at that time were very holy men and the confessors I go
to these days are equally saintly, they spoke to me very harshly and
scolded me when I most needed their compassion and support.

When I told these men afterward how I felt about the way they had
treated me, they were very surprised and claimed they were powerless to
refrain from acting this way. They felt very sorry about the pain they
caused me and tried not to do it again. Knowing how I had suffered in
body and soul, they were determined to comfort me the next time I came
to them with these problems, but they couldn't do it.

They didn't exactly use bad words. That would have been an offense
against God. But they used the strongest possible language allowed a
confessor. Apparently, they meant to mortify me. And there were times
when I was ready and willing to suffer that kind of mortification. But
when I was undergoing this particular trial, I couldn't bear it.

I also used to worry that I was misleading my spiritual directors. So I
went to them and warned them that I was quite capable of deception.
Of course, I knew that I would never deliberately lie to them, but I was
so afraid of everything that I thought I might inadvertently say the
wrong thing and they would end up with the wrong idea.

One of these men was familiar with the kind of temptation I was struggling with. "Don't worry," he said. "Even if you wanted to deceive me,
I'm too smart to let myself be deceived." This was very comforting to me.

I almost always felt at peace after receiving Communion. Sometimes simply approaching the Sacrament made me feel so good in body and soul that I was truly amazed. It felt as if all the darkness in my soul was lifted in a single moment, and by the light of that radiant sunshine, I could clearly see how foolish all of my negative thoughts had been. At other times, a single word from my Beloved cured me completely. Such as the time I told you about, when he said to me, "Do not grow weary; do not be afraid." Or sometimes after seeing a vision it was as if there had never been anything wrong.

I rejoiced in the Lord. And I also complained to him about all the torments I suffered. But he always repaid me afterward by pouring his mercies upon me with great abundance. My soul would emerge from this crucible like gold, purified and refined, shining with a new radiance that enabled her to see God inside herself.

And so, although our trials may seem unbearable, they eventually grow light. We are willing to suffer them all again if it means we will serve God in this way. From this perspective we understand that there will be more persecutions and tribulations ahead, but if we endure them serenely, without forsaking God, everything will work out for the best. I must admit, I have not always handled my own trials quite so perfectly.

There are times when I seem to be utterly incapable of thinking a single good thought, let alone putting one into action. My body and soul feel heavy and useless. The other temptations and worries I told you about are replaced with a deep sense of dissatisfaction with everything and everyone. When I have suffered from this sort of temptation, I have tried to force myself to perform some good works just to keep myself occupied, but I felt powerless to do anything in the absence of grace. This was not as painful as other trials, because the awareness of my own unworthiness brought me some relief.

There are other times when I cannot seem to formulate any concept of God. Even if I am alone, I am unable to practice prayer. Yet I still feel that I know God. The faculties of reason and imagination cause the trouble. The will remains inclined toward all that is good. But the intellect is out of control, like a lunatic no one can hold down. I can't even control my wild mind for the amount of time it takes to recite the creed.

Sometimes I have the ability to witness my own misery and laugh at myself. I watch this inner madman to see what he's going to do. Glory be to God! To my surprise, my thoughts do not rush after evil but turn to neutral things. My mind wanders here, there, and everywhere in search of something to think about. This makes me realize what a great favor his Majesty is doing me when he holds the madman bound in perfect contemplation.

I'd love to see what would happen if all those people who think I'm so holy could witness this insanity. I actually feel compassion for my poor soul when she's in this state. I see that she's in bad company, and I long to set her free. I turn to the Lord. "When, my God?" I ask him. "When will I finally see the whole of my soul unified in praise of you? When will all my faculties come together to enjoy you at the same time? Do not allow my soul to be fragmented any longer. Each shard seems to pull me in a different direction."

The scattering of the faculties happens to me often. Sometimes it seems obvious to me that this is the cause of most of my health problems. I also think that the legacy of original sin has something to do with our inability to enjoy all blessings in an integral way. Plus, my own transgressions exacerbate the problem. If I hadn't been so unconscious in the past, I would be more integrated now.

Here is another terrible trial I suffered. I had read all the books on prayer and felt I understood them because the Lord had already given me such favors. I concluded that I did not need these books, so I focused on the lives of the saints instead. I considered myself severely deficient in the ways these men and women served God, and I hoped to gain wisdom and encouragement from them.

Then it struck me that thinking I had attained any kind of advanced spiritual states demonstrated a shameful lack of humility. But since I could not persuade myself to dismiss the reality of these states, I was very distressed. Finally, the blessed Father Pedro de Alcantará came along and told me not to worry about that.

It is clear to me that I haven't begun to be of service to God. His Majesty has already granted me the kinds of blessings he gives to much more advanced souls. I am the very embodiment of imperfection. But I am well endowed with good desires, and my heart is full of love. I think the Lord has favored me with love-longing so that I might have some way of serving him. I really do believe that I love him, but all my imperfect actions make me very sad.

Then there are times when my soul suffers from what I can only call stupid attacks. I don't seem to be doing any harm, but I'm doing no good either. I'm just going along with the crowd, as they say. I'm not walking in pain, but I'm not walking in glory. I don't care if I die, but I don't mind if I keep living. Nothing pleases me, but nothing burdens me. I don't feel anything.

My soul in this state is like a little dumb donkey grazing in a pasture. It is nourished because its food is provided, but it eats without even noticing that it's chewing and swallowing. The soul cannot help but feed on God's grace. She is content to live this humble life. But she doesn't experience any impulses or other effects that help her to understand herself.

It seems to me now that the soul is drifting on a gentle breeze. She travels great distances without knowing how. In other stages of the spiritual journey, the effects can be so dramatic that the soul has no doubt that she is growing as a result. Her desire surges, but nothing satisfies her. It makes me think of small, flowing springs I have seen; they never cease heaving up the sand all around them.

This is what it's like for souls who reach this state. Love is continuously stirring inside them. They cannot stop thinking of all the things they will do for love. Just as the water in a spring does not seem to fit in the ground and so the earth casts it out of itself, the soul cannot contain the love inside her. She is soaked in its waters. Since she has such abundance, she wants others to drink and join her in praising God.

Oh, how many times have I remembered the living water that Christ told the Samaritan woman about! I have always been very fond of that Gospel passage. From the time I was a little girl, I often begged the Lord to give me that living water, long before I understood how good the water is. I kept a picture with me of the Lord coming to that well with these words inscribed beneath it: "Sir, give me this water."

This love is like water and also like fire. The fire is vast and always needs fuel to consume so that it will never go out. No matter how arduous the task may be, souls in this state will keep carrying wood so that the fire will not be extinguished. I'm even content if I only have pieces of straw to toss in. Often, that's all I have to offer.

Sometimes I laugh at myself. Other times I grow so weary I could cry. An inner impulse moves me to offer some service, but I'm not good for much. I arrange branches and flowers before holy images. I sweep a hallway or tidy the chapel. There are a few other tasks, but they are so trivial that it embarrasses me to mention them. Even when I performed some small penance, I knew it was meaningless unless the Lord counted the intention behind the act and discounted the act itself. I couldn't help but make fun of myself for my petty efforts.

When God so bountifully gives the fire of his love to a soul who lacks the physical strength to do anything useful for him, it can be a terrible trial to her. Her grief is intense. If she is not strong enough to throw a little wood on that fire, she is terrified that it will go out. She is dying with longing and cannot do anything about it. I think a soul in this state consumes herself and turns to ash. She dissolves in tears and melts away. It is a severe torment, yet it is also a delightful one.

Let the soul who has evolved to this point praise the Lord with all her heart, especially if he gives her the strength to sacrifice herself a little for his sake. Those to whom God has given the education, talents, and freedom to teach and bring other souls to him have no idea what a blessing this is unless they have experienced what it's like to be unable to do these things and yet still be the recipient of such lavish gifts from God. May he be blessed forever and may the angels glorify him! Amen.

I'm not sure if I'm doing the right thing to put down so many details here. Ever since you sent me your most recent message, telling me not to worry that I'm saying too much and to be sure not to leave anything out, I'm writing everything I can think of, as clearly and truthfully as I can remember. I can't help but leave out a great deal, but I would be wasting even more time if I covered every little detail, and I have so little time available as it is. Even if I had more time to write, I doubt I could add anything worthwhile.

XXI ✠

HOLY WATER

THE TEMPTATIONS I've been telling you about were internal and private. Now I'd like to describe some of the more public ways the spirit of evil chose to torment me. It was impossible not to recognize his presence in these incidents.

One day, when I was in the oratory, the spirit of evil appeared to me in a hideous form at my left side. Since he was speaking to me, I couldn't help but focus on his mouth, which was terrifying. A huge flame leapt from his body. It was very bright and cast no shadow.

"Truly, you have freed yourself from my clutches," he roared, "but I will seize you with them again!"

I was very frightened. The minute I began to cross myself, he disappeared. But he immediately came back again. This happened twice. I didn't know what to do. Then I noticed a vial of holy water. I threw some in his direction, and he never returned.

On another occasion, he tormented me for five or six hours with racking external physical pains and harrowing internal mental anguish. I didn't think I could bear it for a minute longer. The sisters who were with me had no idea how to help me, and I was totally incapable of helping myself. Normally when I am ill or in pain, I make it a practice to offer up my suffering to the Lord. If what I am going through might be of any service to his Majesty, I ask him to give me the patience necessary for me to endure it until the end of the world. The agony was so severe that day that it was all I could do to maintain my resolve to give it to God.

The Lord must have wanted me to recognize that the devil was causing this trouble, because suddenly there appeared an abominable, dark creature beside me. He was snarling, as if frustrated that he had lost what he had been trying so hard to win. When I saw him, all my fear drained away and I laughed.

But the sisters who had witnessed my suffering didn't understand what was going on. They couldn't figure out how to alleviate my pain, and they felt helpless. The spirit of evil made me thrash around and bang my head and limbs against the floor. I was powerless to stop it. The inner turmoil was even worse. I wanted to ask them for holy water, but I was afraid they would realize what was going on, and I didn't want to alarm them.

In my experience, there is nothing more frightening to demons than holy water. It makes them run away and never come back. They flee from the cross too, but they return. Holy water must be incredibly potent. It has a powerfully refreshing quality that I could never adequately describe. I notice a singular consolation in my soul whenever I come into contact with holy water. It is an inner delight that thoroughly permeates my being.

This is something that has happened to me not once but many times. I have paid close attention to its effects. It's as if a person were very hot and thirsty, and someone handed him a cup of cold water. His entire being feels refreshed. Everything that is blessed is important, but I think there must be something especially sacred about the prayer that so vastly differentiates ordinary water from water that is blessed.

That particular day, the torment just wouldn't let up, so finally I said to the sisters, "If you wouldn't laugh at me, I'd ask you for some holy water."

They brought the holy water and sprinkled it on me. But it didn't do any good. I threw some in the direction of the evil spirit, and he vanished. In that moment, all the sickness left me, as if someone had scooped it out of me by hand. The only lingering symptom was a pervasive ache, as if I had been severely beaten with a stick. It made me think about what the spirit of evil would do to a soul he managed to capture for his own. Look at how much harm he did to one who does not belong to him! It renewed my desire to distance myself from such negative forces.

This happened to me one other time, not long ago. I was alone, but I cried out for help. Two nuns rushed in with holy water. The evil spirit had already departed, but the sisters smelled a foul stench like sulfur in the room. I didn't smell anything, but these women are both very trustworthy, and they would never tell a lie. The odor lingered long enough that other people detected it too.

Another day, I was in the choir when I felt a strong urge toward recollection. I left the choir so that the other sisters would not notice the state I was entering, but they all heard a loud crash in the place where I had just been kneeling. I heard the sound of nasty voices close to my ear, as if the evil spirits were plotting something, but I couldn't make out the words. By that time, I was so absorbed in prayer that I didn't perceive anything else and I was completely unafraid. This kind of thing also happened every time the Lord granted me the favor of guiding some soul along the path that leads home to him.

I am about to tell you something that I can assure you really did happen. There were several witnesses. One of them is my current confessor. He saw it described in a letter and knew exactly to whom it pertained without my even telling him.

A certain person came to me who had been engaged in grave spiritual error for two and a half years. It was one of the most serious transgressions I have ever heard of. He had not confessed his sins or made amends during this entire time, yet he continued to say Mass.

"How could I confess something so ugly?" he asked me.

This priest had a deep desire to give up his sinful behavior, but he couldn't help himself. I felt deep compassion for him, and it caused me great sorrow to see how he was forsaking God in this way. I promised him that I would beseech God with all my heart to help him and that I would recruit some other people who are more spiritually evolved than I am to pray for him also.

I sent letters to the priest through a certain person whom he trusted to deliver them. As it turns out, as soon as he read my first letter, he went to confession. I suppose having all those pious people praying for him had some effect. I am a miserable wretch, but I approached his problem with tremendous care. It seems that God wanted to grant this soul his mercy. The priest wrote to me that he was doing much better. "I haven't sinned for days," he said.

Yet temptation continued to torment him so severely that it sounded as if he were living in hell. He asked me to keep praying for him. I, in turn, asked my sisters to pray for him, and they took his situation deeply to heart. Still, nobody could guess the identity of this secret sinner. I implored his Majesty to take away his torment and send those demons to me instead, as long as they would not cause me to offend my God. It was during that month that I suffered from the severe afflictions and diabolical intrusions I just described.

I wrote to tell him what I was going through during this time, and he wrote back to tell me that it was working. The evil spirits had left him, his soul was fortified, and he felt truly liberated. He could not thank me enough, although he had nothing for which to thank me. And he praised God with all his heart. Knowing that God had granted me spiritual favors seemed to inspire him. When he read my letters and saw what I had suffered so that he could be saved, it motivated him to change for good. I was amazed myself. I would gladly have endured years of pain if it meant that this beautiful soul would be set free.

May the Lord be praised for everything! The prayers of souls who serve him, like the sisters who live in this house, are powerful. I suppose it enraged the spirits of evil to see me seek these prayers and they made me pay for it. I'm sure my own wickedness had something to do with my torment as well.

Another strange thing happened during this period. One night I woke up and couldn't breathe. I thought they were choking me. The sisters came and sprinkled a lot of holy water all around my cell. Suddenly I saw a large crowd of evil spirits rushing past, as if they were on their way to throw themselves off a cliff. There are many times when these demons still try to torment me, but I am no longer afraid. I know that they have no power except what God allows them to have. It would bore you to hear about the many little ways they have beleaguered me. I would bore myself to recount them.

I pray that what I have written so far is of some help to the true servants of God. Pay no attention to the scarecrows the spirit of evil sets up to frighten us. Remember, every time we ignore them, they grow weaker and we gain more mastery. We always benefit in some way from these encounters. I won't elaborate on that now or I'd be off on another long tangent. I'll just tell you about one thing that happened to me on the night of All Souls.

I was in the oratory and had just finished reciting a nocturn. I was starting to repeat the deeply devotional prayers that come next in our prayer book. Suddenly a demon swooped down and actually landed on my book so that I couldn't finish reading the prayer. I crossed myself, and he went away. But the minute I began praying again, he came back. I think this happened three more times. It wasn't until I threw holy water at him that I was finally able to complete my prayer.

At that moment, I saw several souls emerge from purgatory. Their period of purification must have been almost up, and the spirit of evil had been trying to prevent their release. I have not seen the devil in physical form many times, but I have often perceived his presence.

I want to tell you about another thing that really frightened me. One day on the Feast of the Holy Trinity, I was sitting in the choir of another monastery and had slipped into rapture. In this heightened state, I witnessed a great battle between angels and devils. I did not understand what the vision meant at the time. But less than two weeks later, a bitter conflict erupted between some sisters who were deeply devoted to the practice of prayer and some who were not at all prayerful. Suddenly that vision made sense. This dispute caused a great deal of harm in the house. It lasted for a very long time and shook everyone up.

There were other times when I saw a crowd of evil spirits gathered around me, but I was enveloped in light and they could not touch me. I could tell that God was watching over me and keeping them away so that they could not make me forsake him. Knowing who I am, this was a real danger.

Since then I have come to understand that as long as I do not set myself up against God, the spirit of evil has almost no power and I have very little to fear. Unless they encounter cowardly souls who give in to them, demons have no strength. Sometimes I suffered from such compelling temptations that it seemed as if all the vanities and weaknesses of my past were reawakening inside me. I had to pray hard to get through it.

This experience made me question all over again whether the favors I had received from God actually came from the spirit of evil. It seemed to me that someone who had experienced the blessings I had experienced shouldn't have the tiniest twinge of a bad thought ever again. But my confessor set my mind at peace about this.

Another thing that tormented me then and continues to torment me now is when people put me on a pedestal. It especially disturbs me when highly prominent people speak of me with great respect. I have suffered terribly from this kind of esteem. Look at the life of Christ! Look at the lives of the saints! Did they evolve through flattery? No! They attained their station by being subjected to contempt and insults. My life is the opposite of theirs.

I'm like someone who does not dare raise her head for fear of being noticed. I feel better when I am being persecuted. Then my soul walks with her head held high. My body may suffer and I may experience certain kinds of emotional pain, but my soul is master of herself. I don't really understand how this works, but that's how it is. At times like this, the soul seems to be ruler of her own kingdom; everything rests beneath her feet.

There is another temptation I have grappled with. Sometimes it lasts for many days. It tries to disguise itself as the virtue of humility, but a very learned Dominican friar clearly explained to me that it is a trap. Whenever I considered the possibility that the favors the Lord was granting me might become public knowledge, I suffered intensely. My soul became so disturbed that I would have preferred to be buried alive than have people find out about my spiritual experiences. Since I was incapable of resisting recollection and rapture, even when they happened in front of other people, I would always emerge from one of these deep states feeling so ashamed that I was reluctant to go out where anyone might see me.

Once, when I was especially worried about this, the Lord spoke to me. "What are you afraid of?" he asked. "Only one of two things could come of it. People will either criticize you or praise me." He explained that the people who believed in the experience would praise him, and those who didn't would condemn me. It wasn't my problem. Either way, the outcome would benefit me, so I shouldn't be anxious.

This calmed me a great deal. I still feel comforted when I think about it. But at that time, the temptation reached such an intense degree that I wanted to pack up and move to a place where nobody knew me. I had heard about a convent that was far more cloistered than the one in which I was living. I had heard great things about that community. It belonged to my own order, and it was many miles from Ávila. I would have felt much better being anonymous, but my confessor wouldn't let me leave.

This fear seriously encumbered my freedom of spirit. I finally realized that it was not a sign of true humility; it caused too much anxiety. Besides, the Lord taught me this truth: his blessing is not some good thing reserved for me alone; it belongs to God. I must be absolutely certain of this. Am I sorry when I hear other people praised for their holiness? On the contrary, it gives me comfort and joy to see that God has revealed himself in them. And so I should never be troubled if he displays his works in me.

Whenever a person seemed to see something good in me, I had a tendency toward another extreme. There was a special prayer I had composed for just such an occasion in which I beseeched his Majesty to reveal my sins to that person. That way, the person wouldn't mistakenly believe the favor I was receiving correlated with any merit on my part. It is very important to me that people understand how undeserving I am of God's abundant grace.

My spiritual director advised against this special prayer. But until very recently, I found it difficult to stop. I always seek roundabout ways to advertise my transgressions when it looks like someone is starting to think highly of me. Even though it gives me relief to do this, my confessor does not approve, and he has made me more circumspect about this behavior.

It turns out that these feelings did not arise from humility but were a subtle kind of temptation. I was obsessed with the notion that I was deceiving everyone. And while it is true that they were mistaken about my goodness, I certainly did not intentionally delude them. The Lord had his own reasons for making them think such things. I even tried to stop discussing the issue with my spiritual guides unless it really seemed necessary, because I recognized that I had a tendency to make too much of it.

Now I understand how these guilty little fears that masquerade as humility come from a lack of spiritual development. A soul who has surrendered herself into God's hands doesn't care whether people say good things or bad things about her. God has given her the gift of understanding that nothing she has belongs to her alone.

Let the soul trust in the One who has given her this gift, and she will discover why he has given it to her. Let her be ready for persecution. For in times like these, it is guaranteed that the minute people begin to hear that a certain person is being granted divine favors, the person will be condemned for it. There are a thousand eyes fixed on such a person, while a thousand other people go entirely unnoticed.

There are perfectly valid reasons to be afraid, but my qualms stemmed from simple faintheartedness. A soul whom God leads along an open path before the eyes of the whole world should be prepared to be martyred; if she does not willingly die to the world, the world itself will surely kill her. There is nothing in this world that pleases me except its basic refusal to tolerate faults in good people. By criticizing them, it perfects them.

I say that it is easier to suffer a quick martyrdom than to follow the way of perfection. Unless the Lord chooses to grant the special privilege of perfecting a soul all at once, perfection generally comes very slowly and requires tremendous courage. When the world sees that someone has started out on that path, it demands that she be perfect right away. The world thinks that it detects a fault in someone from a thousand miles away, when what it perceives might actually be a virtue. Maybe that same behavior is actually a vice in the person who condemns it, and he judges others the way he should be judged himself.

Souls on the path to perfection are hardly allowed to eat or sleep or even breathe. The more highly they are esteemed, the more they are expected to forget they have a body. No matter how perfect a person's soul might be or how successfully she may have trampled the world under her feet, she still lives on this earth and is subject to its miseries.

Such a soul must be very brave. She has barely begun to walk, and they are trying to make her fly. She still hasn't conquered her passions and they are insisting that she be unmoved in the face of great temptation. They have read how the saints behaved after having been confirmed in grace, and they expect this poor soul to act the same way.

There is great cause to praise the Lord here, but there is equally ample reason to grieve. Many souls turn back at this point because they don't know how to help themselves. I believe my own soul would have turned back if the Lord himself, in his mercy, hadn't done everything for me. Before that, as you will see, all I could do was fall down and get up and fall again.

I wish I knew how to express this. I know I have used this comparison before, but I think it's worth repeating because I see so many souls suffering unnecessarily. They have been deluded into thinking they are supposed to fly before God has even given them wings. They start off with fervent desires and powerful determination to evolve in virtue. Some of these souls have severed all their worldly attachments.

Then they notice other souls who have grown in perfection and engage in highly virtuous actions. They read all the books on prayer and contemplation and hear about the things we need to do to rise to that exalted state. And they become thoroughly dejected as a result. There is someone who seems to be happier when people speak badly about him than when they speak well of him; he doesn't care about his reputation. There's another who has distanced himself from all of his old relationships because the people are not interested in prayer and it wearies him to converse with anyone who isn't on a spiritual path. This troubled soul doesn't realize that God is the one who gives us these gifts; we cannot cultivate them independently.

These virtues are supernatural; that is, they transcend our natural inclinations. Let these souls drop their anxiety. Let them trust in the Lord. Let them simply practice prayer and do the best they can. His Majesty will take their highest desires and turn them into action. Our nature is weak. It is very important to cultivate confidence and not lose heart. We should not give in to the doubt that our sincere efforts will lead to victory.

Since I have so much experience in these matters, I'd like to offer a little advice. Don't think that you have gained virtue unless you have been tried by its corresponding vice. We must always be vigilant and never take our growth for granted as long as we live. We have not yet been given the grace to understand the true nature of everything. There are many dangers in this life, and it's easy to get attached to worldly things.

A few years ago, I thought I had achieved the virtue of detachment from my relatives. Since many of them did not practice prayer, distancing myself from them was not difficult. The truth is, I could hardly stand to have a conversation with them; they bored me. Then a very important business matter came up, and I had to go stay with my younger sister, Juana, for a while. I had been very fond of her before, but now I didn't feel any rapport between us, even though she was a better person than I. She was married, and we had very little in common. We didn't talk about the things I would have liked to discuss. So I spent most of my time alone.

I noticed, however, that listening to her marital troubles upset me and worried me far more than they would have if I had been hearing about the tribulations of a neighbor. I came to realize that I was not as free as I thought. I saw that if I wanted the seed of virtue the Lord had begun to give me to flower, I would have to avoid the opportunity to be attached. With his help, I have tried to do this ever since.

When the Lord begins to instill a certain virtue in the soul, she should tend it well and never take the risk of losing it. This is especially true of attachment to what other people think. Do not assume that those of us who believe we are detached actually are. We have to be exceedingly careful about this.

Anyone who wants to make progress on the path but is concerned about his reputation needs to listen to my advice. Strive to detach. Attachment is like a chain no file can cut. Only our sincere prayers and earnest efforts, combined with God's grace, can set us free. Attachments are like shackles on the spiritual path. I am astounded by the harm they can cause.

I see certain people who impress everyone with the righteous and sacred acts they perform. God help me! Why are souls like that still on earth? Why haven't they reached the summit of perfection? What is this? What would be holding someone back who has done so much for God? I'll tell you: attachment to what other people think. What's even worse is that these men have no idea they are attached. This is because the spirit of evil sometimes makes us think that we are entitled to receive honor.

Let these men believe me! Let them, for the love of God, believe this little ant who has something to say. The Lord wants her to say it. If you do not pick off the caterpillar of attachment, it probably won't destroy the whole tree because other virtues will compensate for it, but the tree will be worm-eaten. It will not flourish. It will not be beautiful. It won't even allow the trees around it to thrive. The fruits of good example they offer to others will not be healthy and will quickly wither.

I often say that no matter how small a point of honor may be, it is not worth fighting for. Concern about what other people think is like striking the wrong chord on the organ or playing a song when the timing is off; the music is dissonant and ugly. This attachment to reputation is a problem in any context, but it is especially toxic on the path to perfection.

We are striving for union with God. We are seeking to follow his teachings, which have come through Christ, who was falsely accused and burdened by his wounds. And we also want our honor and reputation to remain intact? These two desires are mutually exclusive. If we take different roads, how can we expect to meet God? The Lord comes to the soul when she has made a voluntary effort to surrender her rights in every possible arena.

"But I don't have any opportunities to practice detachment from my rights," you might say. Or "I have nothing to give up." Remember, the Lord wants you to attain the highest good. If you are determined to break your attachments, I do not believe he will stand in your way. His Majesty will arrange so many occasions for you to practice detachment that you may wish you had never asked. All hands to the task!

I'd like to mention some of the little nothings I used to care about when I first embarked on the path. Among my many other faults, I neglected to learn all the prayers in my prayer book or the various duties we were expected to perform in the choir. I was too busy engaging in vanities and trivialities. But there were other novices who were capable of teaching me these things.

Did I ask for help? No. I was afraid they would discover how little I knew. Plus, I didn't want to set a bad example. What a cheap excuse! Soon enough, God opened my eyes a little. Then, even when I actually did know what I was doing, I would ask the youngest girls for guidance. I didn't lose any honor or credit by doing this. In fact, the Lord seemed to give me a better memory from then on.

I didn't know how to sing very well either. Whenever they entrusted me to lead a song and I failed to practice adequately, I panicked. It wasn't that I was afraid of making a mistake in front of the Lord. That would have been a virtuous qualm. I was concerned about the opinions of the people who were listening to me. And so, for purely egotistical reasons, I became so agitated that I ended up doing far worse than I should have.

Later, whenever I was unsure of my part, I took it upon myself to ask someone. This was very painful for me at first, but eventually I came to enjoy it. It turned out that the less I came to care about what people thought of what I knew, the better I sang. Whereas the more I tried to protect my miserable honor, the more I failed in performing what I considered to be a true honor. *Honor*—that word means different things to different people.

With the combined energy of all these little nothings, which really do amount to nothing, and the utter nothing that I am, since such nothings bothered me so much, my efforts began to pay off. His Majesty values every little thing we do for him. Then he helps us do bigger things.

So I was thinking about the problem of humility. I could see that everyone in the house was making progress in this area except me. I had always been good for nothing. It occurred to me to gather up all the sisters' mantles after they had left the choir. This made me feel like I was serving the angels who were praising God there.

This went on for quite some time. Then somehow, and I will never know how, they found out what I was up to. This embarrassed me terribly. Not because I had grown so virtuous that I was willing for people to know my secrets. Nor was it a matter of humility. Rather, I was afraid they would laugh at me because the things I was doing were so trivial.

O my Lord! I am ashamed of so much wickedness. Here I am, reporting on some grains of sand I still couldn't lift from the riverbed to serve you. Everything I did came wrapped in a thousand miseries. The water of your grace was not yet flowing beneath my sands to raise them up.

O my Creator! Amid so many evils, who could find anything worthy to talk about? What do I have to offer compared to the great favors you have given me? But so it is, my beloved Lord, and I don't think my heart can bear it. I don't know how anyone reading this can fail to hate me. Look how poorly I have repaid such wondrous blessings. And in the end, I shamelessly claim the services I have offered you as my own.

Yes, I am ashamed, my Lord. I really am. But since I have so little to say for myself, I elaborate on my lowly beginnings. My hope is that anyone who actually does great things right from the start will take heart from my poor example. It is clear the Lord took my meager efforts into account; surely he will value theirs all the more.

May it please his Majesty that I not get stuck at the beginning forever. Amen.

XXXII ✢

A GLIMPSE OF THE UNDERWORLD

ONE DAY, while I was in prayer, I suddenly found myself plunged into hell. The Lord had long ago begun to grant me exalted states of prayer. I didn't know how I had ended up here. Then I realized that the Lord wanted me to catch a glimpse of where a life of sin leads. The whole experience only lasted for the twinkling of an eye, but it made such an impression on me that I don't think I could ever forget it even if I were to live for many years.

The entrance to hell looked like a long, narrow alley or a low, dark furnace. The floor was covered with filthy mud that emitted a noxious stench. It was swarming with disgusting vermin. There was a small hole, like a cupboard, scooped out of the wall at the end of the alley. I found myself stuffed into it. Compared to what I felt then, what I had been seeing was pleasant. I cannot exaggerate what it was like.

I experienced a fire in my soul that I could never begin to describe. I have suffered grave physical ailments in this lifetime. During that time when I became paralyzed, all my nerves were constricted. Doctors have told me that the excruciating pain I have endured is the worst a human being can bear here on earth. And the devil has also caused me terrible suffering. But nothing compared to what I experienced in hell. The thought that this pain would go on without end and never cease compounded my suffering.

Yet even this paled compared to the anguish of my soul. I was strangled and suffocating. The agonizing despair was so intense that it's impossible to find words strong enough to describe it. It would be inadequate to say that it's as if the soul were being unrelentingly torn from the body. That would make it sound like someone else was stealing the life from the soul. The truth is, the soul herself is tearing herself into pieces.

I simply don't know how to convey the fury of that inward fire and hopeless misery. It far exceeds the most intense pain and torment we could imagine. I felt as though I were being crushed and scorched, yet I couldn't see who was inflicting this on me. But the worst part, as I said, was the inner fire and despair.

I found it impossible either to sit or lie down in the horrific hole. The walls, hideous and cramped, seemed to be closing in on themselves, blotting out everything. There is no light in that place. Everything is enveloped in the densest darkness. Yet everything that is painful to see was fully visible to me. I don't understand how this can be so.

It was not the Lord's will for me to see any more of hell at that time. Since then, I have had other frightening visions that depicted what would happen if I continued to indulge in certain vices. But even though these things seemed more dreadful, they were not accompanied by that racking physical pain, so they did not terrorize me as much. In the vision of hell, the Lord wanted me to experience the spiritual torments and afflictions in a visceral way, as if my body were actually involved. I don't know how such a thing can be true, but I believe the Lord was doing me a big favor by giving me this glimpse of the underworld and letting me see with my own eyes the fate from which his mercy had delivered me.

Reading an account of this is nothing compared to the reality of the experience. Sometimes I have purposely tried to think about certain torments, like demons tearing off my flesh with their pincers or various other forms of torture I've read about. But I don't do well with fearful thoughts. Still, nothing comes close to the excruciating pain I felt in hell. It is altogether different from anything that can be experienced on earth. Being burned alive here in this world is nothing compared to blazing in the fires of that world.

This experience left me terrified. I still feel horror now, almost six years later. As I write about this, a chill creeps into my bones and makes me tremble.

Looking back, I cannot think of a single trial I have experienced in this lifetime that can measure up to that fleeting taste of the underworld.

We have no reason to complain about mundane problems! The Lord did me a big favor when he plunged me into hell. It helped put the tribulations and contradictions of this life into perspective for me. It gave me the strength to suffer these things. It also renewed my gratitude toward God, who liberated me from everlasting torment. Everything else seems easy now.

It astonishes me that even after I had read books that described the horrors of hell, I didn't take them seriously. What was I thinking? How could I possibly have found pleasure in anything that was leading me to that dreadful place? O my God, may you be forever blessed! It is clear to me now that you loved me more than I loved myself. How many times, my Beloved, have you freed me from that dark prison, only to have me defy you by locking myself up all over again?

This is what makes me so sad for all the souls who have fallen into disgrace. I want to help them return. Especially those who have been baptized and are already lovers of Christ. I would willingly suffer a thousand deaths if it meant I could set even one such soul free from such terrible torture. Think about it. Whenever someone we love in a special way suffers here on earth, our very nature moves us to compassion. If their trial is severe, we ourselves suffer. Who, then, could bear to see any soul suffer the never-ending fires of the underworld? No heart could possibly endure this without breaking!

In this world, we know that life is finite and any affliction will eventually be relieved by death, yet we are still moved to deep compassion by the suffering of others. How can we rest knowing that so many souls are facing endless agony in that other world? How can we stand by while the spirit of evil carries away so many souls every day?

This vision also makes me wish that we would all do everything in our power to avoid this outcome for ourselves. Let us neglect nothing. And may it be the Lord's will to give us the grace to serve him in all ways.

It strikes me that no matter how badly I sometimes behaved, my intentions were always good. I cared deeply about being of service to God. I didn't do certain things that I see other people do so carelessly, as if they didn't mean a thing. Plus, I have suffered grave illnesses very patiently. Of course, the Lord himself gave me this patience. I was not inclined to gossip or criticize other people. I never wished anything bad on any-body. And I don't remember ever being so envious that my feelings would be offensive to the Lord. There were several other good things I did. Because even though I was wretched, I was always in awe of God.

Yet in spite of all this, look where the evil spirits took me! And my transgressions probably earned me an even worse fate than the one I glimpsed. The torture was unbearable. It is a dangerous thing to become self-satisfied. It's too easy to fall into grave error with every step. For the love of God, we constantly need to be vigilant about missing the mark.

The Lord will help us. He helped me. May it be God's will never to release me from his hand; we know where I will end up. Being who he is, may he keep me from falling. Amen.

The Lord, in his mercy, showed me this and other secret things. It was his will for me to understand the glory he gives to the good and the pain that the wicked must endure. I was anxious to find out how I could make amends for the bad things I had done and earn back the goodness I may have forfeited.

I had this urge to get away from people and completely withdraw from the world. My spirit was restless, yet it was a delightful kind of dis-quiet and not a disturbing one. It was obvious that this gentle anxiety came from God. His Majesty was heating up my soul so that I could more readily digest the tough meats he was feeding me.

I was thinking about what I could do for God. It occurred to me that one of the first things would be to follow the call to the monastic life his Majesty had given me more authentically and try to honor my vows as perfectly as possible.

There were many servants of God at the Incarnation who were sincere-ly dedicated to him. Nevertheless, to the extent that was appropriate to their religious vocation, sometimes they needed to stay somewhere else for a while. Our community was poor, and the sisters endured constant hardship. Also, our convent did not strictly observe the rules of our order. But then, neither did the rest of the order!

It seemed to me that our monastery was quite comfortable. It was spa-cious and pleasant. I think the ease of life there was a disadvantage. I was just as inclined to leave as anyone. But this was because there were cer-tain nuns our superiors found it impossible to refuse and they liked to have me near them. When the superiors were cajoled into it, they would often order me to go along. Thus, as a result of my vow of obedience, I wasn't home very much. I suspect the spirit of evil had something to do with this. Since I was sharing the things I was learning about the spiritual path with some of my sisters, he was trying to thwart the good that came from this.

One day, I was talking with a small group of women about the lack of spiritual depth at the Incarnation. We expressed our yearning to live and practice prayer like the ancient desert fathers and mothers.

"If we can't go to the desert," Maria said, "why can't we found a little monastery of our own with just a few sisters, where we could live an austere life of prayer together?"

Maria's question echoed my own desires. I began to discuss the idea with doña Guiomar, the widowed lady I have mentioned, because I knew she shared this vision. She immediately set about trying to secure the funds necessary to establish the new house and provide it with a modest income.

I see now that our initial plan did not have much chance of materializing, but our longing made us think it was a viable one. The truth is, I was perfectly content at the Incarnation. All my needs were met, and my cell was just the way I liked it. So I think I was holding back a little from making such a radical move. Still, we agreed to pray about it with deep intention and see what God had in mind for us.

One day after Communion, his Majesty spoke to me. "You must strive with all your might to make this dream of a new monastery come true," he said. "I promise it will not fail to thrive, and it will be of great service to me." He told me we should call it Saint Joseph's. "Saint Joseph will keep watch over one door," he said, "and our Lady at the other. Christ will live among you. This place will be a star that will radiate its light everywhere."

The Lord went on to remind me that even though we were correct to strive for radical simplicity, conventional monasteries were not bad places. They served him too. "What would become of the world," he asked, "if there weren't people willing to detach from material pursuits and assume a life of prayer?"

Finally, he commanded me to tell my confessor what he had ordained.

He said I should make it clear that God did not want Father Baltasar to go against the plan or prevent me from acting on it.

12. This vision had a powerful effect on me. God's voice was so clear that I could not possibly doubt he had really spoken to me. He had partly revealed the severe trials and trouble that founding a new monastery would cause me, and the thought of facing all this caused me intense pain. I was very happy at the Incarnation. Until this vision, I had treated the idea somewhat casually. I had not approached it with the determination and confidence necessary to bring it into being.

I felt as if a heavy burden was being placed on my shoulders. When I realized that my calm life was about to be shattered, I didn't know what to do. But the Lord returned again and again to speak to me about this new monastery. He gave me so many clear reasons and explanations that I could no longer doubt that it was his will for me to carry it through. This gave me the courage to write a letter to my confessor, telling him everything that had happened.

13. Father Baltasar did not dare tell me to forget the whole thing, but he did not consider it feasible. From a strictly rational standpoint, he did not believe it would work, since doña Guiomar, who had offered to support the new house, did not have the practical means for doing so. He told me to speak with the provincial of Castile about the matter.

My companion, doña Guiomar, spoke with the provincial instead. The provincial of Castile was very sympathetic to the contemplative life. He loved the idea and offered her his unconditional support. He said he would be happy to have such a monastery under his jurisdiction. They discussed the income the house would require. For a number of reasons, we decided our monastery would never have more than thirteen residents. Later we ended up lifting the restriction on numbers.

Before we went any further, we consulted the holy friar Pedro de Alcantará. We informed him of everything that was happening. "Do not give up on this," he urged us. He offered his advice on how to found a monastic community.

14. No sooner did word of our plans spread through the city than persecution came raining down on us. It was so intense that I cannot begin to describe it. People spread all kinds of gossip about us. They ridiculed us. They declared the idea absurd. They said I should just leave things as

they were. And they gave my companion such a hard time that it completely wore her down. I didn't know what to do. I couldn't help but wonder if they were right. Weary to my core, I prayed to God. And his Majesty began to console and encourage me.

"Now you can see the suffering the saints who founded religious orders had to endure," he said. "There is much more persecution still to come. You must not let it bother you." And then he told me some things to convey to my companion.

What amazed me most was how his words instilled such deep comfort in us that we found the courage to stand up to all the abuse. There was hardly a person throughout the greater spiritual community who was not hostile to our cause. In fact, the whole city seemed to be against us. Everyone seemed to think the project was completely foolish.

The outcry and negative talk from my own monastery was so excessive that the provincial decided it would be imprudent to oppose them. So he changed his mind and withdrew his support.

"The income is too small," he explained. "And the opposition is too great."

All things considered, he seemed to be right. So our most influential advocate abandoned the project and refused to sanction it. For those of us who had already been the target of violent blows, this was a painful rejection. Especially for me. With the provincial behind me, people had taken me seriously. As for my companion, they threatened that unless she abandoned the idea, they would refuse to give her absolution. They blamed her for creating a "scandal."

Terribly upset by these accusations, doña Guiomar confided in a very learned Dominican, named Pedro Ibañez. Actually, she had been giving him a full account of our plans and soliciting his advice from the beginning, even before the provincial turned his back on us. He was one of the only people who did not dismiss our project as a mere whim.

Doña Guiomar shared all the details with Father Ibañez, including how much income she could expect from her estate. She told him she had nowhere else to turn, and she fervently hoped he would help us. After all, she said, he was the most learned man in all of Ávila.

Then I told Father Ibañez all the things we were thinking of doing and explained the reasons behind them. I avoided mentioning anything about my revelations and relied on the rational arguments for our case. I saw no cause for complicating things with the supernatural source of my impulse.

"I will give you an answer in eight days," he told us. And then he asked, "Are you determined to do whatever I tell you?"

"Yes," said doña Guiomar.

"Yes," I said.

I agreed to this because I knew there was no other way to go forward with the project. But in truth, I never doubted for a moment that the monastery would be founded. My companion had even more faith than I. Nothing anyone said could have dissuaded her from our cause.

I simply found it impossible to consider the notion of giving up. Since the vision did not in any way go against sacred scripture or break any of the religious rules we were compelled to observe, I believed it must be a true revelation. Although I was certain we were dealing with a divinely ordained venture, I'm also certain that I would have obeyed the Dominican if he had come to the conclusion that we would be offending God by following through on our plan. All he would have needed to do was tell me we were doing something that defied the demands of good conscience, and I would have sought some other way to respond to the urgings of my Lord. But my Lord did not offer any alternative.

This great servant of God later admitted to me that he was fully determined when we came to him to insist that we give up the foundation. He had heard too many rumors and was convinced that the project was untenable.

"When a certain important gentleman found out that you had come to me," he went on, "he warned me to be careful of you and advised me to refuse to help you."

But as Father Ibañez began to search his own soul and consider what kind of answer he would give us, he reflected more deeply on the matter and turned his attention to our true motivation. He realized how determined we were to live a deeper spiritual life and saw that our foundation could not help but be of great service to God.

So after the eight days, Father Ibañez said, "Go ahead and found that monastery. And do it quickly!"

He told us how to bring the project to fruition. "Your resources may be limited," he said, "but you have to trust in God for something." Then he said, "If anyone tries to stop you, send them to me. I'll deal with it." And Father Ibañez never did let us down.

His reply was very comforting to us. A number of very pious people who had been in opposition to us revised their attitude because of Father Ibañez's support. Some of them even helped us. Among them was that saintly gentlemen, don Francisco, who changed his mind and decided that the impetus could come from God. His only concern had been one of practicality. He couldn't see how we would pull it off. But he knew that prayer was our entire basis for wanting to found this monastery. Because he was so holy, he recognized that even though it was likely to be terribly difficult, our plan carried the potential for great perfection.

It seems that the Lord himself transformed don Francisco's opinion. And he did the same thing for the learned cleric Gaspar Daza. Father Daza is one of the men I mentioned with whom I had spoken at the beginning. Everyone in Ávila looks up to him. God keeps him there as a positive example to help guide many souls. He, too, stepped up to help me with this endeavor.

Now, with the assistance of many prayers, we had arrived at a crucial junction. We made an offer on a house in a good section of town. It was small, but that didn't trouble me. His Majesty had told me to get started and simply do the best I could. "Soon you will see what I will do for you," he said.

And how well I have seen it! So although I was well aware that we had almost no money, I believed the Lord would help us and arrange other ways for us to thrive.

XXXIII ✠

DIVINE DISOBEDIENCE

THE BUSINESS of founding a new monastery was about to be concluded. The deeds were drawn up and ready to be signed. Suddenly, our father provincial changed his mind again. In retrospect, I see that this was meant to be. Powerful prayers were being offered up for this foundation. The Lord seemed to be using these prayers to perfect the work and bring it about in another way.

Once the provincial refused to sanction the new monastery, my confessor ordered me to let the whole project go. Only the Lord knows the hard labor and suffering it had cost me to bring things to this point. It was the provincial himself who had commanded me to do everything I had done so far. Yet the prevailing opinion seemed to be that this notion of a new monastery was nothing more than the foolishness of women. When the project was so abruptly dropped, it intensified the rampant criticism and gossip about me.

My desire to found a more strictly enclosed house made me very unpopular throughout the Incarnation. They accused me of many things. I was insulting them. I could serve God just as well where I already lived, since there were many women here who were much holier than I. I had no loyalty to my own convent. I should be busy raising funds for my own house rather than founding a new one. Some said I should be thrown into a prison cell. Others tentatively defended me, but not many.

I accepted the possibility that my opponents were right in many respects. Sometimes I tried to explain myself to them. But mostly I remained silent because I could not mention the most important factor:

that the Lord himself had charged me with this task. I didn't know what to do next. So I simply waited for his guidance.

God granted me the grace to be unperturbed by all this. I gave up the plan with ease. I was as content as if the whole thing had cost me nothing. No one could believe this, not even my companions in prayer. They were sure that I must be very upset and ashamed. Even my confessor was puzzled by my calm.

The truth is, I knew that I had done everything I could to fulfill what the Lord had ordained for me to do and that I was under no obligation to do more at this time. So I stayed at the Incarnation and was satisfied there. Still, I never stopped believing that the monastery would eventually happen. I just couldn't see the means or the timing.

What did cause me terrible anguish, however, was a letter my confessor wrote to me. He spoke as if I had opposed his will. I suppose the Lord noticed that I hadn't been tested enough in the area that was the most painful to me, and he sent me this trial. I had always counted on Father Baltasar to comfort me in the midst of persecution. Instead, when I needed him most, here he was scolding me.

"From what has happened, you must realize by now that the whole project was a dream," he wrote. "You should make amends and not speak about this thing or act on it again. You see what a scandal you have caused."

He said many other things, all equally painful for me to hear. This letter distressed me more than everything else put together. Had I really led other souls astray? Had I offended my God? Had these visions of a new monastery been delusions? Had all the prayer I had experienced been nothing more than self-deception? Was I utterly lost? These self-doubts weighed on my heart and plunged me into confusion.

But the Lord did not let me down. He consoled and strengthened me throughout my many trials. There's no reason to enumerate them all here.

"Do not be troubled," he told me. "You have been of great service to me and have not offended me in any way. For now, do what your confessor tells you. Remain silent. The time will come to return to our task."

This message left me deeply comforted. I felt so happy that the criticism being hurled at me seemed like nothing at all.

Through this suffering, the Lord taught me what a blessing it is to endure persecution for his sake. I watched the love of God blossom in my soul to such an extent that I was amazed. It made me desire even more trials. My silence made people think that I was deeply ashamed. And I would have been ashamed if not for the fact that the Lord was showering me with his grace.

The impulses of love for God began to surge more powerfully in my soul, and the raptures grew more intense. Still, I stayed quiet and didn't mention these blessings to anyone. Father Ibañez, the holy Dominican friar, remained as certain as I was that the monastery would come into being. He understood that I didn't wish to go against my confessor by involving myself in any plans, so he conferred instead with my companion, doña Guiomar. They wrote to Rome and started negotiating for the foundation.

Around this time, the spirit of evil began to spread the word from person to person that I had received some kind of revelation about this work. People who cared about me were alarmed. They reminded me that we were living in treacherous times and that I was at risk of being reported to the Inquisition. This amused me and I laughed. I was not afraid of being denounced. I knew myself. And anyone who paid attention would see that I would rather die a thousand deaths than go against a single ritual of the Church or article of faith in holy scripture.

"Don't worry about these accusations," I reassured my companions. "It would be pretty bad for my soul if she harbored something that would make me fear the Inquisition. If I believed I had something to fear, I myself would seek out the Inquisitors and turn myself in. And then, even if they found me guilty, the Lord would free me and I would gain from the experience."

I discussed this with my Dominican father. He knew so much about so many religious matters that I felt fully confident with whatever he told me. I disclosed all the details of the visions and voices. I described the nature of my prayer and the great gifts the Lord had given me.

"Please," I begged him, "consider all this carefully and tell me what you think. Let me know if there is anything in it that is opposed to sacred scripture."

Father Ibañez relieved me of all my concerns, and something about our exchange seemed to benefit him as well. He had always been a good man, but from then on he devoted himself almost exclusively to the inner life. He retired to a secluded monastery of his own order where he could maintain more solitude and engage more deeply in the practice of prayer. He remained in that place for more than two years. But because he was so badly needed by so many souls, obedience called him back into the public sphere, to his grave disappointment.

I missed Father Ibañez terribly when he went away. But even though his leaving was a great loss to me personally, I did nothing to prevent him from going. That's because when I was feeling sad about losing him, the Lord consoled me.

"Do not be troubled," he said. "Father Ibañez is being well guided, and his soul is flourishing in the place where he has gone."

Indeed, Father Ibañez made such dramatic spiritual progress that when he returned, he told me he would not have given up his time there for anything in the world. I couldn't help but affirm the beneficial effects. Before his retreat, he had consoled me through his intellectual knowledge, but now he did so through the things he had learned from spiritual experience. He was beginning to receive an abundance of supernatural blessings. And God brought him back to me at the precise moment when he could be of most help in the work of founding the monastery his Majesty wanted.

Well, I kept quiet for five or six months. I did not speak about the matter to anyone and avoided getting involved in any of the details. The Lord gave me no further guidance about what to do, so I did nothing. I wasn't sure why, but I could not get it out of my head that this foundation was eventually going to happen.

At the end of this period, the director of the local Jesuits was transferred and replaced by a deeply spiritual man named Gaspar de Salazar. Father de Salazar had great courage, profound understanding, and an impressive background in theological studies. He brought all these things into my life during a time when I was in dire need of them. Since my confessor, too, was a member of the Society of Jesus, that made Father de Salazar his superior.

The Jesuits share this extreme characteristic: they do not dare move a muscle unless it conforms to the will of their superior. So although Father Baltasar thoroughly understood my soul and wanted it to grow, he was reluctant to take any action on his own—and for good reason. My spirit was weathering tremendous impulses of love at this time, and although the effort to hold myself back made me feel like I was in jail, I did not disobey his orders.

One day, when I was especially distressed about the fact that my confessor did not believe in me, the Lord spoke to me. "Don't worry," he told me. "Your troubles will be over soon."

I rejoiced deeply, because I thought this meant that I was about to die. It made me happy to think of it. Afterward, it became obvious that these words were referring to the arrival of the new Jesuit director who greatly alleviated my distress. Father de Salazar did not restrain my confessor with regard to my soul but instead told him to console me. He told Father Baltasar that there was no reason to fear and that he should not lead me by such a restrictive path. He insisted that my confessor allow the spirit of the Lord to work in me. Sometimes these spiritual impulses took my breath away.

This new director came to visit me at the Incarnation. My confessor had advised me to feel free to speak to him with perfect candor and directness. Normally, I was repulsed by the prospect of talking about myself. But the moment I entered the confessional, I experienced something that I don't remember having felt with anyone else before or since. I don't know how to describe the experience either literally or metaphorically.

A wave of spiritual joy washed over me. A certainty burgeoned within my soul that his soul would completely understand mine and mine would be in perfect harmony with his. I don't know how such an experience is possible, but that's what happened to me. I had never spoken to the man before and had heard nothing about him in advance. There was no logical reason for my heart to be filled with such hope.

Later I discovered that my spirit had not been deceived. My conversations with Father de Salazar have greatly contributed to the growth of my soul. He works skillfully with people whom the Lord has already brought fairly far along the path. Instead of forcing them to keep walking step by step, he encourages them to run. He does this by getting them to detach in every possible way. The Lord has given him a great gift for this, as well as for many other things.

When I started to converse with Father de Salazar, I quickly understood what kind of person he was and the special way he has of guiding souls in his care. I saw that his own soul was pure and holy and that this gave him a unique talent for discerning spirits. He was very consoling to me.

Not long after I met Father de Salazar, the Lord once again began to urge me to take up the monastery project. He armed me with plenty of reasonable arguments to present to my confessor and his rector about why they should not stand in my way. Some of these reasons frightened them. Father de Salazar had never doubted that I was being prompted by the spirit of God. His concern was about practical aspects of the plan, which he had considered carefully. Ultimately, neither of these two men dared to prevent me from going through with it.

My confessor gave me permission to throw myself back into this task with all my energy. I felt very much alone and had no income of my own. I entertained no illusions: this project would bring me severe hardship. We agreed that it would be best if we pursued this work in total secrecy. So I prevailed upon my sister Juana to procure a house for us and fix it up as if it were for herself. Juana lived outside the city of Ávila in Alba. We used the money the Lord had pulled together to buy something modest.

How did the Lord provide for us during those early days? It's a long story. I had to be careful not to violate my vow of obedience. I knew if I mentioned anything about our project to my superiors that we would lose everything all over again, only this time it would be worse.

I made arrangements to procure the money, sign the contracts, acquire the house, and furnish it. Looking back, I am amazed that I was able to endure the many trials and problems I suffered during this process. I did some of it completely by myself, although my companion tried to help where she could. But there wasn't much she could do besides lend her name to the transaction and give her approval. All the details fell on my shoulders.

Sometimes I called out to God, "My Lord, why do you command me to do things that seem impossible? If only I were free, even if I am a woman. As it is, I am thwarted on every side. I have no money and no means of raising any. I can't obtain the required papers or anything official. What can I do, Lord?"

Once, when I couldn't pay some workman for a job we desperately needed done, I was feeling particularly helpless. That's when Saint Joseph, my dear father and lord, appeared to me. He revealed that I should hire the men and the resources would not be lacking. So I did. I didn't have a penny at the time, but my brother Lorenzo, who was living in Ecuador, sent me some money just when we needed it.

The house seemed too small to me. I didn't see how we were going to turn it into a convent. I wanted to buy the house next door, which was also very small, and make it our church. Of course, I had no money for this. So I wondered what to do.

One day after Communion, Christ spoke to me, "I have already told you, move ahead as best you can." Then to emphasize his message, he said, "Oh, the greed of humanity! You think there will not be enough room for you on this vast earth! How many times did I sleep out in the open because there was no other place for me to lay my head?"

His voice brought me to my senses, and I realized he was right. I went to the little house, really looked at it, and drew up the plans. I saw that even though it was small, it was perfect for a convent. So I gave up the idea of buying more property. Instead, I arranged to have the place fixed up so that it was livable. It was rough and simple, but it was adequate for a healthy lifestyle. Things should always be approached with an open mind.

On the feast day of Saint Clare, I was on my way to Communion, and the saint appeared to me in all her dazzling beauty. "Have courage," she said. "Continue what you have begun. I will help you."

A profound devotion to Saint Clare blossomed in my heart that day. What she told me has since come to pass. A nearby convent of Poor Clares helps to sustain us even to this day. Not only that, but this blessed saint has contributed to refining and perfecting my desires to such a degree that we now practice in our house the same rule of poverty observed in their order. We are living on alms.

This has not been easy. Living simply is not the hard part; it's convincing the Holy Father to back up our vow of poverty with his authority so that no one can change it or force us to collect revenue. But the Lord is doing this and even greater things for us now, thanks in part, I am certain, to the intervention of this sweet saint. For his Majesty provides everything we need without our even having to ask. May he be forever blessed. Amen.

Around that same time, I was celebrating the Feast of the Assumption of Our Lady at the Dominican monastery of Saint Thomas here in Ávila. I was sitting in the Christ Chapel, reflecting on all the sins of my past that I had confessed in this same church and thinking about how wicked I have been for most of my life. All of a sudden, I was seized by a rapture so intense that it nearly lifted me out of myself. I sat down. As I recall, I could no longer see the altar or hear the Mass. Later I felt a little ashamed of this.

I seemed to see myself cloaked in a great white robe of shimmering light. At first I couldn't see who was dressing me in this radiance. Later I saw our Lady on my right side and my father, Saint Joseph, on my left. They were putting this robe on me. In that moment I understood that they were cleansing me of my transgressions.

After they had finished clothing me in this way, I felt the most marvelous joy and glory. Then our Lady took my hands in hers. "You make me very happy by serving Saint Joseph," she said. "Please believe that what you are striving for will come to be. This new monastery will be of great service to our Lord Jesus Christ, to Saint Joseph, and to me."

Then the Blessed Mother told me that even if obedience was painful to me at this time, I had nothing to fear, for the three of them were watching over me. "Hasn't my son already promised you he would be with you?" she reminded me. "As a symbol of this truth," she said, "I give you this jewel."

Then she seemed to slip an exquisite gold necklace over my head. A very valuable cross dangled from the chain. This gold is incomparably more precious than any gold that can be found on this earth, and the stones far exceed the worth of any gems that have ever been seen. Their beauty is completely different than anything we can imagine here.

As for the robe, the intellect could never grasp its nature. The imagination cannot conceive of its whiteness. Any attempts to compare it to anything here on earth would amount to nothing more than a sketch made with ashes.

Even though I could not make out many details, I could see that the beauty of our Lady was extraordinary. I was able to perceive the general form of her face and the amazing splendor of her garment. It was not a blinding white but rather a soft luminosity. I did not see the glorious Saint Joseph as clearly, although I knew he was definitely there, as in those visions I told you about where one sees without seeing.

Our Lady appeared to me as a very young girl. They stayed with me for a little while, and I basked in a state of grace. I had never experienced any joy quite like it and wanted it to last forever. But then it seemed to me that I saw them ascend to heaven with a vast multitude of angels.

Their departure left me feeling profoundly alone. At the same time, however, I was so comforted and uplifted that I entered a state of deep recollection in prayer and was unable to stir or speak. I was beside myself, overcome by a passionate yearning to melt into God. No matter how hard I tried, I could not doubt that this vision came from the spirit of God. Among its many glorious effects, it left me deeply consoled and in great peace.

It had been troubling me to withhold my allegiance from my order, but the Lord had told me when it was not appropriate to obey my superiors. This is what the Queen of Angels meant when she mentioned obedience. Christ had given me clear reasons why it would not be suitable to obey my superiors in the matter of the new monastery. But he gave me a particular way to petition Rome directly and assured me that he would take care of the results.

And so it came to be. I made the petition to the bishop, don Álvaro de Mendoza exactly the way the Lord had taught me, and it was granted with ease. Until that time, we had been entirely unsuccessful in obtaining permission through our own efforts! It turned out to be very fortunate that we had obeyed the bishop. But at the time I was not acquainted with the man and had no idea what he was like.

As it is, don Álvaro was a wonderful person. It was the Lord's will for this bishop to be very supportive of our foundation. This was important, since we were faced with such violent opposition to our cause. He helped bring our house to its current state.

May the One who really does everything be blessed. Amen.

SECRET PREPARATIONS

NO MATTER how much I tried to keep this work secret, there were always people who managed to uncover something. Some believed what they heard; some did not. I was very worried that someone would inform the provincial about what we were up to when he next came to town. That would have been the death of the whole project. But the Lord circumvented this danger in an unexpected way.

It turns out that a grieving widow who lived in Toledo, more than sixty miles away from Ávila, had called for me. Doña Luisa de Cerda was of high nobility. The death of her husband nearly a year earlier had plunged her into a state of inconsolable sorrow from which she could not seem to recover. Her grief had reached such an extreme degree that her loved ones feared for her life.

Somehow doña Luisa had heard of this miserable little sinner and had taken it into her head that I would be able to help her cope with her loss. The Lord had arranged things so that she heard only good reports of me. As it turns out, many blessings flowed from that favorable beginning.

Doña Luisa was well acquainted with the provincial. She knew that I lived in a convent where the nuns were allowed to come and go. Her urge to see me was so powerful that she found it irresistible. And since she was a person of the aristocracy, she knew she could arrange to bring me to Toledo. So she wrote to the provincial, who was far away, to initiate the process. On Christmas Eve, I received an order from him. "Go immediately," he wrote, "and take a companion with you." Because I was under a vow of obedience, I had no choice but to do as I was told.

The only thing that bothered me was that this woman was under the illusion that there was something good about me. Knowing the truth about myself, I could not bear this thought. I prayed earnestly to God about it, and my prayer triggered a deep rapture that lasted throughout matins.

"Go," the Lord said to me. "Pay no attention to all the opinions on the matter. Very few people have wise counsel to offer." He told me that even though this journey would not be without trials, God would be well served by it. He said that it was appropriate for me not to be home when the contract for the new monastery arrived. The spirit of evil was preparing a cunning plot for the provincial's homecoming.

"Do not fear," the Lord said to me. "I will help you with this."

These words very much strengthened and comforted me. I told the Jesuit director about it. "Then do not hesitate to go," he said.

Other people were insisting that I not go to Toledo. They advised me to ignore the provincial's letter. They warned that this whole trip was a ploy of the devil and that something terrible was going to happen if I left. They urged me to write back to the provincial and inform him that I wasn't going.

But it was Father Ibañez I listened to. Strengthened by what I heard in prayer, I went without fear. I continued to feel embarrassed about why they had called me to Toledo, however, since I knew they were mistaken about what I had to offer. All I could do was beg the Lord to be with me. It made me feel better to learn that there was a Jesuit house founded by Father Francisco de Borja there, and that I could rely on the priests to guide me away from home.

It was the Lord's will for doña Luisa to improve dramatically within a short time of my arrival. For some reason, my presence consoled her. She seemed to be more at peace every day. Her grief had been such a heavy burden that this improvement was a great relief to her. I'm sure it helped that there were a lot of pious people praying for my success in this matter.

Doña Luisa was a deeply spiritual person who was in awe of God. Her goodness and her love of Christ seemed to compensate for my shortcomings. She developed a great affection for me. When I saw how much integrity the woman had, I became very fond of her in return.

But everything else was a cross for me to bear. The comforts I was given were nothing but a torment, and the way they all fussed over me made me nervous. My soul had such misgivings about all the luxury and kindness that I grew hypervigilant. But I did not need to be so watchful, since it turned out that the Lord himself was watching over me.

While I was in that house, God granted me the most sublime blessings in prayer. They released me of any attachments to material things and gave me contempt for the opulence I saw all around me. The greater the favors, the more I despised these things. Although I knew it was an honor to serve such great ladies, I never treated them as anything other than equals. That's how free God made me feel.

I had an important insight there, and I shared it with doña Luisa. I realized we should not envy the nobility, because noblewomen are human and therefore just as much subject to passions and weaknesses as the rest of us, only they are expected not to succumb. The higher their status, the greater their trials. I observed how careful these women had to be to maintain their composure under all circumstances. It was as if their station did not allow them to live!

I saw that the ladies were forced to eat in accordance with prescribed timetables and not in harmony with their physical constitution. And the foods they ate had more to do with their rank than with their actual appetite. Why would I ever want to be a lady of nobility? God deliver me from phony composure.

The truth is, I have met few women as humble and as deeply simple as doña Luisa, who happens to be one of the most noble in the kingdom. Whenever I saw how she was forced to go against her own inclinations to fulfill the duties of her state, I felt deep compassion for her. Her servants were no help. She had some good ones, but most of them could not be trusted. God forbid that you spoke to one more than another! Everyone else started to hate the one you favored. Aristocracy is nothing but subjugation. It is a lie to call these people "master" when they are slaves to a thousand things.

It was the Lord's will for the people who lived in that house to be of greater service to God when I was around. Of course, the love the lady bore me caused some envy and brought me some trials. There were people who seemed to think I was vying for some personal advantage. I suppose the Lord challenged me in this way, as well as in other ways, to keep me from becoming enchanted by all the luxury I experienced there. To my soul's great profit, he chose to extricate me from all this.

While I was in Toledo, a very noble person showed up in that city. He was a priest, and we had been in touch many times over the years. I was attending Mass at a monastery of his order near the house where I was staying when I caught sight of him. I had this overwhelming urge to speak to him. I wanted to know the condition of his soul, since I longed for this man to be a great servant of God.

So I got up to talk to him. But since I was in a deep state of recollection in prayer, this impulse suddenly struck me as a waste of time, so I sat down again. Who was I to meddle in his interior life? I think I went through these motions three times: rising, returning to my pew, standing again, sitting back down. Finally, the good angel won out over the bad. I went to him and asked him to meet me in the confessional.

It had been many years since we had seen each other, and we began to ask each other questions about our lives. I mentioned that there had been innumerable trials that had plagued my soul.

"Tell me about them," he urged me.

"No one is supposed to know about these things," I said. "I probably shouldn't have brought it up in the first place."

"Don't worry," he said. "Pedro Ibañez, the Dominican father you mentioned, is a good friend of mine. I will get the story from him."

But the truth is, this priest could not resist the temptation to keep pressing me for details, and I could not resist sharing them. I didn't feel any of the characteristic shame and terror I usually experienced when I spoke of these things. Rather than suffering distress, I felt unburdened.

I discussed these matters within the privacy of the confessional. I had always believed that this priest had a very good mind, but now he seemed wiser than ever. I recognized the special talents and gifts he had and saw the good he could do if he gave himself entirely to God.

I have had this experience many times over the years: whenever I like someone very much, I am filled with nearly unbearable longings. I want to see this person utterly surrender to God. While I want everyone to serve God, my yearning is especially acute when it comes to the people who please me most. Thus, I fervently beseech the Lord on their behalf.

This is what happened to me when I met with the priest I am speaking about.

He asked me to pray wholeheartedly to God on his behalf. But he didn't need to ask. I was already so filled with prayers for him that I could not have done otherwise. I went to my usual place for solitary contemplation and became instantly and profoundly recollected. I began to talk to the Lord in that silly way of mine. I don't know what I'm saying when this happens. It's love that's talking. My soul becomes so transported that I can no longer tell any difference between her and God.

Love knows that it already possesses the Beloved. It forgets all about the individual soul and thinks she is one with him. Free of all distinctions, she speaks pure nonsense. I remember that day when I tearfully begged God to take the soul of that priest into his committed service. I already considered him a good man, but this wasn't enough for me. I wanted him to be even better.

"Lord, you must not refuse me this favor," I said to his Majesty. "I have a feeling it is going to be very important to have this good man as our friend."

Oh, the great goodness and loving-kindness of God! You do not look at our words but at the desires and the will that animates them. How do you put up with someone like me who speaks so boldly to your Majesty? May you be blessed forever and ever!

I recall that at one point during that night of fervent prayer, a great sadness washed over me. I started wondering if I had alienated myself from God. How could I tell if I was in a state of grace or not? It wasn't that I wanted to know. It's just that I wanted to die. Only in death would I find myself in a life where I wouldn't wonder whether or not I was dead, since there was no death more terrifying to me than not knowing if I had forsaken my Beloved.

The pain of wondering overwhelmed me. I was overflowing with tears. Dissolving in tears. "Please, God," I beseeched him. "Do not let me be separate from your grace."

Then it struck me that the sure sign that I was in grace was the boundless love for him that filled and spilled from my soul. This consoled me immeasurably. Look at all the divine favors and holy feelings he had given me in the past few years. Could such blessings coexist in harmony with a soul in mortal sin? Of course not!

I rested in the confidence that his Majesty would do what I asked him to do for the priest. Then the Lord gave me some words to tell the man. I hate it when God does this. I don't know how to convey these things. It embarrasses me to deliver messages from the Lord to a third party. Especially in this case. I didn't know how this priest would take it. Maybe he would make fun of me. I became very distressed about it. But God was so persuasive that I finally agreed to tell the man what God said. To mitigate my shame, I wrote it down and gave it to him in a letter.

Well, the words definitely seemed to come from God, because they had an amazing effect on this man. He resolved to dedicate himself wholeheartedly to the practice of prayer, even though it took him a while to follow through on this intention. The Lord used me as a conduit to transmit some truths to this man because he wanted his soul for his own. Without my even knowing it, these things were so relevant that it astonished him. The synchronicity convinced him that the messages indeed came from God.

Wretch though I may be, I earnestly implored God to transform this man completely in himself and make him reject the shallow gratification and petty things of this world. It worked. May God be praised forever! The priest turned so completely toward God that every time he opens his mouth to speak to me now, I am in awe. If I had not witnessed this myself, I would have trouble believing that God would have granted any soul so many and such powerful favors in such a short time. He is so full of God that he seems to be empty of any worldly attachment whatsoever.

May his Majesty protect him. This man seems to be so well grounded in self-knowledge that if he continues to advance at this rate, he will become one of God's most cherished servants and lead a multitude of souls to the way of perfection.

This man has gained a great deal of spiritual experience in a very short time. These are gifts God gives when and how he wills. They do not depend on time, and they are not compensation for services rendered. It's not that time and services are unimportant. It's just that sometimes the Lord gives the grace of contemplation to one person within a year of starting out on the path and does not give it to another person who might have been practicing prayer for twenty years. His Majesty knows the reason why.

Here's where we make our big mistake. We think that years of study should yield an understanding that can only come through direct experience. Many guides are mistaken in believing that they can discern spirits without having spiritual experience themselves. I'm not saying that someone who has not had spiritual experience should refuse to direct a soul who has, as long as the director is at least a man of learning. But he should limit himself to making sure that when he is dealing with both interior and exterior matters, he is following the natural path of reason. When it comes to supernatural experiences, all he needs to do is check to see if they are congruent with sacred scripture.

As for the rest, he shouldn't kill himself trying to figure it all out. He should never presume that he understands it either. Above all, he must not repress the spirit. The soul is being guided by another greater Master, and he has no authority in that case.

O you spiritual directors, do not be surprised by this. Don't think that such things are impossible. All things are possible for the Lord. Your only task is to humble yourselves and bolster your faith. So what if the Lord gives some little old woman deeper knowledge of this sacred science than he gives to a very learned man? Continuously cultivating humility will make that man much more useful both to other souls and to himself than trying to be a contemplative if he is not one.

I'll say it again: if he has neither direct spiritual experience nor the humility to admit that he does not understand the experience of the soul he is guiding, he will be of little benefit to himself and even less to the people he's dealing with. Just because he doesn't understand something doesn't mean that the thing is impossible! If the guide is humble, he should not fear that the Lord would allow either of them to be deceived.

The Lord made this Dominican friar very humble in a number of different areas. He has dedicated himself to finding out everything he can about the things he has not experienced. He is a great scholar, so if he doesn't know something, he investigates and finds someone who does. The Lord supports him by giving him a deep faith. He has grown immensely in this way and has been a big help to other souls, including mine.

As it was, his Majesty was about to call home to himself a couple of great men who had been guiding my soul: Pedro of Alcantará and Pedro Ibañez. But he replaced them with other guides to help me through some very difficult times, and they did me a great deal of good, like the priest I am telling you about.

God has transformed this man almost completely. He hardly recognizes himself. Where he used to be weak and sickly, the Lord has given him the strength to undergo rigorous penances. He has the courage to do things he never dared try before. He seems to have received a very special calling from God. May he be forever blessed.

I believe all these benefits have come to him through the blessings he has been receiving in prayer. Such goodness cannot be counterfeited. The Lord has already challenged him in certain areas, and he has emerged from these trials like an adept who knows the blessings that come through persecution. I hope that great good will come through him to members of his order and to the whole of the order itself.

Actually, people are already beginning to realize who this priest is. I have seen great visions and the Lord has told me some very important things about this man, as well as about the Jesuit director of whom I have spoken and two Dominicans. God has already revealed some great things about one of these Dominicans in particular; before that, I was the only one who knew about the dramatic spiritual progress he had been making. But the one God has told me most about is this priest of whom I've been speaking.

Now I want to tell you about something. One day I was sitting with this man in the parlor. My soul became aware of such a powerful love of God burning inside his spirit that it almost transported me beyond myself. Simply reflecting on the glory of God, who had elevated that soul to such a high state in such a short time, was enough to send me into rapture.

But it also embarrassed me. There he was, listening with such humility to the things I had to say about prayer. Who was I to be speaking of such things to a person like this? I guess the Lord put up with it because of the passion I had to see this soul make ultimate spiritual progress. Being with him did my soul so much good that it seemed to revive the flames of my own longing to serve the Lord.

O my Jesus! How much a soul can accomplish when she is on fire with your love. How highly we should value such a soul and how fervently we should pray to God to let this soul remain with us here on earth. Anyone who shares this love-longing should follow such souls wherever they go.

Isn't it a wonderful thing when a sick person encounters someone afflicted with the same malady? How comforting it is to know that you are not alone. The two wounded souls become a powerful help to one another. They inspire each other to risk a thousand lifetimes for God. In fact, they welcome the opportunity to die and die again for him. They are like warriors willing to go into battle because they know they will come away with great treasure. They cannot become rich unless they fight. It is their supreme duty to labor and suffer and triumph.

Oh, what a marvelous thing it is when the Lord sheds his light on the mind so that we realize how much we gain when we suffer for him. Until we abandon everything for him, we will not understand this. Clinging to something is a sign that we are attached to it. If we are attached, it causes us grief to give it up. This clinging only leads us astray.

Remember the saying "He who goes after what is lost gets lost himself"? That fits perfectly here. What greater spiritual ruin is there, what greater blindness, what greater misfortune can there be than to cherish something that is nothing?

Well, to get back to what I was saying. As I sat contemplating that soul, I was filled with deep joy. It seems that the Lord wanted me to see clearly the treasures he had placed there. When I realized the favor he had granted me by making me the instrument of this spiritual blossoming, I knew I didn't deserve it. But I valued the blessings the Lord had given to this soul more than if he had given them to me. In fact, I considered them to be more my own than those that were actually mine. I praised his Majesty for hearing my prayer and fulfilling my great desire that he awaken souls like this.

And then my soul reached its full capacity for joy and went out of itself. Lost in this way, I had all the more to gain. All reflections evaporated, and I forgot them. Now the Holy Spirit was doing the talking. Hearing that divine language, my rapture deepened. It only lasted a short time, but it almost made me lose my senses. Then I saw Christ.

Radiating awesome power and glory, he expressed his pleasure over what was happening.

"You see?" he said. "I am always present in conversations like these." He wanted me to understand the great delight it gives him when people find their great delight in speaking of him.

Another time, when this priest was far away, I saw him lifted up by the angels in great glory. This vision taught me that his soul was making excellent progress. Soon after this, someone spread cruel slander against the priest's honor. He had provided a remedy for his accuser's soul at a time when the man's own reputation was at stake. The priest cheerfully endured this betrayal. He performed other acts and suffered other persecutions that were of great service to God.

I don't think it makes sense for me to say anything more about this now. You know all the details yourself. If you think it is appropriate, you can write them down later for the glory of God. By the way, everything I said about the prophecies concerning this monastery, as well as other prophetic visions I'll tell you about later, were fulfilled. Some of them came to pass three years after they were revealed. Others took more time, still others less.

I always shared these prophecies with my confessor and with doña Guiomar, in whom I had permission to confide. I know that she told them to other people, so I have proof that I am not lying. May God never permit me to speak anything but the whole truth on any subject, especially in such a serious matter as this.

Around this time, a brother-in-law of mine died suddenly. I was deeply grieved because he hadn't gotten a chance to go to confession before he died. Then I was told in prayer that my sister, too, would die this way, and I should go to her immediately so that she could prepare herself. When I told my confessor about it, he didn't let me go. So the message kept coming to me from God. When my confessor heard about this, he told me to go there, since he couldn't see that any harm would come of it.

Maria lived in that little village where I had stayed during my illness so many years ago. Without mentioning the spiritual voices, I enlightened her as much as I could on every relevant subject. I got her to tend her soul with the greatest care and to confess frequently. Maria was a good person, and she did all this willingly. She was conscientious, and these customs soon became ingrained in her.

Four or five years later, my sister also died alone without the opportunity to cleanse her soul formally. Fortunately, since she had developed the habit of confessing her transgressions, she had taken care of her soul in this way only a week before she died. It brought me great joy to hear news of her death. She did not linger in purgatory. Within a week, the Lord appeared to me after I had received Communion. He wanted to show me how he had brought Maria to glory.

In all those years, from the time the Lord predicted my sister's death until the day she died, I never forgot what he had revealed to me. Neither did my companion. When Maria died, doña Guiomar came to me amazed about how the revelation had been fulfilled.

May God be praised forever! He takes such good care of souls so that they won't get lost.

XXXV ✠

HOLY POVERTY

WELL, I STAYED with doña Luisa for more than six months. While I was there, a lay sister of our order found out about me and decided to come and meet me. She lived two hundred miles away and went substantially out of her way to speak to me. It turns out that God had inspired this woman to found a radically simplified convent during the same month of the same year he had first spoken to me about it! As soon as his Majesty gave her the summons, she sold everything she had and walked barefoot to Rome to obtain the required documents.

Sister Maria de Jesús is a woman who practices rigorous austerities and deep prayer. Our Lord has granted her many favors. Our Lady appeared to her and commanded her to perform this task. Sister Maria was so far ahead of me in serving God that I was ashamed to sit in her presence. She showed me the letters of endorsement she had brought from Rome. During the fifteen days she stayed with me, we planned out the details of the monasteries.

Until Sister Maria brought it to my attention, I didn't realize that our order had drifted away from the Primitive Rule. We were originally never meant to own anything. Although I longed for the simplicity reflected in that ideal, it had not occurred to me to found a monastery without any money. My goal was that the sisters not be distracted by worrying that our needs would be met. I hadn't taken into consideration the serious distraction it can be to own property.

This blessed woman did not even know how to read and yet she understood very well what I, who had read our constitutions many times, did not. This is because the Lord himself taught her what is important.

What she told me made a great deal of sense to me, although I was not at all confident that our superiors would agree to it. I was afraid they would say that not only were we, the founders, being foolish, but that we would make others suffer.

If I had been alone, I wouldn't have hesitated for a moment to embrace poverty. It would have brought me great joy to follow the advice of our Lord Jesus Christ, who advocated living simply and had already given me a profound desire for poverty. I did not doubt that this was the best path for me personally. I had been wishing for a long time that I could give up my house and all my things and go begging for love of God.

But I was afraid that if the Lord did not give this desire to others, they would indeed be miserable under such circumstances. I had also observed that in certain poor monasteries, scarcity of resources became the primary focus and people were not becoming recollected in prayer. I failed to realize as I reflected on this that their absence of recollection was not an artifact of their poverty, but the other way around: a lack of prayer impoverished them. Distraction does not make us rich, and God never fails anyone who serves him. My faith was weak compared to the clear convictions of this holy sister, Maria.

Of all the men I had consulted, I found no one who really thought the path of poverty was a good idea. They leveled so many arguments against the notion that I didn't know what to do. Now that I knew it was a sanctioned element of the Carmelite tradition, I believed more than ever that observing poverty as a community would be a more perfect practice. I couldn't persuade myself to arrange for an income.

Every once in a while, they managed to convince me of their position, but the moment I returned to prayer, I came back to my senses. All I had to do was contemplate Christ on the cross, so poor and so naked, and I could not patiently bear the idea of being rich. Tearfully, I begged him to ordain things so that I could be poor like him.

It became so clear to me that having an income would be a serious impediment to our cause that all I did was argue with learned men. I strongly felt that possession of revenue would create nothing but disquiet and distraction. I wrote to Father Ibañez, the Dominican who was helping us. He sent back a two-page letter enumerating his objections—

on both sides of the paper—and giving me complex theological reasons why I shouldn't do it.

"I have studied the matter very carefully," he told me.

I answered that I wasn't interested in theology if it didn't support my vocation. I had taken a vow of poverty. I had a calling, and I intended to follow the counsels of Christ. In this case, he was doing me no favors with all his learning.

It made me very happy whenever I found anyone who was willing to help me. Doña Luisa, for instance, was very supportive. There were people who would tell me they thought it was a good idea at first and then change their minds. They claimed that when they reflected on it, they saw too many disadvantages, and they reverted to trying to talk me out of it.

"Since you are so quick to alter your opinion," I responded, "I think I'll just stick with your original one."

My hostess had never met the holy man, Pedro de Alcantará, so I took it upon myself to make arrangements for him to visit to her house while I was there. Father Pedro knew the treasures that lay at the heart of poverty. He was a great lover of this practice and had observed it for many years, so he was a big help to me.

"You must not fail by any means to go through with your plan," he insisted.

I valued his opinion above all others, since he had lived our ideal through vast experience. I made up my mind not to go seeking any more points of view on the matter; his was sufficient.

One day, while I was praying intensely to God about this, the Lord spoke to me. "Don't let anything stop you from founding this monastery in poverty," he said. "This is not only my will, but the will of our Father. I will help you." This encounter with Christ was accompanied by such deep rapture and so many other remarkable effects that I could not doubt that the impulse came from God.

On another day, he told me that money disquiets the mind. He said other things in praise of poverty and assured me that whoever observes this holy practice will not lack what she needs to live. As I said, I never feared deprivation for myself.

Eventually the Lord changed the mind of the Dominican who had been advising me, the one who had written to me with all the reasons why I must not found a monastery without income. I was thrilled to hear this. Various other opinions in my favor began to come in. It seems to me that I was being rewarded for my determination to live by the love of God. My heart was so filled; I felt that I truly possessed all the riches in the world.

Around this time, there was a pending election at the Incarnation. My provincial lifted my vow of obedience to stay with the noblewoman in Toledo and let me decide whether to return to Ávila or remain with doña Luisa for a while. Someone sent word that many of the sisters were recommending that I be chosen as their prioress. The mere thought of such a thing was a terrible torment to me. Yes, I was determined to suffer any martyrdom for my Beloved, but please, not this one!

It's not only that it would be a tremendous amount of work to be the superior of a convent with 150 nuns, but there were other reasons I resisted the idea of holding a formal office. For one thing, I thought that being a superior would not be healthy for my conscience. I praised God that I was away. I wrote to my friends in Ávila and told them not to vote for me.

When I was feeling most satisfied that I was not there in the midst of all the turmoil, God spoke to me. "You must go home," he said. "You have professed a desire to carry the cross. A perfectly good one is waiting for you back in Ávila. Do not reject it. Go with courage. Go right away. I will help you."

I became very upset, and I couldn't stop weeping. I thought the cross meant that I was about to be elected superior. I knew that holding such a station would not be good for my soul. I didn't think I was qualified for the job either.

I talked to my confessor about all this, and he told me I should try to get back to Ávila. "It would be the most perfect thing to do," he said. "But it's very hot right now for traveling. Why don't you wait a few days so that you don't get sick? You'll still get there in time for the election." But it turned out that the Lord had something else in mind.

I was extremely restless inside. I couldn't practice prayer. I was afraid that I was forsaking my Lord's command to me. Here I was in this luxurious place, taking advantage of its comforts, when there was real work to be done at home. Was I only good for lip service? I had to ask myself, if Ávila was the more perfect place for me to be, why was I hesitating to go there? If I was going to die, then I would die.

Along with this inner turmoil, a heavy oppression fell over my soul. The Lord dried up all the gratification I had grown to expect in prayer. My spiritual condition worsened to such a degree that I finally asked the lady if she would be good enough to let me go home. When my confessor saw me in this state, he concurred that this would be a good idea. God moved him as he moved me.

Doña Luisa was so reluctant to see me go that her sorrow became another torment for me. It had not been easy for her to bring me there in the first place. She had gone through a great deal of trouble to get permission from the provincial to have me stay with her, and it was just as difficult for her to let me leave. She was terribly sad. But she also loved God, and I told her that my departure might enable me to render greater service to the Beloved. I also told her that I might be able to come back and see her again. With brave resignation, she released me.

I was no longer sorry to go. I realized that I could be of more perfect service to God in this way, even if only through my joy, since it made me so happy to serve him. This gave me the strength to endure the regret in leaving that lady who seemed to feel the pain of separation so acutely. It was also hard to leave other people there in Toledo to whom I owed a debt of gratitude, especially my Jesuit confessor, who had become a true friend.

The more aware I became that my suffering was for the sake of God, the more easily I embraced it. I didn't understand how it was possible that losing my consolation made me so happy. Why would I be happy and pleased and consoled about something that weighed so heavily on my heart? Weren't these two feelings mutually exclusive?

I had been very content in doña Luisa's house. I had time for long hours of contemplative prayer there. I knew that I was about to plunge into the fire back in Ávila. The Lord had already told me that I was going to have to bear a great cross. That cross turned out to be far greater than I had ever imagined. Still, I was happy to move on. Since the Lord had wanted me to go, I felt badly about delaying the battle as long as I had. So his Majesty sent his strength to bolster my weakness.

I thought more about the seemingly contradictory feelings that filled my soul and came up with an analogy. Say that I owned a jewel or some other treasure that gave me great happiness. Then I found out that someone I love and want to please more than I want to please myself desired that object. If giving that thing to the person I loved made him happy, then my happiness in living without it would far exceed the pleasure I derived from owning it. Because the happiness I experienced in pleasing my beloved would surpass my original happiness, it would cancel out any pain I might have felt in sacrificing the cherished object.

I wanted to feel upset about leaving the people I had grown so close to. I hated the idea of being separated from them. I am, by nature, a grateful person. Ordinarily it would cause me terrible distress to walk away from a place where the people had been so good to me. Yet now, even though I wished I could feel those qualms, I couldn't.

The business of this holy house was so important that I don't know how I would have pulled it off if I had delayed a minute longer. Oh, how great God is! I am perpetually amazed when I reflect on all the specific ways his Majesty wanted to help me found this little dwelling place of the Divine. That's what I think it is: an abode in which his Majesty takes great delight. Once, when I was in prayer, he said to me, "This house is a paradise of glory for me."

It seems as if his Majesty has selected the souls he wants to live in this monastery. I am humbled just to be in their presence. I would never have known how to ask for such companions, so prayerful and so pure, so dedicated to silence and simplicity. They bear their poverty so joyfully and with such genuine gratitude that not one of them can believe she deserves to be in this house.

The Lord called some of them out of a world of pomp and vanity where it would have been so easy for them to conform to the laws of the world and be perfectly satisfied. But the Lord has doubled their delight by bringing them here. They clearly see that for every pleasure they left behind, he has given them a hundred joys. They cannot thank him enough.

Many were already good, and God made them better. To the young, he gives fortitude and knowledge. He helps them see that detaching from all their worldly desires gives them a life of deep calm and helps them maintain equanimity in earthly affairs. To the elderly, he gives vitality and strength. He helps them bear the same austerities and penances as the rest.

O my Beloved! Your power is boundless! We have no need to find reasons to justify your will. You transcend all natural reason and make all things possible. Over and over, you show us that all we have to do is love you and leave all the rest up to you. That's when you make everything easy, my Beloved. They say that you pretend to make your law difficult, Lord, but I don't see it that way. They say that the path home to you is narrow, but that's not my experience.

What I see is not a rough trail but a royal road. It is safe for any traveler to take this road—much safer than not taking it. The pitfalls of sin are in the distance. Those are the narrow mountain passes and loose rocks that make us fall. Worldly paths have a deep gorge on one side and a precipice on the other into which the soul can plummet the minute she loses focus and then shatter into a thousand pieces.

He who truly loves you, my Supreme Good, walks securely on a broad and royal road. The abyss is far away. As soon as he begins to stumble, you steady him with your own hand. If he loves you more than he loves this world, then falling down from time to time will not do him any harm. Even falling a lot will not hurt him. He travels through the valley of humility. I cannot understand why people hesitate to set out on the way of perfection.

May the Beloved, being who he is, help us realize how illusory the security of following the crowd really is. The perils of that path are so obvious. May he help us realize that our safety lies in striving to walk on God's road. Let us turn our eyes to him and not be afraid of the setting of the Sun of Justice. If we do not abandon him, he will help us walk safely, even through the darkest night. We will not go astray.

What the world calls honors and pleasures, I call lions. People are not afraid to walk among such wild beasts, any one of which would be more than happy, it seems, to tear off a piece of them. Yet here on this royal road, the spirit of evil makes us afraid of mere field mice.

This misplaced trepidation has amazed me a thousand times. And my own blindness and wickedness has amazed me ten thousand times. I long to cry myself empty. I yearn to shout the true story of my unconsciousness from the rooftops if doing so would wake other souls up. Please, through God's great goodness, open your eyes! And may he never allow mine to close again. Amen.

XXXVI ✠

FOUNDING SAINT JOSEPH'S

AFTER LEAVING Toledo, my spirits lifted, and my journey back to Ávila was pleasant. I was determined to accept God's will in whatever forms it manifested. The same night I reached the city, the documents authorizing the new foundation arrived from Rome. What a coincidence! I was amazed by the timing. So was everyone else involved in this project, for they knew how the Lord had made me return very quickly, and now it was clear why. I was needed here.

The bishop was waiting for me, along with the saintly Pedro de Alcantará and a gentleman with whom the holy friar was staying, who was also a great friend to God. This gentleman regularly gave protection and support to God's servants. The two men convinced the bishop to sanction the new monastery. This was not easy since the poverty issue was such an unpopular one. But anyone who was determined to serve God was dear to this bishop's heart, and we soon won his support.

It was really Father Pedro who made everything happen. The elderly holy friar believed so strongly in this foundation that he went around gently urging all the right people to help us. If it hadn't been for the extraordinary coincidence of my arriving on that very night, I don't think the monastery ever would have been founded. As it turned out, Father Pedro was not going to be with us for much longer. He was very sick at that time, and God brought him to himself eight days later. It seems that his Majesty purposely preserved Father Pedro until this business was taken care of. He had already been dying for almost two years.

We did everything under a veil of secrecy. Otherwise, I don't think we could have pulled it off. So many people were against our project, which became increasingly evident later. Around this time, the Lord ordained that my brother-in-law Juan, who was in Ávila to finish negotiations for the house they had purchased for our new monastery, become ill. Since my sister Juana was not there, it fell on me to take care of him.

With this excuse, I was able to leave the Incarnation and attend to the business of the foundation without anyone suspecting anything. Well, that's not exactly right. Some people were accusing me of hatching a plot, but my superiors did not listen to them. The amazing thing is that my brother-in-law's illness only lasted as long as it took to complete our business with the new foundation. As soon as I needed to be free of my duties as caregiver, Juan got better and moved back to Alba. This also freed up the house he had procured for us. Juan himself was amazed by how the Lord brought all this about.

I had a lot of trouble at different times from different people who opposed the foundation of this new monastery. I also had trouble with my sick brother-in-law. Then there were the workmen. There was so much to do to convert the house into a convent, and it all needed to be done quickly. Plus, my companion, Doña Guiomar, was away at Toro. That was intentional, though; it seemed to us that we would have more luck concealing our activities if she was not there.

For many reasons, I saw that everything needed to be taken care of in a hurry. One reason was that with every passing hour I was away from the Incarnation, I was afraid they were going to demand that I return. There were so many challenges happening at the same time that I couldn't help but wonder if this was the cross to which the Lord had referred. But it all seemed like a light burden compared to the heavy one he had led me to expect.

It was August 24, Saint Bartholomew's Day. Everything was ready. The Blessed Sacrament was in place. The first group of sisters received the habit: Antonia del Espiritu Santo; Maria de la Cruz; Ursula de los Santos; and Maria de San Jose. Thus, with all due authority and power, this monastery of our most glorious father, Saint Joseph, was founded in 1562!

I was present for the receiving of the sacred robes, along with two other sisters from the Incarnation. Remember, my brother-in-law had bought the house we converted into the monastery so that we could keep our project a secret while we were fixing it up. So I had permission to be there. Plus, I had consulted so many learned men along the way that I was confident I had not compromised my vow of obedience one iota.

The men who supported me saw many reasons why this foundation would be beneficial to the whole Carmelite order. They told me to proceed with the plan, although I did everything in secret so that my superiors would not find out. If they had discovered a single real imperfection in anything I was doing, I would have willingly given up founding a thousand monasteries, let alone one. This is beyond question. Even though I was dying to radically withdraw from everything and live simply, focusing exclusively on prayer, what I wanted most was to be of service to God. If I had found out that I could have served him better by not living in strict enclosure, I would have abandoned the entire project with complete peace and calm, as I had done before.

Well, it was like heaven for me to see the most Holy Sacrament reserved in our new monastery and four poor orphans, who happened to be four great servants of God, come together to support each other in following the way of perfection. This is what I had always envisioned: that the people who would join this community would live by their example of prayer and integrity. They would be the foundation on which we could build to attain our goal. All I cared about was that we would work together to achieve what I knew in my heart would be of service to the Lord and would honor the Blessed Mother.

It also made me happy to have followed the directions of my Beloved and dedicated a new church to our glorious father, Saint Joseph. Not that I ever thought I really had anything to do with it. Everything was the work of God. What small part I played, I performed so imperfectly that I found far more cause to blame myself than to congratulate myself. Still, it gave me great delight to see that he would use someone as flawed as I am to be an instrument of his wondrous work. My joy was so intense that it transported me beyond myself and put me into a state of profound prayer.

But then, around three hours later, the spirit of evil paid me a little visit and instigated a spiritual battle within me. "Maybe what you have done is wrong," he said. "Maybe you actually did violate your vow of obedience to make a foundation without your provincial's consent." He hit a nerve here. I was concerned that the provincial might be angry that I hadn't told him what I was doing ahead of time and that I had arranged things so that the bishop would be in charge of us. On the other hand, he was the one who had refused to sanction it, but I had never changed my plans. Why should he care that we went ahead without him?

"Maybe the sisters who live in this house will be unhappy with such rigorous austerity," the spirit of evil went on. "What if they don't get enough to eat? Isn't this venture simply foolish? What business is it of yours, anyway? You already have a convent to live in—and a perfectly good one."

All the commands the Lord had given me, all the good advice I had solicited and received, all the unceasing prayers of the past two years vanished from my memory as if they had never happened. I could only remember my own decisions. My faith and all my other virtues were paralyzed. I had no strength to reactivate my useless virtues or defend myself against these unrelenting blows.

"How can you even think about shutting yourself up in a strictly enclosed monastery when you have so many health problems?" the spirit of evil demanded. "How could you leave such a pleasant and spacious monastery where you have been so content to live where you will have to endure such penance? And what about all your friends at the Incarnation? What if you don't like your new companions? And you have taken on so many obligations. It's a setup for despair."

Maybe the spirit of evil was trying to steal my inner peace and quiet so that I wouldn't be able to concentrate on prayer and would then lose my soul. He mixed up all these thoughts together in my mind so that I was powerless to think of anything else. I cannot possibly exaggerate this state of confusion. It plunged my soul into deep darkness.

Finding myself in this wretched condition, I made my way to the Blessed Sacrament. I was incapable of praying, so I just sat there in my pain. I felt like a person must feel in the death agony. And there was no one I could speak to about it because I had not yet been assigned a spiritual director.

O God, help me! What a hard life this is! There is not a single joy that lasts and nothing that does not change. Only a short time ago, it seemed to me I would not trade my happiness with anyone on earth. Now the very reason for this happiness so thoroughly tormented me that I didn't know what to do with myself. Oh, if only we would consciously observe the events of our lives. We would see what little cause they really give us for either happiness or unhappiness.

I truly think this was one of the most difficult episodes of my life. It was as if my soul were having a premonition of everything I was going to have to endure. Still, none of the trials to come would prove to be as severe as this night of suffering would have been if it had continued unabated. But the Lord did not let his poor servant suffer for very long. He never does. He always gives me comfort in my tribulations. In this case, he cast a little light to help me see that the spirit of evil was causing all the trouble. I realized that the spirit of evil was using lies to try and scare me away.

Once I saw what was going on, I was able to remember my powerful resolution to serve God and my desire to suffer for him. I realized that if I were to act on these lofty intentions, I couldn't go around seeking ways to rest. If trials came my way, I would earn merit by withstanding them. If I experienced unhappiness and offered it up in service to God, it would purify my soul. I had nothing to fear. The greater the opposition, the greater the gain. Why didn't I have the courage to serve the One who had given me so much?

With the help of these reflections, I got myself back under control. I vowed before the Blessed Sacrament to do everything in my power to obtain permission to come live in the monastery I had founded. I promised I would commit myself to a strictly cloistered existence as soon as I could do so in good conscience.

The moment I made this vow, the spirit of evil fled. I instantly felt calm and happy and have remained that way ever since. All the seclusion and austerities that we practice here have turned out to be extremely easy for me. My joy is so complete that I wonder sometimes what else could possibly bring me this much delight. I am starting to think that this life of radical simplicity is also contributing to the general increase in my health.

Maybe the Lord wants to give me this consolation so that I can observe the austerities required of those who live here, since it is necessary and correct for me to do whatever everyone else has to do. Sometimes these things are hard for me, but for the most part, I feel better than I've ever felt in my life. All the people who know about my chronic health problems are amazed by my ability to adhere to these standards. Blessed be the One who gives us all things and by whose power all things can be done.

This conflict with the spirit of evil left me utterly exhausted. But I chuckled to myself to see that it had all been an illusion. This was the first time in my twenty-eight years of being a nun that I had regretted my monastic vocation even for a moment. I think the Lord allowed this conflict to help me see what a favor he had granted me and what torment he had saved me from. Also, now I wouldn't be surprised if someone who was unhappy as a nun were to come to me. Instead, I would have compassion for her and know how to console her.

After the turmoil had passed and we had eaten dinner, I wanted to get some rest. I had hardly slept all night, and I had been working late or else worrying for many other nights. Plus, my days were so filled with work that I was almost always tired. But then my superior sent for me to return to the Incarnation immediately.

Word of what we had done had spread through the city and created a public outcry. This negative reaction seemed to bear considerable weight with the prioress of the Incarnation. As soon as I received her orders, I left my nuns, who were very sad to see me go, and returned to the Incarnation. I could tell that I was going to be confronted with many obstacles, but I wasn't too worried because at least our new monastery was now established.

I prayed to the Lord to protect me. I prayed to my father, Saint Joseph, to bring me home to his house very soon. And I offered up to God whatever suffering I might yet have to endure. I was pretty sure they would throw me in a prison cell the moment I arrived at the Incarnation. I was quite happy about the upcoming opportunity to suffer for my Beloved and to serve him. Actually, I thought it might be pleasant to be incarcerated for a while. I wouldn't have to talk to anyone, and I could get a little solitude for some badly needed rest. I was worn out from having to deal with people so much.

When I gave an account of our activities to the prioress, she was somewhat placated. They resolved to send everything to the provincial and let him decide. When he came, I went willingly to receive whatever judgment he had for me. I was happy to know that I would be suffering something for the sake of my Beloved. I couldn't find it in my heart to believe that I had committed any offense either against his Majesty or against the Carmelite order. On the contrary, I was doing everything in my power to contribute to the positive growth of that order. My desire for our order to fulfill its mission perfectly was so intense that I would have eagerly died for it.

I thought about Christ's trial and saw that my own persecution amounted to nothing at all. I accused myself of being at fault and acted as if I were very much to blame. To anyone who didn't know the reasons, this appeared to be perfectly true. The provincial reprimanded me severely, although not as severely as the transgression deserved, at least according to what so many people had told him. I had no desire to defend myself. I had been determined to do what I did. I simply asked for his forgiveness and invited his punishment.

"Please don't be angry with me," I added.

It was clear to me that some of the things they blamed me for were not my fault. For instance, they said I founded the monastery so that I would become famous and people would revere me, which was far from the case. But in other matters, they were speaking the plain truth, as when they said I was no better than anybody else and, in fact, much worse.

"If you couldn't even observe the monastic rule of your own house," they asked me, "what makes you think you'll be able to keep an even stricter one?"

They accused me of creating a scandal and promoting innovation. None of this bothered me that much, but I acted as if it did. I didn't want to give them the impression that I was not taking what they were telling me to heart. Finally, the provincial ordered me to go explain myself to the nuns, which I did.

I felt a sense of deep inner peace and I knew the Lord was with me. I expressed myself to my sisters in such a way that no one there could find anything for which to condemn me. Afterward, when I was alone with the provincial, I was able to speak more freely with him. He was quite satisfied, and he promised to sanction the new foundation.

"Let's let the commotion in the city die down a little first," he said. "Then if all goes well, I promise to help you."

But the opposition was fierce. After three days of deliberation, some of the city councilmen and the mayor unanimously declared that they could not by any means grant their consent to our new foundation. To do so, they said, would bring significant harm to the greater community. They ordered the immediate removal of the Blessed Sacrament from the house and commanded that all work related to the foundation come to an absolute halt.

Then they convened a meeting between two learned representatives from each religious order so that everyone could voice their opinion on the matter. Some of the representatives condemned the new foundation; others remained silent. The final consensus was that the monastery should be dismantled right away. They were furious.

Only one man, the Dominican Domingo Bañez, spoke up to say that the foundation should not be suppressed, but rather should be more carefully considered. The only thing he objected to was the rule of poverty. He said there was plenty of time to reconsider and that it was really the bishop's business anyway. His words had a calming effect and prevented the group from storming in to shut us down that day.

In the end, the foundation had to continue because the Lord was pleased with it. All those men together couldn't do a thing against God's will. This did not stop them from persecuting me, however. They stated their case with righteous zeal. Without offending God, they managed to make everyone who was associated with the project suffer for it.

The town was in such an uproar that it was all people could talk about. Everyone was condemning me. They were petitioning my monastery and appealing to my provincial. What they were saying about me caused me no more pain than if they hadn't said anything at all. In fact, I think that the negative things people said about me made me very happy. The only thing that concerned me was whether or not they would succeed in having us shut down. Also, even though I didn't care about my own honor, it disturbed me to realize that the reputations of people who were helping me were being damaged.

If I had had a little faith, I don't think I would have felt so conflicted. But a small lack in one of the virtues seems to put them all to sleep. During the two days they were holding those meetings in town, I was deeply troubled. At the height of my distress, the Lord spoke to me.

"Don't you know that I am omnipotent?" he said. "What are you afraid of?" He assured me that the new monastery would not be dissolved.

This was very comforting to me. The assembly sent an official denunciation to the royal council. When the reply came, it simply asked for an account of exactly how the new monastery had been founded. This led to a lawsuit. The city of Ávila sent its delegates to the royal council. Then we had to find someone to go and represent us. But I had no money for legal assistance. I didn't know what to do.

The Lord provided, however, and my provincial never ordered me to give up my involvement with the foundation. This man is so sympathetic to any virtuous cause that even though he didn't actively help us, he didn't stand in our way. But he waited to see what the outcome of the lawsuit would be before he gave his permission to move to Saint Joseph's. So my sisters, those great servants of God, were left on their own in the beginning. They accomplished more through their prayers than I did with all my negotiations. Still, the legal affair demanded a great deal of effort on my part.

Sometimes it seemed that nothing was working. Especially when the prioress of the Incarnation came to me the day before the provincial was scheduled to arrive and ordered me to have nothing more to do with the new monastery. This meant abandoning everything I had worked so hard to achieve.

I went to God and said to him, "Lord, this house is not mine. It was founded for you. Now that there is no one to manage its business, you're going to have to take over." I felt so calm and at ease after this that it was as if the whole world were managing everything for me. From that moment on, I knew I was in good hands.

Father Gonzalo de Aranda, a great servant of God, went to the royal council to advocate for us. This priest was dedicated to the way of perfection, and he had always been very good to me. And that saintly gentleman who had been through so much with me, Francisco de Salcedo, did everything he could to assist us. He suffered innumerable trials on our behalf. But he always treated me as his own daughter and is still like a father to me.

Everyone who helped us found themselves blessed by a sense of deep connectedness to the cause. Each one considered the matter integral to his own life and treated it as if his personal honor depended on it. What mattered most to them was that this foundation was about serving God.

It seemed clear that his Majesty was assisting Father Gaspar Daza, the priest who had been such a tremendous help to me. The bishop sent Father Daza as his representative to a major meeting about our foundation. He stood alone against all the rest and ultimately won them over by recommending certain procedures that would buy us some time. But none of this was enough to throw the men off course. They seemed intent on suppressing the foundation, as if its termination were a matter of life and death.

This priest was the same one who had officiated at the ceremony where the first sisters of Saint Joseph's received their robes. He reserved the Blessed Sacrament there and was vehemently persecuted for it. The attack on us lasted six months. It would take far too long to recount in detail the horrendous trials we endured during this time.

It was amazing to me that the spirit of evil would bother to stir up so much trouble against a few poor little women. And I couldn't believe that the people of Ávila would consider a dozen cloistered sisters and their prioress such a threat to the community at large. If the foundation turned out to be a mistake, it might cause harm to the sisters who lived there, but how could it hurt the city? It just didn't make sense. Not to me, anyway. But it apparently made good enough sense to our adversaries that they fought with all their might to oppose us and felt thoroughly justified in doing so.

They finally offered a compromise position: we could found the new monastery, but only if we had an income. At this point, I was so weary of all the struggles that I considered giving in. I felt worse about the trials of the people who were helping me than about my own. Maybe it wasn't such a bad idea to allow for an income until our opponents settled down. We could always relinquish it later. Maybe this was what the Lord wanted, since it didn't seem as if it would work out any other way. Being what I am, these are the thoughts I entertained.

The night before the matter was supposed to be resolved, I was in prayer. I was already in the process of acquiescing to the demands of the city, and we had begun to discuss the details. Then the Lord spoke to me. "You must not give in to them," he said. "If you accept an income in the beginning, they will not let you renounce it later."

That same night, the holy friar Pedro de Alcántara, who was already dead, appeared before me. Before he died, Father Pedro had written me a letter telling me that he rejoiced in the intense opposition and persecution we were suffering to bring this new foundation into being. He knew what we were going through and considered it a sign that the Lord would be served by it, since the spirit of evil was going to so much trouble to thwart it. In the letter, he also urged me three or four times not to accept an income under any circumstances. "If you follow my advice," he wrote, "everything will turn out the way you desire."

I had seen Father Pedro two or three times since his death and had experienced his great glory, so I was not afraid when he appeared to me that night. Rather, it made me very happy to see him. He always manifested in his glorified body, filled with glory, and it filled me with glory to behold him. I recalled what he had told me the first time he appeared to me. "My joy is utterly sublime," he said. "The penance I performed on earth has yielded an abundant reward."

I think I have already told you about these glorious appearances, so I will not say any more about them here. But this time, his countenance was severe. He repeated that I should by no means accept any revenue. "Why do you refuse to take my advice?" he asked. Then he vanished, leaving me startled.

At my first opportunity the next day, I confided in my old friend don Francisco. Since he was now the man who was most involved in the project, I turned to him with everything. I told him about my vision and instructed him that we absolutely must not accept an endowment. "Let's let them go ahead with the lawsuit," I said. But don Francisco was already more convinced of the importance of poverty than I was! This news made him very happy. Later he told me he had only agreed to that compromise with the most severe reluctance.

Then, just as the negotiations were about to result in a settlement, an overly zealous servant of God stepped forward to say that the entire matter should be placed in the hands of some learned men. This worried me. Some of the people who were helping me actually capitulated to that proposal. This new snarl the spirit of evil tied in our project proved to be the most difficult of all tangles to unravel.

The Lord helped me with everything. It would be impossible for me to describe all that happened in a summary like this. Although the entire two years between the founding of the monastery and the resolution of the litigation was a difficult time, the first and last phases were the most labor-intensive.

Well, once the City of Ávila was somewhat mollified, Father Ibañez, the Dominican who had been helping us from afar, came to our rescue in an important way. The Lord brought him to us just when we needed him most. This priest later told us that he had not intended to come to Ávila but had ended up there by accident. When he heard of our plight, he stayed long enough to convince the provincial to let me come to the new monastery, along with a few other sisters from the Incarnation, to recite the Divine Office and teach it to the sisters here. It was almost impossible to believe that he could pull this off in such a short time, but he did. The provincial granted us his permission.

The day we first went to Saint Joseph's to recite the Divine Office was a day of profound consolation for me. Before I entered the new monastery, I sat outside in the church to pray. As I slipped into a nearly total state of rapture, I saw Christ. He seemed to be receiving me with great love. He placed a crown on my head and thanked me for everything I had done for his mother.

On another occasion, we were all praying in the choir after compline and our Lady appeared to me in all her glory. She was clothed in a white mantle, and it seemed as though she were sheltering all of us beneath it. I saw this as a sign of the high degree of glory the Lord would give the sisters who lived in this house.

Once we had initiated the liturgical practices, people began to grow deeply devoted to the new monastery. We accepted more nuns, and the Lord began to inspire our most vigorous persecutors to become our most enthusiastic supporters. They approved the very thing of which they had disapproved, and they even gave us alms. Eventually they dropped the whole lawsuit. They admitted that the house must be the work of God, since his Majesty had brought it into being against all odds.

There is no one left who thinks the new foundation was a bad idea, and they provide us with charity to keep us going. We don't have to beg or even ask for anything from anybody. The Lord moves them to send us money. We get along very well and do not lack any necessities. I trust in the Lord that we never will. There are so few of us, and as long as his Majesty continues to give us the grace to serve him as he has done so far, I am sure we will never need to be so anxious that we become a burden or a bother to anyone. The Lord will provide for us.

It is a supreme joy to find myself living with such detached souls. All they talk about is how they can serve God better. They take comfort in solitude, and the only people they want to see are those who make the fire of their love for their Beloved burn brighter. Otherwise, the thought of being with other people, even their own relatives, is a burden to them. They do not entertain idle visitors.

And so people do not come to this house unless they come to talk about love. The language of love is the only vocabulary the sisters know. They don't understand anyone who does not speak the same language, nor could anyone who doesn't know that language understand a word these lovers say.

It seems to me now that all the trials we suffered were well worth it. We live with severe austerity, it's true. We follow the original Carmelite Rule. We are strict vegetarians except by necessity. We observe an eight-month fast and other rigors. We engage in some other ascetic practices that we feel help us live the rule more perfectly. But all of these sacrifices feel small to the sisters. All I can do now is hope in the Lord that what has begun to blossom will continue to flower, as his Majesty has promised it will.

The Lord has also showered blessings on the other house founded by the holy sister, Maria de Jesús. Sister Maria, too, was confronted with horrendous opposition and suffered severe trials. Her monastery has been established in Alcala, and they also conform to the Primitive Rule of our order. May it please our Lord that everything we do be for his glory and praise and the glory and praise of his blessed Mother, the glorious Virgin Mary, whose robes we wear. Amen.

I suspect that the long history I have given of the foundation of our monastery may be a little tedious to read. But believe me, in light of the many trials we suffered and the wonders we enjoyed, it's very short. There are many witnesses who can attest to the marvels the Lord worked for us, so I beg you, even if you tear up all the other parts of this account, please preserve anything that pertains to this monastery.

When I am dead, please give this document to the sisters who live here. I have a feeling it will serve as important encouragement to those who come after us. When they see how his Majesty orchestrated so many things to establish this place, using such a flawed creature as myself as an instrument, it will inspire them to be of even greater service to God. May they never let what has been created here fall into decay but rather help it to flourish forever.

The Lord has very specifically blessed this foundation. It seems to me that we would be committing a punishable offense if we were ever to slacken the way of perfection that has been established here. Since we bear this tradition with such ease and everything runs so smoothly, he obviously favors it. The single requirement for maintaining this equanimity is to rejoice in Christ, our Beloved. This must be our sole aim, to be alone with him.

And we must strive to have no more than thirteen members living here. I have been told that this is an appropriate number and have had this confirmed through experience. If we are to preserve our spiritual life and survive on charity without begging, we cannot sustain a large number. Let us always trust the One who, with the many prayers and willing surrender of many souls, made everything work out for the best. We have experienced such happiness and delight during our years here. Our burdens have been light, and our health has been better than ever. These things testify to the correctness of our small numbers.

Anyone who thinks life here is harsh should blame her own lack of spirituality and not our practices. If women who are sickly or have delicate constitutions observe the rule so gracefully, why shouldn't these others be able to endure it? Those who are not ready for this way of life should go to some other monastery where they can find salvation in accordance with their own spiritual natures.

XXXVII ✠

DIVINE FRIENDSHIP

HOW COULD I possibly say any more about the blessings the Lord has granted me? It must already be too much for anyone to believe that he has given such gifts to someone like me. But both the Lord and his earthly representatives have commanded me to write this account, so I will say a few more things in praise of God.

May it please his Majesty that some soul may be inspired to serve him more, simply to see that he has given such mercy to a soul as lost as mine. What, then, will he grant to someone who truly serves him? May everyone everywhere be motivated to please his Majesty who, even in this lifetime, bestows such wondrous tokens of his love.

The first thing to understand is that there can be different degrees of glory in different divine favors. It has amazed me to observe how the consolation and delight in some visions far surpasses the joy that comes from other visions. Sometimes the ecstasy God gives a soul in rapture is so perfect that she cannot imagine that there is anything left on earth to desire so she asks for nothing more.

Ever since God first showed me how even in heaven different souls experience different levels of happiness, I have seen how here on earth, too, there is no limit to what the Lord can give. And so I wouldn't want to measure out what I offer up to the Lord. I want to engage the full extent of my life force, my health, and my strength to serve him. I wouldn't want to risk losing a single crumb of my ultimate reward through some fault of my own.

If someone were to ask me whether I would be willing to bear all the trials in the world until the world itself comes to an end if it meant I would experience a little more glory in the next world, or else live without any trials and so not ascend as high in heaven, I can honestly say I would eagerly choose all the trials. I am yearning to rejoice in the knowledge of God's greatness. I see that whoever understands him best loves and praises him most.

I don't mean to imply that I wouldn't be happy or count myself incredibly blessed to attain even the lowest level of paradise. Since I have deserved the bottom spot in hell, his Majesty will be showing me enormous mercy to bring me to heaven at all. May it be his will that I go there! May he not take my sins seriously! What I am saying is that, with God's grace, I want to work very hard not to lose my chance to go to paradise through my own unconsciousness. Scoundrel that I am, I have already committed so many errors and forfeited such grace.

Fortunately, I have learned something from every mystical favor the Lord has granted me. With each new vision or revelation, my soul has grown. In some cases, the benefits have been remarkable. The vision of Christ left me with an indelible impression of his supreme beauty. I carry this beauty with me always. If one incident has such a powerful and lasting impact, imagine how much more deeply he imprints himself on my soul when he reveals himself to me again and again.

Here is one benefit I derived from my vision of Christ. Before he appeared to me, I had this troubling tendency to become very attached to anyone I thought liked me. As soon as I began to detect that someone had fond feelings for me and I myself found them attractive, I would start thinking about them all the time and recalling every detail of our encounters. I had no intention of forsaking God, but I was very happy whenever I got to see these people. I loved to think about them and reflect on all the positive qualities I perceived in them. This habit was becoming a serious problem and leading my soul astray.

After I had seen the extraordinary beauty of the Lord, no human being could compare with him or take his place in my thoughts. All I had to do was turn my gaze slightly inward to behold the image imprinted in my soul and I was instantaneously free from all mundane attractions. In fact, everything here on earth looked ugly to me compared to the excellent attributes I had glimpsed in this glorious Beloved of mine.

And his speech! There is no worldly wisdom and no human solace I can think of that could amount to anything compared with a single word uttered from those divine lips. Imagine how much more meaningful to hear many whole sentences. Unless the Lord were to punish me for my transgressions by erasing my memory of him, I think it would be impossible for me to become so entangled by thoughts of another person that I couldn't extricate myself with the gentlest effort to return my attention to the Lord.

I experienced this kind of liberation in the case of one of my confessors. I have always had a tendency to develop a deep fondness for the men who guide my soul. I believe they stand in God's place in a very real way, so my thoughts of them are intimately entwined with my thoughts of God. Because I feel safe with them, I express my affection. This often seems to make them uncomfortable. Being God-fearing servants of the Lord, they are afraid that my love for them—even if it is a very spiritual love—might become a dangerous temptation for me, so they have treated me harshly.

It never happens until I enter into a relationship of obedience to them. As soon as I begin to obey them, I grow fond of them. Sometimes when I saw how they were misinterpreting my feelings for them, I would laugh to myself but wouldn't let on to them how unattached I really was to any human being. But I did reassure them, and as they got to know me better, they realized that my primary attachment was to the Lord. These misunderstandings usually only occurred at the beginning of our acquaintance.

Once I had seen this Beloved of mine and discovered how easily and how continually I could converse with him, my confidence in the divine friendship increased. I saw that although he was God, he was also a man, and the frailties of the human condition didn't surprise him. He understood our nature. He knew that our tendency to fall was because of the original fall, and that was exactly what he had come to repair.

Even though he is Lord, I can speak with Christ the way I would talk to a friend. I know he isn't like the lords we have here on earth whose authority is entirely artificial. They have designated times for speaking and designated people to whom they speak. If some poor little person has some business with such a lord, she has to go through all kinds of roundabout routes to get to him. She has to beg favors and endure insults just to have a moment of his time.

Imagine if this person were trying to get an audience with the king! Poor people don't have a chance. Unless a supplicant comes from the upper class, she can't get close. Instead, she has to ask his assistants for help. And believe me, these aids are not men who have trampled the world underfoot. Those who have severed their worldly attachments are not afraid to speak the truth. They are not obligated to anyone. They are not suited for palace life because they cannot be who they are in such places. If a person like this were to see something he thought was wrong in the kingdom, he would have to hold his silence. He wouldn't dare speak out or even think about it for fear he would fall from royal favor.

O glorious King! O Lord of all kings! Your sovereignty is not plagued by trivialities. Your kingdom has no limits. Of course we do not need intermediaries to reach you. All we need is a fleeting glance and we immediately see that you alone deserve to be called "Lord." You don't require an entourage or armed guards to prove that you are King.

Here on earth, a king would not be recognized as king if he were all alone. No matter how much he wanted his status acknowledged, no one would believe him. He would look like everyone else. It is only outward displays of power and authority that convince people of his royal station. Stripped of these trappings, he commands no one's esteem. The appearance of power has nothing to do with the man himself, but with the artificial display of authority that others confer upon him.

O my Lord! O my King! Who would ever know how to describe you? How could we ever fail to see that you are in yourself a great Emperor? A mere glimpse of your majesty strikes the heart with awe. Look how graciously you blend magnificence with humility. The more I see the love you pour on such a miserable creature as I, the more awestruck I become.

Still, once the first wave of fear from beholding your Majesty passes, we feel free to engage in intimate conversation with you. We can say anything we like. Even though the fear of offending you grows stronger, it is not punishment we are afraid of. Punishment is nothing compared to the possibility of losing you, my Beloved.

Here are some of the benefits of this vision. For one thing, a vision that comes from God leaves marvelous effects when its light strikes the soul. But sometimes it's the Lord's will for a soul to remain in darkness and not see the light. There are good reasons for a soul who knows herself as I know myself to be a little afraid.

Just recently, I spent eight days feeling spiritually dry and empty. I lost all sense of gratitude toward God and couldn't get it back, no matter how hard I tried. I couldn't remember any of the blessings he has given me. My soul had sunk into a terrible stupor, and I had no idea how it had gotten there. I wasn't having bad thoughts, but I seemed incapable of having any good ones either.

I couldn't help but laugh at myself. It amused me to see how low a soul can sink when God is not working in her every minute. This trial is not nearly as severe as others I have endured, because I don't doubt that God is still with me. But in a state like this, no matter how much wood the soul piles on the fire, no matter what else she does by her own effort, the flames of love will not burn. Through God's great mercy, she sees the smoke, so she knows the fire is not completely dead. The Lord will come back to rekindle it.

Even though the soul bruises her head trying to blow on the embers and rearrange the wood, all she seems to succeed in doing is stifling the flames even more. I believe the best thing for the soul to do in this situation is to surrender totally. She needs to accept the fact that she can do nothing and occupy herself by being of service to others. Maybe the Lord takes the soul away from her customary state of prayer so that she will engage in charitable works and realize that by herself she can do nothing anyway.

I have to admit, today I was delighting with my Beloved in prayer, and I grew very bold. "Why isn't it enough for you, my Lord," I complained, "to keep me bound to this miserable life? For love of you, I endure all this and resign myself to living in a place where everything hinders me from enjoying you. Here I have to eat and sleep and conduct business and carry on conversations with everyone. It torments me, my Lord, but I suffer it all for love of you.

"In the few moments I have left over to enjoy your presence, how could you hide from me, my Beloved? Is this compatible with your compassion? How can your love for me allow this? I believe, Lord, that if I were able to hide from you as you have hidden from me, your love for me would make it impossible for you to endure it. But you are always with me, and you see everything I do. Do not put up with this separation a moment longer, my Beloved! I beg you to see how much you are hurting the one who loves you so much!"

It occurred to me to say many other things to my Beloved, knowing perfectly well how merciful he has been to me compared to what I deserve. But sometimes I become so crazy with love that I don't know what I'm saying. With the full energy of my mind, I launch these complaints against my Lord, and he puts up with it all. Praise be to such a good King!

We wouldn't dare say these things to an earthly king. We have good reason to be afraid of such a man and of his representatives too. The way the world is these days, our lives would have to double in length for us to have any hope of learning all the fine points of etiquette and all the new social rules and still have some time left over for paying attention to God. When I see what's going on, I bless myself.

The thing is, I still had not learned how to live when I entered the monastery of Saint Joseph's. I failed to treat certain men any better than I felt they deserved. I did not take their social status seriously enough. Important people do not take such carelessness lightly. They consider it a personal affront, and then you have to make an effort to prove that your intentions are good. Even then, please God they believe you.

Really, I did not know how to live. My poor soul was worn out. The men told her that she must keep her thoughts fixed on God. They insisted that her only hope for salvation was for her to devote her attention entirely to him. Yet she also received the message that she had better not miss a single point of worldly honor that might compromise the reputation of people whose status was based on such details.

These rules wearied me. I was constantly apologizing. Although I studied the matter, I couldn't help but make many mistakes. And as I say, in a world like this, errors of etiquette are no laughing matter. Shouldn't monks and nuns be exempt from strict observance of these worldly customs? Well, apparently we aren't. Instead, monasteries are expected to be charm schools. We are supposed to know all the nuances of social etiquette.

I, for one, cannot understand this. I thought the masters had taught us that monastic life is where we learn to be courtiers in heaven. The world has it all backward! Our focus needs to be on pleasing God and rejecting the world. If we care about the spiritual path, how can we be equally careful to keep up with all the ever-changing rules about pleasing important people in the world?

I mean, if we could learn a list of rules once and for all, that would be fine. But the simple task of finding the proper titles with which to address a letter requires a university chair to deliver a lecture on how it is to be done. Sometimes you're supposed to leave a margin on one side of the page, sometimes on the other. Sometimes a man who is not even called "magnificence" is expected to be addressed as "illustrious."

I don't know how any of this is going to turn out. I am not even fifty yet, and I have already seen so many changes that it makes my head spin. I don't know how to live anymore. What's going to become of the people who are being born right now and will live for many years to come? I have deep compassion for spiritual people who are, for one reason or another, obligated to live in the world. All these rules of correct behavior must be a heavy cross for them to bear. If only they could make an agreement among themselves to remain ignorant of this silly science! They should insist on their right to such ignorance. It would save them a great deal of trouble.

But what nonsense I've been talking. I meant to speak of the greatness of God, and instead I've delivered a diatribe about the pettiness of the world. Since the Lord has graciously allowed me to renounce the world, I will leave these things behind now. Let those who are in love with trivial things attend to them. Please God we will not have to pay for these things in the next life, where everything is unchanging. Amen.

XXXVIII ✠

FLIGHT OF THE SPIRIT

ONE NIGHT, I felt so ill that I had to excuse myself from the communal practice of silent prayer. I took my rosary with me so that at least I could occupy myself with vocal prayer. Since I was sitting in an oratory, it probably appeared that I was in a recollected state, but I was trying very hard not to let my mind become absorbed. Such techniques are of little use, however, when the Lord wills otherwise.

I had not been there for very long when such a forceful rapture seized my soul that I was powerless to resist it. It seemed to me that I was carried to heaven where I was greeted by my father and mother. In the short amount of time it takes to recite an Ave Maria, I saw so many wondrous things that I remained utterly transported. The blessing felt too great to bear. Although it seemed as if it was over in a fleeting moment, the experience may have lasted much longer; I'm not sure.

The vision felt totally real, but I started to worry that it might be a delusion. I didn't know what to do. I was embarrassed to go to my spiritual director about it. I don't think this was a matter of humility; I think I was afraid he would make fun of me. "You're a regular little Saint Paul, aren't you, with your heavenly visions?" he might say. Or "Look who thinks she's Saint Jerome."

The fact that these glorious men had experienced similar visions made me worry even more. All I could do was cry. I didn't think I could possibly deserve to see what saints see.

Finally, I overcame my resistance and went to my director. No matter how much I disliked talking about these things, I knew it was dangerous to remain silent about them, since I am often plagued with the fear that my experiences might be delusional. When he saw how distressed I was, he comforted me. He said all the right things to disengage me from my troubled thoughts.

Over time, the Lord showed me other great secrets. He continues to do so. It's impossible for the soul to behold more than God reveals to her. No matter how much she may have sometimes wished to see beyond what God was manifesting, my soul saw exactly what she needed to see every time. And the truth is, the smallest part of what he revealed to me was so vast that it was enough to leave my soul in awe and put all the insignificant things of this life into perspective.

I wish I could say something about even a fraction of what I came to know, but I find it impossible to express. If I try to use the analogy of light, it falls short. There is light here and there is light in that other place, but the latter so totally transcends the former that any comparison becomes meaningless. Next to the divine light, the light of the sun looks dull. However keen the imagination may be, it can never succeed in describing or illustrating this light or in conveying any of the other things the Lord taught me.

Along with the knowledge he gives, the Lord bestows an ineffable delight. It is so sublime that a thousand words cannot describe it. All the senses rejoice. The absolute exultation it produces defies all language. And so, it's better to say nothing.

Once the Lord spent more than an hour revealing these wondrous things to me. It seemed that he never left my side that whole time. Finally, he said to me, "Do you see, my daughter, what those who reject me lose? Please do not fail to tell them about it."

Ah, my Beloved, unless your Majesty gives them light, what good could I possibly do for those who are blinded by their own actions? There are some people who have already glimpsed your light; they may well be in a position to profit from hearing about your grandeurs. But not when the words come from the likes of me. As soon as I mention that you have revealed your mercies to such a flawed person as myself, they will refuse to believe me.

May your name be blessed! May your merciful name be blessed! I, for one, have seen dramatic improvement in myself. After you had blessed me, I wanted to remain in that state forever and never return to the mundane world. Direct contact with you, my Beloved, left me with contempt for everything earthly. The things of this world felt like nothing but dung to me after that. I have seen how easy it is for those of us who dwell here to get caught up in empty concerns.

Once when I was staying with doña Luisa de Cerda, I was suffering from severe pains in my chest. I used to have serious heart trouble, but I don't anymore. Since she was a very charitable woman, she had some elaborate gold jewelry and some very precious stones brought out to show me. One of the diamonds in particular was extremely valuable. She thought it would cheer me up to see them. Recalling what the Lord has in store for us in the next world, I couldn't help but laugh at what people value here. I feel sorry for them. I realized how impossible it would be for me to cherish these objects even if I tried. The Lord would have to expunge the things he has shown me from my memory.

A soul who has been given mastery of her own desires has a huge advantage. But she does not bequeath this dominion to herself. It is a gift from God. Someone who does not have this kind of detachment cannot understand what it's like. It is not a matter of willful self-control; it comes naturally, without any labor on our part. God does it all. And he does it by revealing his truths in such a way that they are imprinted on our souls. It is obvious to us that this detachment is a divine gift, because we never could have acquired it so quickly and easily on our own.

I used to be terrified of death. Not anymore. Since the visions, dying feels like the easiest thing in the world. In the moment of death, the servant of God finds herself released at last from this prison. Finally, she is free to rest. I think these raptures must be similar to the experience of the soul leaving the body. When God transports me like this, he carries my spirit away and reveals such sublime things to me that it seems as if I see everything that is sacred and excellent all at once.

We don't need to talk about the pain that happens when the soul and the body are finally separated from one another. This is insignificant, and it passes quickly. Besides, I have a feeling that death comes gently to those who truly love God and are unmoved by the trappings of this life.

The other thing these visions gave me is the gift of recognizing that we are pilgrims in this world and our real home lies beyond this one. It is wonderful to be given the chance to see the place where we will be living. If someone had to go and live forever in another country, it would make the hardships of the journey much easier for him if he knew that he was going to a place where he would be living in comfort and ease.

The visions have also helped me keep my attention focused on heavenly things. It's easier to keep my conversations on a spiritual track. Cultivating this awareness has many benefits. Sometimes just glancing toward heaven is enough to recollect the soul. Since the Lord has graciously revealed a glimpse of what it's like, the soul has something on which to concentrate.

There are times when the beings that live in that other world are more real to me than those who inhabit this one. They are my companions. They're the ones I turn to for real comfort. They feel truly alive, while those who live here on earth seem so dead! There are times when I think there is no one in the whole world to keep me company. I especially feel this way when the raptures come over me.

Everything I see with the eyes of this body seems to be a dream or a joke. I desire what I have already seen with the eyes of my soul. But it feels so far away, and this life is like death to me. Overall, I know that the Lord is doing us a great favor when he grants us these visions. But even as he is helping us, he is giving us a heavy cross to bear, since nothing in this life pleases us after seeing what he has shown us. Everything here feels like an impediment. Mercifully, the Beloved allows us to forget from time to time. Otherwise, I don't know how we could live.

May God be blessed and praised forever! May it be his will, by the blood his Son shed for me, that what happened to Lucifer never happen to me. That fallen angel lost everything through his own fault. I have already learned something about God's great blessings and have begun to enjoy them. May God, being who he is, not allow me to lose what he has given me. Sometimes I become very afraid about this. But mostly, God's mercy makes me feel safe. He has freed me from so many transgressions that I cannot imagine he would ever let me out of his hands again. I beg you to beg God never to let me go astray.

None of those favors were as powerful as the one of which I am about to speak. Although the greatness of each blessing is incomparable, especially when considered in and of itself, this particular experience is remarkable for the way it fortified my soul.

One day, on the eve of Pentecost, I went after Mass to a secluded place where I liked to pray. I began to read about this holy day in the Carthusian book called *The Life of Christ*. I read about the signs that demonstrate to beginning, adept, and perfect practitioners of prayer whether the Holy Spirit is with them. It made me realize that, as far as I could tell, he was with me.

I praised the goodness of God and remembered that the last time I had read this same passage, I lacked much of what I now had. I had been well aware of this deficiency at the time, just as I was now conscious of how far I had come. So I understood what a great favor the Lord had granted me. I began to reflect on the punishment I deserved for the bad things I had done and gave thanks to God. I could hardly recognize my soul; the changes he had made in me were so radical.

While I was musing on this, a powerful energy abruptly swept over me. It seemed that my soul didn't fit in my body anymore and wanted to get out. She couldn't wait a moment longer to attain such goodness. This impulse was so extreme that there was nothing I could do to help myself. It felt very different from other transports. My soul was so stirred up that she didn't know what had happened to her or what she wanted. I was sitting down, but my natural strength drained out of me so quickly that I had to lean against the wall to keep from falling over.

In the midst of this state, I saw a dove above my head. It was very different from the doves of this world and much larger. It didn't have typical feathers. Instead, the wings seemed to be made of tiny shells that sparkled with intense brilliance. I thought I could hear the sound the dove made with the movement of its great wings.

It fluttered over me for the space of an Ave Maria, but my soul was so transported that as I lost myself, I lost sight of the dove. Ordinarily such a dramatic experience would have frightened and agitated me, but instead my spirit was soothed by the presence of such a good guest, and I relaxed into the vision. My soul lingered in rapture, and I was filled with a joyous quietude.

The glory of this rapture was exceedingly great. For the rest of Pentecost, I remained spellbound and stupefied. I didn't know what to do with myself. I was bewildered by my capacity to receive such an exalted gift. I could hardly hear or see anything, yet I basked in a wondrous interior delight. I noticed that from that day forward I made tremendous progress on the path. My love of God increased dramatically, and my virtues grew much stronger. May he be forever blessed and praised!

I saw that same dove on another occasion. This time it was hovering over the head of the Dominican friar, Pedro Ibañez. Its great wings and the rays of light that radiated from them extended much farther than when I saw it over my own head. I understood that the soul of this man was meant to bring many other souls to God.

On yet another occasion, I saw our Lady drape a bright white cloak over Father Ibañez's shoulders. "I am giving this to him because of the service he has rendered us in helping found this house of prayer," she said. "This cloak is a sign that I will keep his soul spotless from now on. He shall never fall into grave error."

And I am certain this is so. Father Ibañez died a few years later. His life was so pure and his death so holy that insofar as we on earth can know such things, there is no way to doubt the Blessed Mother's promise. A friar who was present at the deathbed told me that just before Father Ibañez died, he told the friar that Saint Thomas was with him. He died with great joy. He was excited to be freed from this exile.

Since his death, Father Ibañez has appeared to me several times in resplendent glory and told me a few things. By the time he died, his practice of prayer had reached such a high level that even though he wanted to avoid contemplative prayer because of his weak health, his raptures kept carrying him away.

Father Ibañez wrote to me shortly before he died. "What should I do?" he asked. "Often, when I've finished celebrating Mass, I slip into a rapture and there's nothing I can do to stop it." At the end of his life, God rewarded Father Ibañez for the great service he had offered throughout his life.

I also witnessed some of the wondrous blessings God bestowed on Gaspar de Salazar, the Jesuit director I've written about. I will avoid mentioning these things here, so that this account will not be too long. Father de Salazar once experienced a terrible trial in which he was being unfairly accused and persecuted. He found himself in a state of deep affliction.

One day as the host was elevated during Mass, I saw Christ on the cross behind Father de Salazar. Christ told me some comforting words to convey to the priest. He said some other things that foretold what was to come and reminded the priest of what Christ had suffered for him, even as he announced that Father de Salazar should prepare himself to suffer. This message gave him courage and solace. Everything turned out the way the Lord had told me it would.

I have seen many other great things concerning the Jesuit order. Sometimes I have seen its members in heaven, carrying white banners in their hands. And the Lord has shown me other wonderful things about them. That's why I admire the Society of Jesus so much. Every contact I have with them further reinforces my certainty that their lives conform to what God has told me about them.

One night while I was in prayer, the Lord began to remind me how bad my life used to be. His words filled me with shame and dismay. Although he did not speak harshly, it triggered an all-consuming regret and grief in me. But a single word from him stimulates more dramatic progress in self-knowledge than many days of reflection on our own wretchedness. The divine message bears the indelible stamp of truth.

The Lord recalled for me the extremely superficial friendships I had cultivated in my youth. He told me that I should be happy that my will, which had been so badly occupied with vanity, was now fixed on him. He promised to honor my desire to be with him.

"Remember when you used to consider it an honor to defy me?" he asked. "While you were dealing me the harshest blows, I was showering you with blessings." The Lord helped me to recognize my debt of gratitude to him.

I am truly blessed; I know I am. Whenever I am doing anything wrong, his Majesty makes me so conscious of it that I am reduced to nothing. Since I have so many faults, this happens frequently. Sometimes after my confessor has chastised me, I seek consolation in prayer. But that's where I receive the real reprimand.

As I was saying, I felt terrible about myself that night. It seemed as though I had made little progress, and this thought made me weep. Then in the midst of my tears, I began to wonder if the Lord was about to grant me some blessing, since he often precedes his favors by humbling me so thoroughly that I have no illusions about being entitled to his grace.

No sooner had I thought this than my soul was swept up in such a powerful rapture that I seemed to be entirely disconnected from my body. I saw the most sacred humanity, clearer and more glorious than I had ever seen it before. With a penetrating understanding, I watched the Father enfold the Son in his heart. I don't know how to describe this! Without seeing anything, I somehow saw that I was in the presence of the Divine.

I was so completely shocked by this encounter that it took me several days to return to myself. It seemed to me that wherever I went, I was accompanied by the majesty of the Son of God. This aftermath wasn't as powerful as the initial experience, but I understood that a vision of this magnitude engraves itself so deeply on the imagination that no matter how swiftly it passes, it leaves its impression for a long, long time. This impression is very comforting. It is a great blessing.

I have seen this same vision three other times. Of all the visions the Lord has granted me, I think this one is the most sublime. It carries marvelous benefits. It seems to purify the soul, removing any attachment to sensual gratification. It is a powerful flame that burns away all worldly desires. For even though I did not desire any typical vain things, glory be to God, this experience helped me to see clearly how all this life is vanity. How vain, how truly vain are the distinctions of this world!

A vision like this becomes a powerful tool for elevating one's desires to pure truth. It fills the soul with a sense of deep reverence that I wouldn't know how to put into words. It is very different from anything we experience here on earth. The soul is awestruck to realize how she or any other soul could dare forsake such an extraordinary majesty.

Remember, different visions have varying degrees of impact on the soul. The beneficial effects of this particular vision are immense. As I approached the altar to receive Communion, I was flooded with the memory of the extraordinary majesty that I had seen. When I considered the presence of the Divinity in the Blessed Sacrament, which I had so often beheld in the host, my hair stood on end. The whole experience seemed to annihilate me.

O my Lord! If you did not hide your greatness, who would dare to keep reaching for union with you? Who could ever consider herself worthy to become one with you? May the angels and all the creatures praise you! You measure out everything according to our weakness. We can rejoice in your supreme blessings without being overwhelmed by your awesome power. You do not scare us away from enjoying you.

What once happened to a certain laborer could happen to us. He found a treasure that far exceeded any value he could comprehend. He became so consumed with worry about what to do with it that his anxiety gradually killed him. What if he hadn't found it all at once? What if the treasure had been handed to him bit by bit? Since he was so poor, it would have sustained him and he would have lived happily. Instead, the discovery cost him his life.

O Wealth of the poor! How beautifully you sustain our souls. You reveal your great riches to us gradually rather than letting us see everything at once. I am astonished to see such extraordinary majesty concealed in something as small and humble as the host. When I reflect on this afterward, I marvel at such profound wisdom and wonder how the Lord gives me the courage to approach him. All I know is that the One who gives me such blessed favors is the One who also gives me the strength to receive them. I cannot possibly hide this knowledge. I cannot resist proclaiming it to anyone who will listen. Listen! God is great!

What will a wretch like me feel when she approaches this majestic Lord, knowing that he has invited her into his presence? I am weighed down with shame. I have wasted my life and forgotten my awe of God. How can a mouth that has spoken so many words against this same Lord receive that most glorious body? He is pure goodness and perfect compassion. Having seen his beautiful face, tender and friendly, my soul feels more sorrow for not having served him than she feels fear of his magnificence.

How can I possibly have experienced what I am about to describe not just once but twice? O my Lord and my Glory! I feel certain that in some mysterious way I have served you by enduring the affliction I will now recount. Oh, I don't know what I'm talking about. I am writing this as if someone else were speaking through me. As I recall these things, I am so disturbed that I am almost beside myself. How could I have just thought I had anything to offer you? That idea did not come from me. Maybe I do have a right to say I have done something for you, but no such notion is even possible unless you put it into my head. There's no reason to thank myself for thinking it. I am the one in debt to you, my Beloved, and you are the one who has been wronged.

Once when I stood up to receive Communion, I saw two abominable devils. They appeared more clearly to the eyes of my soul than to my physical eyes. It looked like they had wrapped their horns around the poor priest's throat. When I recalled that my Lord in all his majesty was within the host that was about to be given to me, now held in the hands of his offender, I understood that the soul of this priest was in mortal sin. Can you imagine, my Lord, what it was like to see your beauty in the midst of such hideous company? The demons seemed terrified in your presence, as if they would flee the second you released them.

This vision so thoroughly upset me that I don't know how I was able to receive Communion. Afterward, I was afraid that the vision did not come from God, because why would he have allowed me to see evil in connection with a priest? But then the Lord himself commanded me to pray for that soul.

"Do you see how powerful the words of consecration are?" he asked me. "However wicked the priest who recites them may be, God does not fail to be present when they are uttered." Christ reminded me of the boundless benevolence he manifests by placing himself in the hands of his enemy and how he does this out of love for me and all beings.

I realized several things from this vision. I saw how much more obligated priests are than the rest of us to be good. I saw what a terrible thing it is to approach the Blessed Sacrament with unclean hands. I saw how much power the spirit of evil has over a soul lost in grave error. All this did me a great deal of good. It helped me to understand more fully what I owe to God. May he be blessed forever and ever.

On another day, I saw a similar vision and it really scared me. I was in a certain place when a man died. I had heard that he had lived a wicked life. But his illness had spanned two years, so he'd had time to make amends for some of the things he had done. Although he died without confession, it didn't seem to me that he would be condemned.

While the body was being wrapped in its shroud, I saw a multitude of evil spirits grab hold of it and start cruelly playing with it. It terrified me to see them drag the deceased with large hooks, tossing him from one demon to another. As I watched while that same body was buried with all the honor and ceremony we bestow on our dead, I reflected on the goodness of God. He conceals the fact that a soul set itself against him. He doesn't allow his enemy to be dishonored.

I was stunned by what I had seen. I did not see another evil spirit during the rest of the ceremony until they placed the body in the grave. That's when another horde of demons jumped in with him and tried to take him away. Seeing this made me frantic, and it took all my courage to conceal it. If they had such dominion over the poor body, what would they be able to do to the soul?

If only souls in a state of grave error could see what I have seen. It's horrible! I think it would be a powerful incentive for them to repair their wicked ways and start living a life of integrity. These visions deepen my awareness of how much I am beholden to God. Look what he has freed me from!

This experience continued to trouble my mind until I spoke to my confessor about it. He assured me that the vision was not a delusion. I had been afraid that the spirit of evil might have been tricking me to discredit the man's soul. It may have been true that he did not have the most pious spirit, but the outcome terrified me every time I thought about it.

Now that I have recounted some of my experiences with the dead, I'd like to tell you about some of the other ways in which it has been God's will for me to see certain souls. I'll just mention a few of these, since it doesn't benefit anyone for me to go into great detail.

I was informed of the death of a man who had once been our provincial, Father Gregorio Fernandez. I had dealt with him on various occasions and he had been very kind to me. He was a virtuous man, known for his many good deeds. When I heard that he was dead, I was immediately worried about his salvation. Father Fernandez had been a superior for twenty years, and I think being in charge of other people's souls can be a dangerous thing.

I entered an oratory with an anxious heart. I offered up all the merit I might ever have accumulated in my life for the good of Father Fernandez's soul. But when I realized that it didn't amount to much, I asked the Lord to draw from his own store of goodness to purify and liberate the priest's soul.

While I was in the middle of petitioning the Lord to the best of my ability, the man's soul seemed to rise up out of the ground on my right side and ascend into heaven. He looked gloriously happy. When I knew Father Fernandez, he was already quite old, but in this vision he looked like he wasn't even thirty. His face was beaming.

The moment passed very quickly, but I felt much better afterward. Father Fernandez was greatly revered, and I saw people suffering severe grief over his loss. But his death never made me feel sad again. The consolation I experienced banished all worry from my mind. I no longer doubted that his soul was safe, nor did I question if the vision was real or a delusion.

Two weeks had passed since his death, and I continued to ask other people to pray for him. But although I kept praying for him myself, I did not do so as desperately as I had prayed before I had been given that vision. It's funny, when someone dies and the Lord shows them to me in this way, praying for them feels like giving alms to the rich. Father Fernandez died far away from Ávila. Afterward, when I heard about the death the Lord had given him, I learned a lot from it. He amazed everyone with his deep wisdom and humble tears.

A nun from the Incarnation died. She had been a great servant of God. A day and a half after her death, another nun was in the choir, reciting the service for the dead for her sister's departed soul. I stood beside her to accompany her. When she was halfway through the verse, I saw the nun who had died. As before, it seemed that her soul rose from my right side on its way to heaven. This was an intellectual vision, rather than an imaginative one like the other, but it was just as reliable.

Around eighteen or twenty years ago, another nun from that same house died. She had suffered from poor health her whole life and had always served God with great devotion. She was dedicated to her choir duties and scrupulous in every way. Since she had endured so many illnesses, I felt certain she had stored up a surplus of merit and would bypass purgatory. Yet four hours after her death, while we were reciting the prayers prior to her burial, I suddenly understood that her soul had been released from purgatory and was on its way to heaven.

While I was at Saint Giles, the Jesuit college in Ávila, I was experiencing one of those great trials of body and soul I've told you about. I was so distraught that I don't think I was capable of thinking a single good thought. That night, a Jesuit brother died in that house. A priest from the Society of Jesus was saying Mass for him and I was praying for him when a deep recollection came over me. I saw him ascend to heaven in great glory, and Christ rose with him. I was deeply blessed to understand that the Lord accompanied him on his journey home.

Another very good friar from my own order, Diego Matias, was gravely ill. While I was at Mass, I fell into deep recollection and understood that Father Diego had died. I saw that he had ascended to heaven without going through purgatory. According to what I learned later, he died at the exact hour I'd had the vision of him.

At first I was amazed that he did not require a period of purification, but then I realized that because he had observed the monastic rule so faithfully, he was saved from a sojourn in purgatory. I don't know why I was given to understand this. It seems to me that it must be because I know that being a friar is not a matter of wearing the right robes. It's about cultivating the state of higher perfection exemplified by a spiritual life.

I don't want to say any more about these things. As I mentioned, they don't really matter. The Lord has granted me the favor of seeing many things. But of all the visions I've received, I never saw any soul skip the purification stage and go straight to paradise except for Father Diego, the saintly Pedro de Alcantará, and the Dominican priest I've talked about, Father Ibañez. It was God's will for me to see the varying degrees of glory allotted to some other souls and the distinct places assigned to them in the afterlife. As it turns out, these differences are far greater than I would have thought.

XXXIX ✠

Beyond Doubt

ONE DAY I was imploring the Lord to restore sight to a certain person. The man had almost completely lost his vision. I felt terrible for the suffering of my friend and started to worry that the Lord would not listen to me because of my transgressions.

Then the Lord appeared to me. He stretched out his left hand and showed me the wound there. With his other hand, he extracted a large nail that was embedded in it. It seemed to me that when the nail came out, it tore out a piece of flesh along with it. I could see the pain on my Lord's face, and it broke my heart.

"You should not doubt the One who has suffered for you," he reminded me. "I will do what you ask, but even better." And then he asked, "Haven't I already told you there is nothing I would not do for you? I know that you would never ask anything that was not for the greater glory of God."

Then, after reassuring me he would answer my prayers, he said, "Please remember that even before you truly began to serve me, you never asked for anything that I did not grant and in a better way than you even knew how to ask. Now that I know you love me, how much more likely am I to fulfill your request? Do not question this."

Not even a week passed, and the Lord gave sight back to the blind man. My spiritual director heard the news right away. Of course, it's possible that my prayer had nothing to do with the man's sudden cure. But since it happened to correspond with my vision, I felt pretty certain that they were connected, and I praised God for his mercy, as if he had granted the favor to me personally.

Once my cousin Pedro was very sick with a severe case of kidney stones. He suffered unbearable pain for two months; the agony made him tear at his own flesh. My confessor went to visit him and felt so sorry for him that he told me I should go to see him myself, since we were related. When I saw my cousin like that, my heart was moved to such pity that I burst into prayer and begged the Lord to heal him. God's favors could not have been clearer than they were in this case. The next day, Pedro was completely cured.

On another occasion, I was very upset because a certain person I cared about was intent on engaging in an activity that would seriously dishonor both God and himself. He had made up his mind; he was going to go through with it. I was so worried about this, and I didn't know what to do to dissuade him. It seemed there was no hope of making him give up his plan. I urged God with all my heart to intervene. But since I didn't see any results from my prayer, I couldn't find any relief for my grief.

We have various secluded retreat spaces here in our monastery. Filled with anxiety for my friend's soul, I went to the hermitage that has the painting I commissioned of Christ bound to the pillar and begged him to remedy the situation. I heard a gentle voice speaking to me as if in a whisper. The voice startled me, and my hair stood on end. I wanted to understand what it was saying, but it passed so quickly that I missed it.

My fear also passed quickly. I felt deep quietude and joy. The inner delight was so pervasive that I was amazed; simply hearing that voice in passing had such a profound effect on my soul. I had actually heard it with my physical ears this time, even though I hadn't understood a word. Somehow I became aware that my prayer would be answered.

Nothing changed externally, yet my inner affliction left me completely, as if what I had asked for had already been accomplished. The pain simply went away. Later I found out that the man I was worried about had changed his mind and abandoned his destructive course of action. I told two of my spiritual directors about what I had gone through. They were both very learned men and good servants of God.

Another person I knew had resolved to serve God with all his heart. He devoted several days to prayer, and his Majesty granted him some favors during this time. But this man was struggling with various temptations, and he gave up prayer and followed his dangerous inclinations instead. This broke my heart. He was a man I loved very much, and I owed him a great deal. I think I begged God for an entire month to bring this soul back to himself.

One day, while I was at prayer, I saw a demon beside me. In a wild frenzy, it was tearing up some papers it had in its hands. It comforted me to see this, because it seemed to me that what I had been asking for had come true and the spirit of evil was frustrated. And so it was. Afterward, I heard that this person had confessed with a contrite heart. He returned to God with such sincerity that I trust he will continue to make tremendous spiritual progress for the rest of his life. May God be forever blessed. Amen.

The Lord has often answered my prayers on behalf of other souls. When I ask him, he draws them away from serious transgressions and leads them on the way of perfection. God has granted me innumerable favors by rescuing souls from the purification stage and releasing them to paradise. He has granted me so many other blessings of this kind that it would exhaust me and bore my reader for me to recount them all. Most of what he has done for me pertains to the health of souls rather than the health of bodies.

There have been many witnesses to these favors, so they are widely known. Initially, I had some misgivings about all this, because I couldn't help believing that I'd had something to do with these amazing cures. Of course, I never lost sight of the most important fact that God was doing this purely out of his own goodness. But there have been so many instances of people radically transforming after I have interceded on their behalf that it no longer bothers me to consider my part in it. Instead, I praise his Majesty even more and see how completely I am indebted to him. These intercessions only quicken my love for him and increase my desire to serve him.

You know what's amazing? When I want something that turns out to be contrary to the Lord's will, I find myself unable to ask him for it, no matter how hard I try to force myself. The thing I want to pray for may seem worthy, but if it is not the Lord's desire, I am incapable of summoning the energy, enthusiasm, and concern to petition God. Yet I find it effortless to pray for the things his Majesty is going to do. Those prayers arise often and with great insistence. Even when I am not intentionally pondering such cases, they pop into my mind.

There is a vast difference between these two types of supplication. I don't really know how to explain it. When a certain outcome is not the Lord's will, I keep trying to force myself to beseech him about a matter that may be very close to my heart, but I don't feel the fervor I feel about those other petitions. I am like a person who is tongue-tied. He wants to speak but nothing comes out. Or if he succeeds in making any sound at all, no one can understand what he's saying.

When the impetus of my prayer conforms with God's will, I feel like a person whose speech flows eloquently and passionately to someone who is eagerly listening to what she has to say. In the first case, I approach the Lord as we do when we practice vocal prayer, with the effort of intention. In the other, I reach out to him from a state of sublime contemplation in which I am nothing but a passive channel. That's when we experience his Majesty revealing himself. He assures us that he hears us, that he is happy we have asked this of him and is glad to grant the favor. May he be forever blessed! He gives so much, and we give so little in return!

What are we to do, my Beloved, if we are not willing to undo everything for you? I stumble and I blunder and I fail. I could repeat this a thousand times. I endlessly fall short of giving it all up for you. My failure to live in harmony with what you have given me makes me want to die. But there are other reasons to keep living. I see so many imperfections in myself. There are so many ways in which I neglect to serve you. Sometimes I wish I could be totally unconscious so that I wouldn't have to face so much that is bad in me. May the One who is able remedy my plight.

While I was staying in doña Luisa's house, I had to be careful about everything I did and maintain constant vigilance about the many vain details such a lifestyle entails. The people there had such esteem for me that they were always praising me and offering me things. If I had been looking out for my own gratification, I could easily have become attached to these extravagances. But the One who sees everything in its true light was looking out for me! He did not let me out of his hand.

Now that I mention true vision, recall the great difficulties people face once God has brought them knowledge of the truth. When we deal with the things of the world, so much seems to be covered up. The Lord explained all this to me once. Actually, many of the things I say here do not come from my own head. The heavenly Master dictates them to me, and I simply write them down.

In the places where I explicitly say, "I was made to understand" or "the Lord said to me," I am exceedingly careful not to add or subtract a single syllable. When I do not remember everything exactly, I claim it as my own thought. Some things actually do come only from me. But I don't attribute anything positive to myself. I already know that there is nothing good in me except what the Lord has put there without my deserving it. When I talk about something "coming from me," I mean that it was not given to me in a revelation.

But why is it, my Beloved, that even in spiritual matters we try to understand things our own way? We approach them as if they were just like the things of this world, and then we come up with a distorted opinion of the truth. For instance, we think we should measure our spiritual progress by how many years we've been practicing silent prayer. In this way, we are trying to put a limit on the One who gives his gifts without any limit. He gives whenever he desires to give. He can give more to one soul in half a year than he gives to another in half a lifetime. I have seen this happen so many times to so many different souls that I'm amazed it's even an issue for anybody.

I strongly believe that anyone with the gift of spiritual discernment will not be deceived in this matter, especially if the Lord has given him humility. A humble person will judge other souls by the fruits he sees in them. He will pay attention to the effects of a soul's prayer and the love he sees in her heart. He will understand that the Lord gives him the light to recognize these things.

God does not care how old we are. He considers only the progress of our souls. That's why one person can gain more in six months than another can in twenty years. The Lord gives what he wants to whom he pleases. He is also more likely to give to those who are ready to receive, regardless of how many years they have been practicing.

I see the young girls entering this house already filled with light. God has touched them and set their hearts on fire with love. They do not sit around waiting for him. They do not tolerate any obstacles in their path to him. They barely remember to eat. For love of him, they shut themselves away forever in a house that has no money, as if they didn't care one bit about their own lives. They give up everything. They don't even want their own will. The thought of being discontent with a cloistered life and austerities would never cross their minds. They offer themselves up whole as a sacrifice to God.

I have no hesitation in admitting their advantage over me. They inspire me to enter God's presence with the utmost modesty. What his Majesty did not succeed in granting me over the course of the many years I practiced prayer, he has given them in three months or three days. With all the favors he has granted me over all this time, I have not accomplished a fraction of what these girls have achieved with far less help from him. But he rewards them generously, and they have no reason to regret what they have done for him.

To those of us who have been practicing prayer for many years, let me offer a reminder: let's not bother those who have made tremendous progress in a short time. Let's not force them to turn around and walk at our pace. Why would I want to make those who fly like eagles on the wings God has given them move instead like fettered chickens? Let us keep our own eyes fixed on God. If these souls are humble, we should not hesitate to hand over the reins. The Lord who grants them these favors will not let them plunge over the precipice.

These young women trust in God, and the truth they know through faith serves them well. We should trust them too and not try to measure them by our own meager standards. If we do not achieve the wonderful results and excellent resolutions they experience, let us not condemn them but rather humble ourselves. It takes experience to understand these things.

By ostensibly looking out for their spiritual growth, we impede our own. Through them, God has given us an opportunity for humility and self-knowledge. He helps us see how much more detached these souls are and how much closer to him. Why else would his Majesty draw them so near?

I do not mean to suggest anything other than this: I appreciate a prayer practiced for a short time if it produces dramatic results. For it takes a powerful love to give up everything for God. A prayer of this intensity is far superior to a prayer practiced over many years that never gives rise to the determination to do whatever it takes to get to God. Sometimes a long life of prayer only yields small acts of love, like grains of salt. They bear no weight. A sparrow could carry them in its beak. We can hardly consider such lukewarm resolutions to be genuine spiritual fruits. What a pity we pay attention to any of the things we do for God, even if there are many.

That's how I am. I forget God's blessings with every step. I'm not saying that his Majesty, who is infinitely good, does not highly value the lowest action we dedicate to him. Of course he does! But I don't want to pay any attention to my own deeds and make a big deal out of small sacrifices. They are nothing.

Excuse me, my Lord. Please don't blame me for seeking minor solace in the things I do. I am well aware that I'm not really serving you. If I served you in great ways, I wouldn't have to latch on to these trifles. Blessed are they who serve you with truly noble deeds. If envying those people and wanting to emulate them could carry me closer to you, I would be almost there by now. But I am worthless, my Lord. Please, since you love me so much, share some of your worth with me so that what I do for you has value.

After we had received the documents from Rome granting us permission to found the new monastery without secure revenue, I started thinking about all I had been through to accomplish this goal. I was glad the matter was resolved and grateful that the Lord had seen fit to make some use of me through these trials. I thought about all the different deeds I had done and noticed that in each of the things I considered worthy, there were faults and imperfections. Sometimes I lacked courage. Often I lacked faith.

Now that I see everything the Lord promised me fulfilled in this house, I recognize that I never fully believed that what the Lord had told me would come true. Yet I could never really doubt that it would either. I can't explain it. Sometimes I thought it was impossible that it would happen; other times I thought it was impossible that it wouldn't. Finally, I sorted it out: the Lord was responsible for the positive parts, and I for the negative. At that point, I stopped thinking about it. I couldn't bear to recall all my faults and stumble over so many imperfections. May the One who desires to draw good out of everything be blessed. Amen.

As I say, I think it is dangerous to keep track of how many years we've been practicing prayer. Even if we are very humble, it's easy for a sense of entitlement to creep in. We start to think we deserve compensation for this service. I don't mean that we don't gain merit from our practice or that the prayer will not bear fruit. But I am sure that any spiritual seeker who thinks he is entitled to certain delights of the spirit in exchange for all the years he has spent on the path will not ascend to the summit of perfection.

Isn't it enough that God has taken him by the hand and guided him away from falling into the kind of error in which he may have engaged before he started practicing prayer? Now he wants to sue God for damages? This doesn't look like profound humility to me. Maybe it is, but I consider it sheer audacity. I don't think even I, who am not very humble, would dare to behave like this. It may be that I have never asked for a reward because I have never really served him. Perhaps if I had, I would want more than anyone for the Lord to give me my money's worth. I don't know.

I'm not saying that if a soul has been humble, she will not grow. God will match the plenitude of her prayer. But I am saying that she should forget about her years of service. Everything we do amounts to nothing in comparison to a single drop of the blood Christ shed for us. What are we asking for, anyway? The more we serve him, the deeper in his debt we are. If we pay one penny toward this amount, he gives us a thousand dollars in return.

For the love of God, let's light these accounts on fire. They are his to judge, not ours. These comparisons fall short even in worldly matters. How much less adequate they are when we are speaking of things only God understands. His Majesty demonstrated this perfectly when he gave as much to those who came last as he gave to those who came first.

You know, I have so little time to write that I've had to walk away from the last three pages and return to them many times over the course of the last three days. I keep forgetting what I was trying to say. Oh yes, the vision!

Well, I saw myself in prayer, standing alone in a field. Many different kinds of people surrounded me. I think they all had weapons in their hands and intended to harm me. Some held spears, some daggers, some swords; others brandished long rapiers. I had no escape route. Any direction I turned would have led me straight into the arms of death.

I was alone. There was no one to defend me. My spirit was gravely afflicted. I didn't know what to do. Then I lifted my eyes to heaven and saw Christ. He was not actually in heaven but high above me in the air. He was holding out his hand to me and encouraging me. I felt totally protected and knew that I had nothing to fear. Those people couldn't hurt me even if they tried!

This vision may not make much sense when considered by itself, but it turned out to be of great benefit to me. Shortly afterward, I was given an understanding of what it meant. I found myself under attack from every side, and I knew that the vision had been a picture of the world. It seems as though everything in the world bears arms to inflict injury on the poor soul.

I'm not talking about ordinary things that ensnare us, such as honor and property and earthly delights. It seems those things are designed to trip us up when we least expect it. No, I'm referring to friends, relatives, and—most surprising of all—some very good people. These very good people oppressed me so much, I didn't know how to defend myself or what to do.

O God, help me! If I were to tell you about all the trials I suffered during that time and add them to those I have already described, it would be a graphic lesson about rejecting all worldly things. This was my greatest persecution so far. Sometimes I found myself beset on every side, and the only relief I could find was to raise my eyes to heaven and call out to God.

I also thought about my vision. This helped me a lot. I remembered not to put my trust in any human being but to turn always to God, who is the only reliable help. His Majesty always sent me one of his representatives to lend me a hand when things were most difficult. It was generally someone who had succeeded in detaching himself from the world, whose only goal was to serve God. This helped me sustain the small flower of virtue I had and to cultivate my own desire to do everything for God. May you be forever blessed, my Lord!

One day I was feeling very distressed. I couldn't seem to recollect myself in prayer. I was at war with my own thoughts, which kept galloping after imperfect things. My customary detachment failed me completely. I started thinking that since I was so wretched, maybe the favors the Lord had granted me had been delusions. A deep darkness fell on my soul.

In the midst of this anxiety, the Lord spoke to me. "Do not be troubled," he said. "Learn from this. Where would you be if it were not for my grace? There is no security as long as we live in the flesh."

He helped me understand that strife is valuable because it generates merit. He seemed to have great compassion for those who live in this world. "Do not think I have forgotten you," he soothed me. "I will never forsake you." With tender mercy, the Lord told me I must do the best I could. And then he said other things that showed me his divine favor, but there is no reason to recount them here.

His Majesty often expresses his love for me. "Now you are mine and I am yours," he says.

"What do I care about myself?" I say. "All I care about is you!" This is my customary response, and I believe it is genuine.

His words embarrass me. Because of what I am, it demands more courage for me to receive these gifts than to undergo the most severe worldly trials. When I experience his grace, it makes me forget any good deed I have ever done. All I can remember is where I have missed the mark. This has nothing to do with the discursive mind. It seems like a supernatural phenomenon.

Sometimes I am overcome by an urgent longing to receive Communion. I cannot exaggerate its intensity. This happened to me one morning when it was raining so hard that it seemed impossible to leave the house. But once I stepped outside, I was already so transported with the desire for Communion that if it had been spears battering my chest instead of raindrops, I would have pushed through them.

When I arrived at the church, a powerful rapture came over me. It seemed to me that I saw the gates of heaven thrown wide open. This time it was not only the entrance I saw, but deep into heaven itself. I was shown a throne, and I could tell there was another one above it. Without actually seeing it, I understood with ineffable knowledge that the Divine himself sat on this upper throne.

It seemed that there were some animals supporting the throne. I think

I have heard a description of these creatures. Maybe they are the evangelists mentioned in Apocalypse. But I couldn't see what the throne was like or who was seated on it. All I could see was a multitude of angels. They looked even more beautiful than the ones I had seen in heaven before. Their glory varied a great deal, and I wondered if they were different orders of being, such as cherubim and seraphim. They seemed to be on fire.

I cannot express in writing the glory I experienced in myself then. It cannot be put into words. Anyone who has not experienced it will not be able to imagine what it was like. I recognized that everything we could ever desire was present together there, yet I didn't see anything.

Then someone, I don't know who, said, "All you can do is understand that you can understand nothing." The voice urged me to reflect more deeply. "Compared to that glory," it said, "nothing else is anything at all." This made me ashamed later. How could we ever be sidetracked by any created thing, let alone become attached to it? The whole world looked like a mere anthill to me.

Well, I attended Mass and received Communion that day, but I'm not sure how I did it. I thought that the glorious rapture had passed swiftly, so I was amazed when the clock struck and I found that two hours had gone by. This fire, I realized, comes from above. It is God's true love. No matter how much I may want it and seek it and strive for it, I cannot obtain a single spark of it unless it is God's will.

It's amazing! When we are united with this fire, it annihilates the old self, with all her cravings and faults, her insipid misery. We are like the phoenix, which is completely burned and then rises again from those same ashes. And so the soul, once she is consumed by the fire of love, becomes something altogether different. She has new desires and tremendous fortitude. She is not what she was before, and she follows the way of the Lord with new purity.

I prayed to God that this would be so with me. I asked to serve him in a fresh new way. Then he spoke to me. "You have come up with a good metaphor," he said. "Make sure you never forget to strive for improvement."

One time when I was struggling with the same doubts about the veracity of my visions, the Lord appeared to me. "O children of men!"

he said in a stern voice. "How long will you be hard-hearted?" He said I needed to look inside myself. "Are you totally surrendered to me?" he asked. "If you are, then believe this, I will not let you go astray."

His reprimand troubled me deeply. But then he came back and spoke to me in the most tender and soothing voice. "Do not worry," he said. "I already know that you are completely devoted to my service. Everything you desire shall be done. Notice how your love for me is growing inside you every day. This is evidence that your experiences do not come from the spirit of evil. Do you think God would allow the spirit of evil to have power over one of his beloved servants? Do you think the spirit of evil could give you the clarity and quietude you've been experiencing or the depth of understanding?" He helped me see that because so many people of such high caliber were assuring me that my visions were from God, it would be wrong of me to doubt them.

One day while I was reciting the Athanasian Creed, I suddenly understood something I had never really understood before. I clearly saw how there is only one God and three divine Persons. I was amazed and consoled by this realization. It enhanced my awareness of God's extraordinary grandeurs and marvelous mysteries. Now when I think or speak about the Holy Trinity, I believe I understand how such a thing is possible, and this makes me very happy.

On the Feast of the Assumption of Our Lady, Queen of Angels, the Lord desired to grant me another favor. In a rapture he showed me the Blessed Mother's ascent to heaven. I witnessed the joy and dignity with which she was received there, and I saw the place where she resides now. I cannot begin to explain how this happened. Simply beholding such glory filled my soul with glory! The effects were magnificent. I was left with a deeper desire than ever to withstand difficult trials. Seeing how worthy our Lady is, I longed to serve her.

Then there was the time I was at the Jesuit college of Saint Giles. As I watched the brothers there receiving Communion, I saw a canopy over their heads. It was very ornate and beautiful. I saw this twice. But when other people were receiving Communion, I did not see it.

SOUL ON FIRE

ONCE WHEN I was in prayer, I felt such profound interior delight that I couldn't help but wonder if I was worthy of such grace. I suspected that what I really deserved was that place I had seen reserved for me in hell. I never forgot the situation in which I had found myself in that vision.

As I reflected on this more deeply, my soul gradually caught fire. I don't know how to describe the spiritual rapture that came over me then. It seemed to me that I plunged directly into the majesty that before I had only understood intellectually, and it filled me completely. Within this majesty, I was given full realization of a truth that fulfills all truths. I don't know how to explain this. I didn't see anything or anyone. Yet I clearly understood that Truth itself was speaking to me.

"This is no small thing I am doing for you," it said. "You owe me a great deal in exchange. All the harm that comes to the world is the result of not knowing the truths exemplified so clearly in the sacred scriptures. Not one iota of this truth shall ever fail us." It seems to me that I had always believed this, that all faithful people believed this.

"Ah, Daughter," Truth said to me then. "How few there are who truly love me! I do not conceal my secrets from my lovers. Do you know what it is to love me truly? It is to know that everything displeasing to me is a lie. By the fruits this knowledge bears in your soul, you will come to understand what you do not yet understand."

And I *have* come to understand this. Praise the Lord! Ever since then, anything that is not directed to the glory of God seems empty and false to me. I don't know how to explain how I know this or how to describe the benefits this knowledge brings to my life. Nor can I express the depth of grief I feel when I observe people in the dark about this truth.

During that rapture, the Lord spoke one particular word to me that blessed me immeasurably. I don't know how this happened. I didn't see anything. But it left me with an indescribable sense of good fortune. I felt fortified with a powerful strength to carry out even the smallest teachings of holy scripture in my life. It seemed to me that there was not an obstacle that could cross my path that I would not overcome.

3 The Divine Truth that revealed itself to me that day mysteriously engraved itself on my heart. It left me with a new reverence for the power and majesty of God. I cannot begin to describe the nature of this knowledge, but it is exceedingly high. After that I had an intense desire to speak only true things that transcend what we generally deal with here on earth. I began to feel the pain of living in the world but was also filled with a feeling of great tenderness, consolation, and humility.

Without my understanding how it happened, I think the Lord gave me many gifts with this one favor. I didn't feel any suspicion that it was a delusion. Even though I didn't see anything, I understood that it is a great blessing to learn to ignore anything that doesn't bring us closer to God. Thus, I came to know what it is for a soul to walk in truth with Truth itself. I understood that God gave me this knowledge.

4 Of all the things I have come to know, some were revealed through spiritual voices and others were not. I comprehended some things more clearly without words. I understood extraordinary truths about this Truth. My understanding was greater than if many learned men had tried to teach me. I don't think they could ever have succeeded in impressing this knowledge upon my soul or helping me see the vast emptiness of this world.

This truth that was taught to me is Truth itself. It has no beginning, and it has no end. All other truths depend on this Truth, just as all other loves issue forth from this Love and all greatness is born of this Greatness. This statement sounds obscure compared to the penetrating clarity God gave me. How mighty is the power of the Lord, who leaves such bountiful growth and marvelous gifts imprinted on my soul in such a short span of time!

O my great Majesty! What are you doing, my all-powerful Beloved? Look at the one on whom you are bestowing such exalted blessings. Don't you remember that this one has been an abyss of lies and a sea of vanities? And it's all my own fault. You endowed me with a natural aversion to lying, yet I have allowed myself to get caught up in a thousand lies. How do you bear it, my God? How can you continue to shower your loving mercy on someone so ill-equipped to receive your grace?

Once while I was reciting the hours with all the other sisters, my soul suddenly became recollected. It appeared to me like a highly polished mirror. There was not a single part of the surface, on the top or the bottom or the sides, that was not totally clear. I saw the image of Christ our Lord in the center. I seemed to see him in every part of my soul as clearly and distinctly as I saw him in the mirror. I don't know how to explain this. This mirror conformed entirely to the shape of my Lord through a loving transmission I cannot possibly describe.

Every time I remember this vision, I notice its benefits, especially after I have received Communion. It gave me a graphic understanding of what it is for a soul to be in grave error. In such a state, the mirror of the soul becomes shrouded in a dark mist so that we cannot see the Lord, even though he is always with us and is the One who gives us our being. I also understood that unbelievers do more harm than simply darkening the mirror; they shatter it.

I cannot adequately describe what I experienced. Seeing it is very different than talking about it. But this vision was very beneficial to me. It also brought me pain to realize the times when I had allowed the mirror of my soul to become so clouded that I could no longer see my Lord there.

I think this vision is especially advantageous to committed practitioners of prayer who know what it is to be recollected. It teaches them that the Lord resides very deep inside their own souls. This notion is much more attractive and fruitful than the idea that God is outside us.

Some books on prayer tell us where to seek this God. The glorious Saint Augustine speaks especially well about this. He could not find God in the marketplace or in pleasures or in any other place he searched for him until he sought inside himself. Absolutely the best place to look for

God is inside ourselves. We don't need to ascend to heaven or reach any further than our own beings. Trying to go beyond our own center only wears the soul out and distracts her. Such efforts do not bear fruit.

7. Here is something I'd like to address, in case this experience happens to you. Sometimes when the soul has been in deep rapture and the faculties have been totally absorbed, the soul emerges from union and yet remains recollected. She has trouble returning her awareness to external things. The two faculties, memory and intellect, are in a state of frenetic confusion. This happens especially in the beginning.

I think this is because our natural weakness cannot bear such spiritual force. It drains our imagination. I know that some people suffer from this more than others. I would recommend that these people stop praying and allow themselves to recover. They can go back and pick up their practice again later, when they have reintegrated. If they push through, they could do some serious damage to themselves. I have personal experience in this matter. I know how wise it is to take your health and disposition into consideration.

8. Nevertheless, personal experience and a spiritual guide are indispensable. Once a soul has gotten this far, she will have many important things to talk about. If you look for a guide and don't find one, the Lord will not let you down. In spite of what I am, he has never let me down. I admit that there are not many people who have arrived at these places themselves. If they have not experienced these things, they have no remedy to offer a soul that has. Lacking direct knowledge, such a guide will only disturb and distress the soul. But the Lord will take this into account as well.

It's best to talk things over with your confessor. This is especially true for women. The confessor needs to be well qualified. I can't remember if I've said all this before; I think so. I'm saying it now because I believe it is very important. The Lord grants these favors to many more woman than men. The saintly Pedro de Alcantará always said this, and I have confirmed it with my own observations. He used to say that women make much more progress along the path than men do. There is no reason to mention all the excellent reasons he gave for why this is so. Suffice it to say that all his opinions favored women.

9 Once I was shown a brief glimpse of how all things are seen in God and how he holds them all inside himself. Although I perceived this with distinct clarity, I did not see any forms, and the moment passed quickly. I have no idea how to express this in writing. But it impressed itself deeply into my soul. It is one of the great favors God has granted me, but it also confuses me and makes me feel guilty in light of all my transgressions.

If only it had been the Lord's will to show this to me earlier and to show it to others who have forsaken him, I don't think any of us would have had the heart to offend him. Even though I am calling this a vision, I have to repeat that I didn't actually see anything. Something must have been there, since I am able to come up with language to describe it. Yet the vision is so subtle and delicate that the intellect cannot grasp it. Visions that are not imaginative are almost impossible to convey. There must be some element of imagery present in them. But since the faculties are transported, they can't recreate a picture afterward of what the Lord revealed to them or how he wants them to rejoice in him.

10 Still, I will try an analogy. Let's say the Divine is like a clear diamond, more vast than the whole world—or else a mirror, so sublime that its purity cannot be exaggerated. We could say that everything we do is visible in this jewel, since it was fashioned to contain all things within itself. Nothing transcends its greatness. It was frightening for me to see so many things joined together in such a short time within this gem, and it made me sad to have seen such ugly things as my mistakes reflected in that pure brilliance. Whenever I recall this, I don't know how I bear it. It leaves me with such a pervasive sense of shame that I don't know where to hide.

Oh, who could explain this to those who commit the ugliest sins! If only such souls could realize that dishonorable deeds cannot be concealed from God. Of course, his Majesty is aware of everything; it all takes place in the middle of his Being. How can we act so disrespectfully in front of him?

I saw how we deserve punishment for a single grave error, yet we just don't seem to understand how dreadfully serious it is to commit this error in the presence of such awesome majesty. Can't we see how far this behavior is from the nature of God? This awareness only increases my perception of his mercy. Even when we understand all this and behave badly anyway, he keeps loving us.

11. If something like this terrifies the soul, then what will the Day of Judgment be like, I have wondered, when this same Majesty will clearly reveal himself to us and we will see everything we have done reflected there? O God, help me! I have walked in such blindness!

I have often been appalled by what I have written in this account. I'm sure it doesn't surprise you. Yet you must wonder how I can keep living after having seen these things inside myself. May he be forever blessed who has put up with so much from me.

12. Once when I was in an especially deep state of recollection in prayer, filled with peaceful delight, it seemed to me that angels surrounded me. I felt very close to God. I began to pray for the Church. Then his Majesty revealed to me that one of the religious orders would do a great deal of good in the future and that its members would uphold the faith with great fortitude.

13 On another day, while I was praying near the Blessed Sacrament, a saint appeared to me. His order had been experiencing a gradual decline. He held a big book in his hands. Then he opened it. "Read this," he commanded. The letters were large and completely legible. "In times to come," they said, "this order will flourish. It will have many martyrs."

14 And then one day while I was at matins in the choir, I saw six or seven members of that same order. They were holding swords in their hands. I think this meant they would be defending the faith, because I saw something similar on another occasion when I was praying. It seemed as if I were carried to a large field where a huge battle was taking place. Those belonging to that order were fighting with tremendous energy. Their faces were radiant, as if they were on fire. They conquered many foes. They either threw them to the ground or killed them. It seemed to me that this was a battle against the unbelievers.

15 I have seen the same glorious saint several times, and he's told me a few things. He thanked me for praying for his people and promised to commend me to the Lord. I'm not going to name this order. If it were the Lord's will for their identity to be known, he would reveal it. As it is, I don't want anyone to feel offended.

Each order should strive for the well-being of the whole. Actually, every member of each group must work to be an instrument of the prosperity of his order. He ought to concentrate on being of service during a time when the Church desperately needs all our help. Lives sacrificed for such a cause are truly blessed!

16 A certain Inquisitor once asked me to beg God to give him a sign by which he could decide whether or not to accept his nomination for bishop. He wanted to know if to do so would serve God. After I received Communion, the Lord spoke to me. "When he understands in complete clarity and truthfulness that real lordship is about possessing nothing," he said, "then he will be ready to accept it." With these words he was teaching that anyone who assumes a position of great power must be far from wanting it. At least he should not strive for it.

17 The Lord continues to grant many blessings to this sinner. It doesn't seem necessary to go into all of them here. I think what I've said is enough to convey something about my soul and the spirit the Lord has given me. May he who has taken such good care of me be forever blessed. Amen.

18 Once the Lord was comforting me in the most loving way. "Don't worry," he said. "Nothing stays the same in this ever-changing stream of life. Sometimes the soul will be passionate, other times dull. Sometimes she will be disturbed and other times serene. She will suffer various temptations. But if she trusts in me, she never needs to be afraid."

19 I was wondering one day if the joy I derived from my relationships with my spiritual guides represented a dangerous lack of detachment. I loved being with these men. I found it deeply satisfying to discuss my soul with such great servants of God. Then the Lord spoke to me. "If a man who had been close to death attributed his recovery to a doctor, it would not be a virtue for him to withhold his gratitude and love from that doctor. And so it is with you. If it hadn't been for these people in whom you have confided, what would you have done? Conversation with good people can never be wrong! If you consider well whatever you say and always speak with integrity, you have no reason to avoid their company. Not only are such conversations not harmful, they are beneficial."

This was very comforting to me. I had been worrying that because conversing with these men gave me such pleasure, it must be an attachment. This made me not want to talk to them at all.

20 The Lord has always given me specific advice. He has told me how to deal with certain people who are weak and with others who have different problems. He never ceases to take care of me. But sometimes I am distressed about not serving him enough. It bothers me that I still have to spend more time than I would like to tend my wretched body.

I was praying before bedtime one night. I was in a great deal of pain, and my customary nausea washed over me. I saw that I was caught by my body while my spirit was longing for more time in prayer. This dichotomy upset me so much that I started to cry.

This was not the only time such a thing had happened. It makes me so angry that I end up hating myself. It isn't usual for me to harbor antipathy toward myself. I can usually see what I need to do and do it. May it be God's will that I never care for myself more than I should. Sometimes I'm afraid that I do.

That night the Lord appeared to me and offered me solace. "Endure these things for love of me," he said. "Your life is necessary to me."

After this, I don't think I ever felt afflicted again. I am determined to serve my Lord and my Comfort with all my strength. Even though he has allowed me to suffer a little, he has consoled me so fully that it is nothing to endure a few trials for him. In fact, it no longer seems that there is any reason for living except to give myself to him in any and every way. I enthusiastically beg God to bring on whatever trials he sees fit.

Sometimes I say to him with all sincerity, "Lord, all I ask for myself is either to die or to suffer." Every time I hear the clock strike I am relieved, because I know I am one hour closer to the end of my life and drawing that much nearer to seeing God.

21 At other times I feel nothing. I don't want to keep living, but I don't actively want to die. Everything seems tepid and dark and difficult. Even though the Lord warned me years ago that he was going to publicize the favors he gives me, this has caused me tremendous suffering, since everyone interprets what he hears about me in his own way.

The only thing that has consoled me is the knowledge that it's not my fault that these things have become widely known. I was extremely careful not to tell anyone but my confessors or people to whom my confessors referred me who understood these experiences. I wish I could claim that it was humility that moved me to avoid talking to my spiritual directors about the divine favors. It simply pained me to disclose them.

Now, glory be to God, people's opinions of me do not bother me very much. I realize that the Lord has used me as an example to many souls. It's true that people still criticize me vehemently. Some men are afraid to hear my confession. Others make up all kinds of stories about me. Maybe the Lord has placed me in this little cloistered corner of the world to protect me from the consequences stemming from public knowledge of these favors. I assumed that once I became enclosed here, it would be as if I were dead and they would forget about me.

But no, things have not turned out quite the way I hoped they would. I am still compelled to talk with certain people. But because I am rarely seen, it seems the Lord has given me some refuge. We'll see.

22 Here at Saint Joseph's, I dwell among a few holy companions, removed from the world. I observe everything as if from above and what people say or think about me doesn't trouble me much. Besides, I would be happy if even one soul could benefit from the things being said about me. Since I have been living in this house, all my desires converge on this desire. Look at how much the Lord himself is willing to suffer for the sake of a single soul!

God has given me a life that is a kind of waking sleep. I almost always feel like I am dreaming now. Everything I perceive seems to be at a distance. I am aware of neither happiness nor sadness in myself. Or if I do feel either of these emotions in any given instance, no matter how intensely, it passes swiftly. I am amazed by how ephemeral these experiences are, and they always leave me feeling like it's all a dream.

This is really true. After the experience passes, I may wish to rejoice in the pleasure or linger in the pain, but I am incapable of doing so. It's like a levelheaded person who finds it impossible to delight or grieve over a dream from which he has just awakened. The Lord has now awakened my soul from the things that used to cause me such feelings before I was sufficiently mortified and dead to the things of the world. His Majesty does not want me to become blind again.

23 This is the way I live now. Please beg God either to take me home to him or else show me how to serve him. May it please his Majesty that what I have written here be of some benefit to you. It certainly wasn't

easy to accomplish, since I have so little time. But the difficulty will prove well worth it if it moves even one soul to praise God more. Then, even if you burn it afterward, I would feel compensated.

2 y But please, I don't want you to destroy this document until you have shown it to the three other men to whom I've addressed it. They have been my confessors and need to have a look at it. If I have done a bad job in recounting the story of my life, then they can give up their high opinion of me once and for all, which would be a good thing. If I have said anything well, these are good and learned men, and I know they will praise God for it because they will understand that it came from him through me.

May his Majesty always keep you in his hands. May he make you a great saint. May the light of your spirit illumine this miserable woman who lacks humility and has been so bold as to take on the task of trying to put such sublime things into words.

And may it please the Lord that I have not made a mistake in writing this. It has been my wish and my intention all along to obey my superiors and be accurate. I have always hoped that through me God would receive some praise. This is what I have begged him for, for many years. Since I have not offered him this praise with my own actions, I have dared to offer this account of a dissipated life as an example of his great mercy. I have only spent as much time composing this as was absolutely necessary to document what has happened to me as clearly and truthfully as I was able.

The Lord is all-powerful and can hear me if he wants. Hear me, Lord. May it be your will that I succeed in doing your will in every way. Do not allow this soul to be lost, your Majesty. You have employed so much ingenuity in so many different circumstances to save my soul over and over. You have pulled me back from the abyss and brought me home to you. Amen!

Epilogue

THE HOLY SPIRIT be with you always. Amen.

In light of what I have revealed here, I don't think it would be wrong of me to ask you to pray for me. Think of what I have gone through to write about myself here and recall all my miseries. Although the truth is, it was far more difficult to recount the favors his Majesty has granted me than to admit my offenses against him.

I did what you commanded and expanded on some of the original material. This was based expressly on your promise that you would tear up whatever seems wrong to you. After I had finished writing the account, you sent for it before I had a chance to read it over. So there could be some things I have not explained sufficiently and also places where I've repeated myself. I wish I had been able to review what I wrote.

I am asking you now to correct this document and find someone to transcribe it before you share it with anyone else. Otherwise, my handwriting might be recognized and give me away.

I desperately want to know what you and Father Juan Ávila think of this. If it is your opinion that I am walking a good path, I will be very much consoled. For then I will have done everything it is in my power to do. Handle this any way you think best, of course, but please remember your responsibility to a woman who has entrusted you with her soul.

I will pray to our Lord for your soul as long as I live. Just do me this favor: hurry and serve God. You will learn from what I've written here that we are best occupied when we give ourselves over entirely to the One who gives himself immeasurably to us. I see that you have already begun to do this.

May God be forever blessed! I hope in his mercy that you and I will see one another in that place where we will know everything with perfect clarity. There, we will behold all the great things he has done for us and praise him forever and ever. Amen.

This book was finished in June 1562.